FIRST NATIONS

in Canada

JAMES S. FRIDERES

ISSUES IN CANADA

OXFORD
UNIVERSITY PRESS

OXFORD
UNIVERSITY PRESS

Oxford University Press is a department of the University of Oxford.
It furthers the University's objective of excellence in research, scholarship,
and education by publishing worldwide. Oxford is a registered trade mark of
Oxford University Press in the UK and in certain other countries.

Published in Canada by
Oxford University Press
8 Sampson Mews, Suite 204,
Don Mills, Ontario M3C 0H5 Canada

www.oupcanada.com

Copyright © James S. Frideres 2016

The moral rights of the author have been asserted

Database right Oxford University Press (maker)

Library and Archives Canada Cataloguing in Publication
Frideres, James S., 1943–, author
First Nations people in Canada / James S. Frideres.

(Issues in Canada)
Includes bibliographical references and index.
ISBN 978-0-19-901535-1 (paperback)

1. Native peoples—Canada. 2. Native peoples—Canada—
Social conditions. 3. Native peoples—Canada—Politics and
government. 4. Native peoples—Canada—Government
relations. I. Title. II. Series: Issues in Canada

Cover image: zack embree / zackembree.com

Oxford University Press is committed to our environment.
This book is printed on Forest Stewardship Council® certified paper
and comes from responsible sources.

MIX
Paper from
responsible sources
FSC® C004071

ANCIENT FOREST ™
FRIENDLY

Printed and bound in Canada

1 2 3 4 — 19 18 17 16

Contents

Contents

Introduction

Until the 1970s, the "Indian problem" was mostly an in-house government issue. Government officials—police, corrections officers, judges, and court workers—were aware of conflicts and issues involving First Nations people, but the problem was not seen as a public one. Provincial schools were not expected to deal with First Nations students unless there was an agreement between the provincial and federal government. Even for those schools, principals and teachers worked on the assumption that the (mainstream) core curriculum was the appropriate curriculum for all students; there were no attempts to modify the curriculum to better fit the needs of First Nations people.

At the time, First Nations people were under-educated, unskilled, and culturally unprepared to enter the urban primary labour resource pool. As such, economic institutions had little contact or involvement with First Nations people except for some occasional involvement in the secondary labour resource pool; there were few other interactions in such areas as health or religion. There was a widespread belief among most non-Aboriginal people that the only "real" culture was the mainstream European one. For example, health officials refused to recognize Aboriginal health care practices, among other longstanding indigenous traditions. Finally, few Canadians had contact with First Nations people. There was little awareness of their living situations.

To be sure, some actions were taken by the federal government. In the 1950s, the Indian Act was revised, removing several particularly egregious sections such as the outlawing of certain First Nations ceremonies as well as the rule preventing lawyers and others from accepting legal cases against the federal government on behalf of First Nations people. Then, in 1966, the federal government authorized a pan-Canadian study to ascertain the social and economic status of First Nations people. The resultant *Hawthorne Report* (1966–67) revealed that First Nations people were marginal in almost every aspect of life. While it received some attention upon publication, by 1970 the Canadian public had by and large forgotten it. It was not until 1973—when the courts ruled that First Nations people had Aboriginal rights—that Canadians began to discuss the "Indian problem."

For most of the twentieth century, many Aboriginal people were marginal participants in Canadian society. There was no official recognition of any contribution to the social, economic, or political development of Canada. In addition, until the mid-twentieth century, most First Nations people resided in rural homelands called reserves. The only time attention was drawn to issues associated with First Nations people was news involving civil disobedience or actions that had an impact on the routine daily life of non-Aboriginal people. However, these events were episodic and short lived; media interest soon dissolved.

Throughout most of Canadian history, First Nations people were blamed for their own marginal plight. If Aboriginal people had low incomes, it was seen as their own fault for not taking better jobs or achieving an education. Public discourse was full of stereotypes such as "lazy," "dirty," "drunk," and "backwards." There was no recognition that the actions of the past and present by government and mainstream institutional orders had any relation to the current status of First Nations people.

A full explanation of why First Nations people have remained the poorest of Canada's minorities has remained elusive. Some history is relevant here. There is a certain mythology associated with early settlers to the "New World" building their institutions upon a *terra nullius*, an uninhabited and undiscovered country. The fact that flourishing cultures pre-existed the French and British "discovery" of the New World violated the vision of *terra nullius*. In 1727, Europeans changed the definition of *terra nullius*: if the country was uninhabited, or if the inhabitants were uncivilized, then the same rules of *terra nullius* applied. In short, ruling officials gave themselves the right to invade and control the country.

By the eighteenth and nineteenth centuries, widely held explanations for the marginal existence of First Nations people centered on their lack of religion. Later it focused on their "innate" lack of ability to understand the complexities of settler society and its administration. Alternatively, Aboriginal culture was "anti-modern." In short, Aboriginal people lacked physical and human capital for success. The focus of the Department of Indian Affairs was on this human capital, detailing the attributes of the people living in the community such as age structure, linguistic abilities, levels of education, and skill level. The goal of Indian Affairs was to understand the reasons behind Aboriginal communities' poor involvement in the labour market and slow economic development. In short, successive governments were mainly interested in removing the "Indianness" of First Nations people to better integrate them into mainstream society.

These arguments have since been discarded. New and preferred explanations focus on the institutional environment in which resource-allocation decisions are made in conjunction with the land and lack of human capital (Anderson and Parker 2006). Today, there is a grudging acknowledgement that successive Canadian governments have used coercion and greed to take over native lands and resources, and this is largely responsible for the marginal existence of Aboriginal peoples. However, even today there is little understanding of how the norms and laws of Canada systematically disempowered Aboriginal people. For example, First Nations people had no legal recourse against illegal actions by government or settlers.

Historical evidence reveals that before and after contact with settlers and colonial governments, First Nations people had developed sophisticated social and economic institutions that enabled them to produce and transport goods, using available resources. However, a new era of colonial–native relations took hold as French sovereignty passed to Great Britain through the Treaties of Utrecht (1713) and Paris (1763). When Canada was established in 1867, the lands and rights were inherited, and further increased with the purchase of Rupert's Land from the Hudson's Bay Company in 1870. The British North America Act became the country's main legal authority. New European–Aboriginal relations came into effect. As such, by Confederation (1867), the Canadian political system developed a bifurcated control system with regard to First Nations people. The British North America Act gave the federal government jurisdiction over Indians and lands reserved for the Indians; for example, First Nations reserves. At the same time it also gave legislative jurisdiction to the provinces over all other lands and natural resources within their own boundaries, outside of reserves and other federal lands (such as national parks). The result is that the province is an important stakeholder in the process of negotiating land claims. Furthermore, with the exception of British Columbia, provinces have the so-called reversionary title to Indian reserves, although they do not have jurisdiction over them. This means that if a reserve is no longer needed or is abandoned by a First Nations community, the land reverts to the province.

Once the treaties were established, institutional autonomy for First Nations was destroyed; colonial powers (and later successive federal governments) began to forge new laws and social norms, imposing these new arrangements on First Nations communities. This began with the control of lands, as well as the debate surrounding what land would be available for establishing reserves. The treaties were explicit in this respect: unwilling to relinquish control, the federal government held the lands "in trust" for First Nations communities. In addition, the government did not believe—or want to believe—that First Nations people were sufficiently culturally advanced to run their own affairs. By 1885, the Commissioner of Indian Affairs (Edgar Dewdney) began to fear an inter-tribal confederacy in the West would counteract federal efforts. As such, he intervened using what can only be described as underhanded measures to disrupt this potential confederacy. He agreed to distribute food rations to First Nations people at the signing of treaties but later began to withhold rations to the communities associated with "troublesome" chiefs, in particular those chiefs who were calling for amendments to the treaties and pushing for an inter-tribal confederacy. In the Cypress Hills area (in what is now Alberta), Dewdney closed Fort Walsh—the distribution centre for rations—thereby implementing a policy of starvation aimed at subjugating the chiefs (Innes 2013). Another example is 1888 legislation passed by Parliament preventing First Nations people from taking out loans for purchasing farm machinery; the reason given by Hayter Reed, the deputy minister of Indian Affairs, was that forcing the Indian to work the soil using only hand implements would help them evolve at the "correct" rate—not "skipping" any development stages—from hunter to peasant, and only then to modern man (Chansonneuve 2007).

Newhouse (2005) points out that for years federal governments took an "extinguishment" approach in the establishment of treaties. The settlement of a First Nations claim through a signed treaty gave the government clear title to land. In addition, this approach allowed the government to develop the time frame for the allocation of the land to be set aside for a reserve. Treaties provided First Nations people with a "one time" land selection that was limited and dictated by the federal government. Finally, it specified and limited surface rights and provided no special rights for First Nations people nor provided any protection for their culture. In short, the entire process was tied to government/private sector development, limited financial compensation, and support only for institutions that were non-Aboriginal in nature. No support was available to First Nations institutions in any form. Finally, the settlement process was both centralized and standardized: all settlements (treaties) were cut from the same template used in the early Robinson Superior treaties in the 1830s.

Historical Trauma

Historical trauma is a term that numerous scholars have used to provide a new lens on First Nations peoples (Brave Heart-Jordan 1995; Duran 2006; Raphael et al. 2008). Duran (2006) defines historical trauma as a cumulative emotional and psychological impact over a lifespan and across generations, emanating from massive group trauma. First Nations people have, for nearly five hundred years, endured emotional, social, physical, and spiritual genocide from European colonialist policy.

The legacy of injustices and suffering brought on by a history of colonialism, forced assimilation, and suppression of religious beliefs and

Types of Historical Trauma Experienced by First Nations People

The following illustrates aspects of First Nations peoples' trauma over the past four centuries, drawing on the work of Duran (2006) and Brave Heart-Jordan (1995).

First Contact (1500–1700)

Environmental and "life-world" shock. Military systematic genocide. Introduction of western ontologies and epistemologies. Establishment of the legal edict of *terra nullius*. Settlers impinge upon First Nations world view and ways of knowing. The introduction of diseases and epidemics throughout Aboriginal communities across the country.

Economic Competition (1600–1800)

Land is defined as a commodity by government and settlers and is to be shaped and used by settlers for profit. Resources on the land seen as being primarily for settlers' use and profit. Control of environment rather than balance. The economic system of First Nations is destroyed with the introduction of capitalism.

Invasion War Period (1700–1900)

The practice of "peaceful subordination" comes into effect. Removal of Aboriginal people from traditional lands; they become refugees in their homeland. Introduction of secondary and primary labour resource pool.

Treaty Period (1763–1930)

Peace and Friendship treaties, Royal Proclamation of 1763. The introduction of the early treaties in 1830. Numbered Treaties until 1923. Refusal to acknowledge land and treaty rights. Aboriginal people relocated to isolated enclaves (reserves) until assimilation. Rupture between old way of life and reserve life. Traditional forms of governance were replaced by Western views of governance.

Residential Schools (1892–1996)

Removal of children from parents and family; children placed into residential schools run by religious orders. Policy of assimilation: "Take the Indian out of the child." Loss of language, Indigenous knowledge, and family. Endurance of abuse by teachers, religious leaders, and other students in the residential school. Estrangement of children from their community, parents, family, and culture. Now into third generation of residential school survivors. Psychological and social pathology emerges from experiences in the residential schools.

Relocation (Ongoing)

The "Sixties scoop" removed children from First Nations families and placed them into unfamiliar "white" families. Community relocation to allow for commercial resource development was sanctioned by successive federal governments. Further loss of culture, language, and family by continued policy of assimilation. Unilateral redefinition of First Nations identity. Federal government policy of encouraging reserve Indians to relocate to urban centres through Indian Act. Refusal to honour Aboriginal rights, land, and treaties. Bill C-31 redefines who is an Indian.

practices has had a devastating impact on the transmission of traditional culture and the well-being of First Nations (National Collaborating Center for Aboriginal Health 2009–10; Smylie 2008). For example, in 1885 the assistant Indian commissioner, Hayter Reed, instituted many policies including a new farming policy that reduced the area under cultivation for each family on the reserve to one acre. Moreover, as described above, he banned the use of machinery on reserves to cultivate this one acre (Innes 2013). The ongoing lack of interest in First Nations history and culture has served to prolong the negative impact of trauma.

Today, First Nations communities remain resilient in spite of this trauma. Many have dealt with the trauma, becoming healthy and economically self-sufficient. However, a significant proportion of First Nations people are not faring as well (Duran et al. 1998; Evans-Campbell 2008; Raphael et al. 2008). Research has shown that the effects of historical trauma include many of the following injurious behaviours: unsettled emotional mental health, depression, high mortality rates, high rates of alcohol abuse, and child abuse and domestic violence.

The impact of each one of these historical "events" is enough to produce some trauma for a people experiencing them. First Nations people have suffered a massive accumulation of traumatic events. In addition, the loss of culture that might have given some expression to their grief undermined their ability to address the trauma. Today, the refusal of the federal government to engage in a pan-Canadian review of the 1,181 missing and murdered First Nations women and girls from 1980–2012 (see www.nwac.ca/2015/02/national-roundtable-on-missing-and-murdered-aboriginal-women-and-girls-framework) provides a more contemporary example of a traumatic event in the lives of First Nations people.

Leadership in Aboriginal communities was undermined as a result of changes in governance structure, historical trauma, and the loss of culture. The historic trauma events also led to the "gender" wars now evident on reserves. In the end, there were many elements of both culture and identity that did not survive; even so, as we will see below, First Nations people have remained resilient.

Resiliency

There are three forms of resilience:

1. positive outcome despite adversity;
2. sustained competence under stress; and
3. successful recovery from trauma.

Resilience means a greater-than-anticipated recovery in the wake of exposure to risk or adversity. First Nations people have shown a high degree of resilience in respect of all three types described above. Aboriginal communities have, over the years, suffered from the following: forced relocation, limited access to resources and land, and denial of access to traditional ways of living. Recent research by Mosby (2013) has brought to light the involvement of medical professionals—with the permission of the federal government—in carrying out "experiments" on First Nations children to test the impact of malnutrition over a sustained period of time. Other abuses were rife at residential schools. Nevertheless, some children who survived have become leaders in their communities, another demonstration of First Nations resilience. As Lalonde (2006) observes in his thirteen-year study of First Nations communities in BC, First Nations people have maintained a flourishing culture in spite of significant adversity.

Marginal Existence

Successive Canadian governments have tried to improve the social and economic position of First Nations people. These different approaches may be categorized in two ways. The first we may call "Jobs and Income," where money is seen as the solution. In this approach, Aboriginal Affairs and Northern Development Canada (AANDC) offers the First Nations community a sum of money to carry out a project. The band council or other groups in the community agree, hoping for job creation or other economic development. This approach is marked by little, if any, concern about the long-term impacts or sustainability of any given project. Fostered by the federal government, there have been many "pilot" projects that AANDC and other federal departments support. All are short-term; when the funding timeline is completed, the project grinds to a halt. New and often unrelated pilot projects are suggested.

A second and more recent approach has been adopted by First Nations communities, focusing on sustainability and "nation building." Advocated by the Harvard Project on American Indian Economic Development, this approach also focuses on issues such as jobs and income. However, it is different in several respects. First, money is not seen as the sole solution to the marginalization of Aboriginal people. Second, the focus on economic development emerges from the community's strategic plan and not that of an external agent with money. The emphasis for the community is to create a social, political, and economic environment that will sustain business in the long term. The community also deals with economic development as a "political" problem that requires sound institutional structures and strategic plans to bring about long-term community benefits. In short, it is the role of the band council and other community leaders to set policy and long-term vision. Others in the community then implement this vision. This creates a "firewall" between community politics and the business programs designed to create sustainable, long-term economic development.

Researchers have noted that in order to implement a successful "nation-building" approach, three fundamental building blocks have to be in place. First there must be some recognition of First Nations self-government in many different forms. This does not mean that First Nations communities have sovereignty in the legal international sense of the word, but it does mean that the community has the right to make economic decisions that reflect their vision and culture. As Cornell and Kalt (2000) note, placing full responsibility on the federal government for improving the economic position of First Nations people may be good rhetoric but it is a bad business model. First Nations communities must take responsibility for themselves and their economic development.

A second condition is that the First Nations community, with the support of federal, provincial, and territorial governments, must build and sustain stable institutions and policies. The creation of such institutions will ensure that all parties—both the community and outsiders who may be investors—are aware of the "rules of the game." In addition, embedded within this process are clearly articulated dispute resolution processes, such that all parties know how to proceed. These effective institutions also reveal a separation of politics from daily economic business decisions (Orr 2013). As described above, the band council and other leaders in the community set policy and strategic plans for economic development, and those policies are then implemented with minimal intervention by the band council. The community hires and retains competent individuals to implement and operate the projects. The proposed economic development projects, then, must "match" the prevailing values of the community from the start.

A third condition is that the First Nations community must develop a vision as well as a strategic plan to achieve that vision. This requires community participation. It is important that the entire community have a voice in development projects, as well as the parameters by which they are implemented and sustained. Once this has been determined, those competent individuals who have been chosen to run the programs will move forward with making decisions (Orr 2013).

In summary, the action of the federal government toward economic development for First Nations people has in the past been based upon a government-mandated third-party legal system. This process has meant that the economic development of First Nations land is driven by the private sector, with the support of the federal government. In turn, when conflict between First Nations and the developer emerges, the resolution of the conflict is referred to a third party, the courts. The new approach to economic development has recently changed due to the courts' insistence that the federal government has a "duty to consult and accommodate" First Nations people when it involves economic development that might have some impact on their Aboriginal rights. For example, the licensing of fisheries has long been an established practice and nearly all the licences were awarded to non-Aboriginal people. More recently, however, the courts have ruled that Fisheries and Oceans must change these actions. This has affected those non-Aboriginal people who have held these licences for nearly a century; they have strenuously objected to the change. The change comes about because First Nations people, traditionally excluded from obtaining these licences, now have an Aboriginal right to fish. In addition, in other cases the courts have ruled that their exclusion was discriminatory and that it had to cease. In the end, the revised policies may improve the economic situation of First Nations people, given that they will now be eligible to hold these licences.

Recent Changes

First Nations people have been able to use various sections of the 1982 repatriation of the Constitution and the enactment of the Charter of Rights and Freedoms as a springboard for obtaining justice and equality. As such, since the 1980s some changes in the relationship between First Nations and the federal government have emerged. For example, First Nations people have been able to enshrine their rights (yet undefined) in the Constitution. They also have used the courts to intervene in conflicts between the federal government and First Nations. While the courts have not always sided with First Nations positions, there has been a remarkable change in the federal government's attitudes toward First Nations people. This is partly based on Supreme Court of Canada decisions over the past thirty years. Land settlements, for example, have incorporated some elements to protect First Nations culture and rights; they have also implemented limits of development by outsiders within claimed lands. Moreover, a process has been developed to take into consideration the unique circumstances of each claim, such that a single template is no longer used. Finally new land claims have not been based on the "extinguishment" philosophy but allow for self-government and control of lands by First Nations communities. In the end, the courts have forced governments to recognize their fiduciary duty as well as the overall "duty (honour) of the Crown" to consult with First Nations people when development activities are undertaken that may affect the land.

In spite of these changes, however, federal governments have still insisted on "certainty" in dealing with First Nations communities. This means that it only allows one-time land claims as well as limits on the development of natural resources within those lands. While certainty is an important element in the settlement process, First Nations people understand changes that come with time, and are much less willing to "finalize" settlements once and for all. They understand the uncertainty of political and social events and thus are much more interested in making tentative settlements in favour of renegotiating at some later time when circumstances dictate the need. First Nations have learned that over time, governments change. Policies, programs, and promises also change. For example, Guimond (2003b) argues that the Indian Act has been amended nearly 11,000 times since it was first enacted in 1876. It is no surprise that First Nations' trust in any government is very low, and that mistrust permeates all the relationships between the two parties (Alcantara 2013). Governments have a history of broken promises over agreements, powers, and incentives for First Nations communities (Kulchyski 2005; Samson 2003). Nevertheless, federal governments, upon the prodding of the private sector, have resisted any approach to settling conflicts that still leaves many questions unanswered or open ended. The private sector demands certainty in decisions before they make a commitment of time, money, and other investments in various projects. Such a philosophy fits nicely into our tort system of law in which there is always a "winner" and also a "loser." In short, the private sector requires that negotiations with First Nations people end with agreements; such agreements do not allow for future revisions on the part of First Nations people. Nevertheless, if the negotiated agreement bodes ill for the private sector in the future, companies—including mining, oil and gas, and timber—feel they can go back to the government and demand (and get) changes that are in their favour. In short, the private sector views its relationship with First Nations as contractual; such a relationship can be changed or broken at any time with few consequences. In other words, the reality is that these contracts are a one-way process; First Nations people do not have the option to renegotiate while the private sector does.

The Charter of Rights and Freedoms

One of the major lessons learned by First Nations people is that federal government decisions must always be tested in the courts. First Nations people know that most of the recent changes initiated by federal governments have originated with the Charter of Rights and Freedoms. It has only been in the past twenty years that federal governments have found themselves forced to revise old policies and legislation to address the discriminative nature of these policies (Gallagher 2013). Finally, we also note that the myriad of programs created to address the objectives and goals of the new policies are generally short-term projects lasting between one and four years. The assumption is that the "problems" will be mediated in a short span of time, thereby achieving the federal government's mission. A good example is the creation of the Truth and Reconciliation Commission, dealing with residential schools. The government apologized to Aboriginal people across Canada and set aside operating money to support the Healing Foundation for six years; the implication is that its obligations and responsibility for First Nations people is now over and that in six years all of the historical trauma impact will be neatly resolved. Likewise when it agreed to "pay" students who attended residential schools, the federal government was clear that once the payments were made, the issue was closed.

Conclusion

The term "traditional culture" refers to the knowledge, attitudes, beliefs, customs, and values that have been passed down from generation to generation within a particular group of people. Culture may be expressed through song, dance, ceremonies, spiritual beliefs, games, and other activities. Moreover, cultural traditions tend to be carried out by elders, traditional healers, and other individuals designated by the community (Kreuter and McClure 2004; FNIGC 2012). First Nations people have a cyclical understanding of life: a view that all things work together simultaneously, interconnected with complex interdependencies. The need for balance and the connection with the creative and spiritual world are key elements that underpin this world view, which contrasts strongly with the hierarchical, logical, linear, and rational viewpoints of most non-Aboriginal Canadians. Moreover, cause and effect are not perceived by First Nations people in the same way as in scientific, positivist, rationalist theory.

These world views have a significant impact on behaviour and learning. Their unique ethos has provided First Nations people with a resilience that has enabled them to rise above the troubled relations of the past. The extinguishment policies of successive governments led to the expectation that First Nations culture would have disappeared by the beginning of the twentieth century. As history shows, this did not happen. Instead, First Nations people have maintained a reverence for native traditions and land (Ali 2009).

James Anaya, a United Nations Special Rapporteur on the Rights of Indigenous Peoples, visited Canada in the summer of 2013. After meeting with federal, provincial, and Aboriginal leaders across the country, he came to some tentative conclusions with respect to the fate of First Nations people in Canada. He first observed that Canada has enacted some positive efforts, such as being one of the first countries globally to offer extensive constitutional protection to First Nations peoples. This protection established a firm ground for dealing with First Nations peoples' rights over the past three decades. In addition, the courts have been able to use the constitutional protection to make reasoned decisions on a variety of First Nations issues. Anaya noted that federal and provincial governments have attempted to address treaty claims, as well as improve the social and economic well-being of native peoples.

Anaya also made criticisms of government handling of relations with First Nations people. He observed that the Auditor General has consistently identified major funding differences between services provided to First Nations people living on reserve and those available to other Canadians (Anaya 2013). The Canadian Human Rights Commission has agreed with the Auditor General's observation, stating that the social and economic conditions of First Nations peoples are a significant human rights problem.

There have been other positive actions taken by the federal government toward the goal of reconciliation between First Nations people and non-Aboriginal Canadians. As noted above, the federal government created the Aboriginal Healing Foundation, made a public government apology in 2008 for the residential schools, and created the Truth and Reconciliation Commission. The government also has increased investment in building the self-governing capacity that First Nations people argue is essential to creating sustainable, healthy, and self-sufficient communities. However, over a century of Indian Act policies continue to undermine many First Nations peoples' self-governance capacity (Anaya 2013). There also is agreement that the government must enhance economic development opportunities.

Anaya (2013) argues that the federal government must establish a partnership with First Nations communities. The two parties must arrive at a common understanding of objectives and goals, based on respect and understanding of First Nations peoples' culture as well as their constitutional and treaty rights. When First Nations people are reassured of continued respect, friendship, and acknowledgement, a level of trust will emerge. At that time, they will have a willingness to share resources as interpreted in the treaties and will look to future relationships with the federal government.

A series of questions arise in response to the federal government's handling of relations with First Nations people. How has a government department that has wielded considerable control over a group of people for more than a century done so little to improve their social and economic position in society? How could the expenditure of over $10 billion each year for the past decade not have brought about substantive changes in the lives of First Nations people? How has the Department of Indian Affairs been able to exist for so long with so little to show for its efforts?

The following chapters will explore the position of First Nations people in Canada as well as the political and economic situation that has led to their marginal status. We also will consider how the resiliency of First Nations people has enabled them to sustain their cultural identity in spite of great obstacles.

Chapter 1

Identities

Introduction

This chapter begins with a discussion of how Aboriginal people are identified (or identify themselves), specifically those people who have been called Indians or more recently First Nations people. This is a question that has fascinated the public, vexed politicians, and frustrated Aboriginal people for many years. Nevertheless, little agreement has emerged. Even the federal government's own official data collectors—such as Statistics Canada and Aboriginal Affairs and Northern Development Canada (AANDC)—have not agreed on a single definition. In the end, the federal government (through AANDC) has unilaterally created the criteria for those who may claim Aboriginal or Indian status. Aboriginal people argue that they are the only ethno-cultural group in Canada whose membership is defined in law through a unilateral action of the federal government.

This book will focus on First Nations people with the understanding that this term refers to the legal concept of "Indian" as defined in the Indian Act. The term First Nations is used in deference to those who object to the term "Indian." In addition, the term "First Nations" is now used in the media, in government reports, and elsewhere. However, at times in the book I will use the term "Indian" as this term carries historical meaning that is enshrined in the Canadian Constitution. As such, the term "First Nations" will refer to those people recognized by the federal government as "Indians." If the discussion warrants a more general discussion of indigenous people in Canada including Inuit or Métis, I will use the term "Aboriginal." The term "Aboriginal people" is now embedded in the Charter of Rights and Freedoms and is furthermore defined in section 35(2) of the Constitution Act, 1982, as a legal entity comprising three groups: Indian, Métis, and Inuit. And, even though the existence of these groups is recognized by the Constitution, the actual definition continues to evolve, sometimes in favour of the Aboriginal people themselves and sometimes in a manner dictated by the federal government.

Some argue that cost and liability issues force the Crown to establish this definitional criteria. For example, Indians can apply for post-secondary tuition support, as well as on-reserve social programs that mirror provincial programs, such as income assistance and assisted living. However, the federal government limits the number of people who are legally defined as "Indians" as a cost issue. Reducing the number of legally defined Indians reduces the federal government costs. At the same time, provinces grow concerned: if these individuals are no longer the responsibility of the federal government (under the Indian Act), they then become the responsibility of the provincial governments.

Certainly there are costs involved with Indian people, but at the same time there are benefits accrued both to the federal government and non-Aboriginals in defining this segment of the population as Indian. History reveals the extent to which non-Aboriginal people have created wealth from the land and resources taken from First Nations people over the years far outweighs the costs. For example, the Cobalt mine land, purchased from Indian people for $40,000 in 1905, went on to generate $230 million between 1907 and 1937. In the end, federal government's insistence on controlling and defining Aboriginal people emerges out of both the colonization process as well as the belief that First Nations people are incapable of managing their own affairs. This belief continues to underlie legislation today.

The history of First Nations–government relations begins with the creation of an Indian Department in 1755 by British administration. This department was transferred to the military and remained there until 1830. At that time the administration was divided territorially into departments for Upper and Lower Canada. By 1860, the authority of Indian Affairs was transferred to the colonies, culminating in the British North America Act that specified the role of the federal government with regard to First Nations people. While the Department of Indian Affairs was created in 1880, until 1966 Indian Affairs was demoted to simply a branch within various larger departments such as Interior, Mines and Resources, or Citizenship and Immigration. In 1966, Indian Affairs and Northern Affairs were merged to create the Department of Indian Affairs and Northern Development. In 2011, Aboriginal Affairs and Northern Development Canada (AANDC) was created and is now the federal department that deals with Indians, Inuit, and Métis as well as "non-status" Indians. Its mandate and responsibilities have been shaped by history as well as unique demographic and geographic challenges.

However, it is worth noting that AANDC is just one of thirty-four federal departments and agencies involved in providing Aboriginal people with programs and services.

The Origins of Aboriginal Peoples

The Beringia theory maintains that between 11,000 and 12,000 years ago, the two glaciers along the continental divide began to separate; a corridor emerged that allowed people to move southward from the Bering Strait. This ice-free corridor enabled hunters to follow ice age mammals as they migrated south.

A more recent theory is known as the North-West Coast route, which maintains that early migrants travelled in watercraft such as skin boats, and moved southward from the Siberian coast along the land bridge of Alaska and then down to the south of North America. This process may have taken place as recently as 16,000 years ago. According to this theory, people might have reached southern North America long before the glaciers melted. Because of the lower levels of sea waters at this time, much more of the continental shelf would have been exposed; these early migrants could have gone to land at various points along their migration. Research shows that along coastal areas of British Columbia (13,000 years ago) and along the coast of Alaska, the inter-continental shelf was not covered by ice at the end of the last ice age. The remains of large land animals such as caribou and bears have been found along this coastal area. Moreover, we have some evidence that humans occupied ice-free regions along the continental shelf between 13,000 and 14,000 years ago (Dixon 1999).

Today new evidence suggests an alternative theory. Some of the oldest known artifacts in North America—13,000-year-old rods buried with Clovis tools and human bones unearthed at the Anzick site in the state of Montana—are made from elk antler (Hoffecker et al. 2014). The radio-carbon data show that elk had pushed into northwestern Beringia by at least 50,000 years ago, but did not advance into North America until 15,200 years ago. Hoffecker et al. (2014) suggest that Beringia, about the size of Alberta, could have been more welcoming than expected during the Last Glacial Maximum, a period of intensely cold temperatures from about 17,000 to 28,000 years ago. This fits well with one idea about the peopling of the New World, namely that the ancestors of the first Americans remained in Beringia for 10,000 years during the Last Glacial Maximum before continuing into North America.

Archaeological evidence for this scenario remains scarce, but some clues come from the Yana locality in the far west in Siberia. This locality, the earliest known in Beringia at 32,000 years old, has yielded several carved ivory ornaments and bone tools such as sewing needles (Hoffecker and Elias 2007). This evidence suggests a culture well adapted to life in the Arctic interior. The data also reveal that Yana's broad-based hunters and foragers hunted diverse game such as the steppe bison, reindeer, horses, polar foxes, and birds (Hoffecker et al. 2014). However, archaeological evidence after Yana remains elusive. In fact, Swan Point, Alaska—the site that has been most closely dated to Yana—has been given a much later date of 14,400 years ago. However, like Yana's occupants, the earliest Alaskans were broad-based hunter-gatherers, targeting everything from horses to hares.

Regardless of when these people arrived we still do not know why they came to North America. Clearly there are both "push" and "pull" factors that drive people to migrate, but in this case the specifics remain unclear and we can only speculate. Nevertheless, there is no refuting that the "first peoples" arrived in what is now Canada millennia before European settlers.

Population Size

Regardless of the origin of these people, what knowledge do we have of the "pre-history" population on this continent? First of all, we know that the period of 800 to 1200 CE experienced a "climatic optimum," in which climatic conditions in North America, particularly in terms of agriculture, were extremely favourable. As such, the food base for these early peoples was revolutionized: they began to plant and harvest crops of beans, squash, and corn. These excellent climatic conditions allowed for a long-term generation of food, such that the new world could support a population well beyond what has been widely believed (Daschuk 2013). The archaeological site at Mantle, Ontario has revealed that the Aboriginal population was extensive, with plant cultivation as the main food source. At the same time, there is agreement that around 1259 CE a huge volcanic eruption brought an end to the "climatic optimum" period, generating deteriorating conditions for these early peoples. Daschuk (2013) observes that the subsequent eruption of Mount Kuwae (near Fiji) in 1453 further compromised agricultural conditions. Overall, demographers estimate there were between 3 million and 100 million Aboriginal people in North and South America at the beginning of the sixteenth century (Dobyns 1966); numbers vary because of different projection models and different assumptions about the ecological carrying capacity of a locality. Nevertheless, all agree that a substantial population of Aboriginal people lived in North America prior to its discovery by Europeans.

Many have argued that the higher end of the population estimate is not a tenable number to use as a baseline. However, there is more of a consensus that about 3 million Aboriginal people were living in North America. Moreover, all agree that no matter what the baseline, the indigenous population decreased at a rate of about 1.5 percent per year for the 500 years following contact (Daschuk 2013). In short, over that period of time, about 95 percent of the Aboriginal population died off so that in Canada, the Aboriginal population by the beginning of the twentieth century was just over 100,000.

What brought about such a decline in the population? We noted above that the climatic conditions began to undermine the carrying capacity of the land. In Canada, the early impact of settlers on indigenous people was minimal. It was not until the mid-seventeenth century that war, disease, and the fur trade began to irrevocably change the lives of indigenous people and their culture. The introduction of the horse around 1730 also revolutionized the western Aboriginal social structure and economy.

As more settlers entered the country in the eighteenth and nineteenth centuries, the effect of invisible new microbes wrought massive loss of life (Daschuk 2013). Settlers introduced a range of diseases, which by the mid-1700s had effected major demographic changes within Aboriginal communities in the eastern part of North America. The death of old people through disease meant that the old social structure operated less efficiently. The death of young men and women, the providers of food and procreators, also had significant effects.

Ironically, the impact of major diseases in Canada was good news for the settlers and the colonial government. As Aboriginal communities decreased in size, new lands became available for settlers. Disease was also linked to more "intermediate" impacts. For example, traders were able to utilize the clothes of indigenous peoples who had died from disease or famine. Merchants who collected furs discovered that to make fine beaver hats for the European market, they had to have furs that did not have the long, exterior "guard" hairs. When First Nations people used furs, they required roughly between five and eight skins per coat and they did not mind these guard hairs of the fur. Over time as the clothes were worn by First Nations peoples, these guard hairs wore off, leaving only the soft under-wool of the pelt that hat makers desired; at the time they did not have technology to remove the guard hairs. Hence, the epidemics benefitted fur traders as well-worn coats could be obtained free (Daschuk 2013).

The period of 1700 to 1900 was two centuries of continual disease epidemics that decimated the Aboriginal population with a range of diseases including smallpox, whooping cough, measles, influenza, and scarlet fever. Moreover, these diseases recurred over time and in different locations as the fur traders and settlers—mostly immune—moved from one location to the next, infecting new First Nations communities. Colonial governments were aware and understood the magnitude of the impact of these diseases, but failed (or were not able) to organize a preventive strategy.

During the years between 1877 and 1882 famine also took hold, leading to further decline of First Nations populations in Western Canada. According to Daschuk (2013), the colonial government refused to supply rations to First Nations people; hunger was used to leverage treaties and reserves. In 1885, the assistant Indian Commissioner, Hayter Reed, instituted many restrictive policies on First Nations people, including the pass system (a requirement that First Nations people living on a reserve had to seek permission from their local Indian Agent to travel beyond its boundaries). Daschuk further notes that Prime Minister John A. Macdonald sought to starve Indians onto reserves. And even when treaties were signed, the government ignored its promises to support First Nations people in times of need. As First Nations people were settled onto reserves, new diseases such as tuberculosis (unknown to First Nations people until 1870) became a major cause of death in the First Nations communities; no help was provided to them.

The end result of this tumultuous period was the four "Ds" that brought First Nations people to their marginal niche in today's society: Disease, Disorientation, Disempowerment, and Discord. By the beginning of the twentieth century, the government believed its policies of extinguishment were meeting with success since the size of the First Nations population had decreased to around 100,000, the use of Aboriginal languages was on the decline (with commensurate increases in the use of English and French), and traditional cultural activities were also in decline.

Defining "Indian"

The answer to the question "who are you?" should be straightforward. We all have various dimensions to our identity, and so the context of the question will influence the answer. From a cultural perspective, most groups have the right and ability to define their own membership. Social boundaries are set and criteria are presented to define who falls within a particular social category. The criteria might be language, phenotypical traits, geographical location, or other cultural traits. However, as we shall see, there has been no continuous definition of First Nations people over the years.

All of this has been circumvented by the introduction of the consolidated Indian Act in 1876. Guimond (2003b) describes "fuzzy definitions" and "changing identities" used by the Indian Act to define the Aboriginal peoples of Canada.

"Indian" is a legal term and has specific meaning embedded in law as well as in the Constitution. By contrast, the term First Nations—now in wide usage—is a social term with no legal definition. It was introduced in the 1970s when the National Indian Brotherhood (now the Assembly of First Nations) sought to identify their members in such a way as to clearly demarcate a difference between them and other non-Aboriginal Canadians; the Brotherhood found the term "Indian" offensive. While the term First Nations is used by three levels of government, it has no legal standing and the definition remains unclear. However, as we shall see below, this is not the case for the term "Indian."

The first European settlers named the Indigenous peoples "Indians." They did not understand nor wish to understand the complexities of tribal affiliation, cultural or linguistic differences, or regional variations. Settlers simply lumped all Indigenous people into a single category regardless of different languages, clothing, phenotypical traits, and cultural attributes. It made little difference if an individual was Ojibwa, Cree, or Blood. Over the course of several generations, a degree of biological mixing between Indians and non-Indians led to the emergence of a new group of Aboriginal people—the Métis. Local non-Aboriginals could still distinguish among themselves, Métis, and Indians. However, strangers entering the community often found the distinction more difficult, although they would soon learn the boundaries of the categories.

Prior to the early 1800s there was enough European settlement that the colonies began to implement legislation pertaining to Indians and the land they occupied, for example, the Royal Proclamation. British North Americans' initial definitions generally focused on cultural or linguistic attributes although at times "blood quantum" factors were used. Inheritance rules had to be established to ensure that individuals from the next generation were properly identified. Thus, the first rule of legislation was that inheritance and heritage would pass down through the male line, as with the British and French traditions, even though many Indian societies traced their inheritance and heritage through the female line. If a given individual wished to opt out of his or her legal identification as an Indian, there was a means to do so, although the change would be irreversible. In fact, the government introduced the process of enfranchisement. Innes (2013) describes how an "enfranchised" individual would be paid $400 to have his or her name removed from the Indian Roll. In the case of such a redefinition, individuals lost their legal status and any accompanying rights and responsibilities. For example, if an Indian wanted to own a piece of land "fee simple," he or she had to renounce his or her Indian status. Alternatively, government officials could coerce individuals into becoming non-Indians through the process of enfranchisement. If an individual Indian had obtained a certain education level, spoke English or French fluently, served in the armed services, or was integrated into the economic system, he or she would unilaterally be struck from the Roll. This involuntary process was particularly active in the early 1920s, although it was enforced until the 1980s. During this period, the Superintendent General was given power to declare any Indian over the age of twenty-one fit for enfranchisement (Taylor 1983). It is now estimated that nearly five thousand people were both voluntarily and involuntarily enfranchised. Moreover, enfranchised individuals' offspring (and their offspring) who wished to be "Indians" could never obtain Indian status, meaning that about 250,000 Indians subsequently were denied status through the enfranchisement process over the years.

In the original Indian Act, the term Indian meant any male person of Indian blood who belonged to a particular band as well as any child of such person and any woman who is or was lawfully married to such a person. Then in 1906, the Indian Act was amended to define a "qualified person" as a male individual other than an Indian. It would not be until 1951 that amendments to the Indian Act redefined the term Indian and defined Indian women as legal "qualified persons."

However, Indian Affairs (which itself has undergone numerous name changes over the years) has chosen to use the Indian Act as the sole criteria for determining identity for legal purposes. Long ago Indian Affairs implemented a register that identifies all those people who are legal Indians; this has become the basis for determining status today and in the future. This "Indian Roll" was established in 1876 and is part of the Indian Act, explicitly defining a specific subset of people known as Registered Indians. As such, the term "status Indian" is redundant: an Indian is by definition status. However, there are lots of people who culturally and personally identify themselves as Indian but given that Indian Affairs does not recognize them as such, they are known as—and call themselves—non-status Indians. Recently the courts have suggested that there is no difference between Métis, status, and non-status Indians, but this decision has been appealed and it will take some time to see the outcome of this appeal.

Until the 1950s, the federal government maintained poor records in regard to the Indian Roll in addition to various treaties. As such, over time, thousands of people have been added, omitted, or struck from the Indian Roll held in Ottawa. As noted in the Introduction, there is plenty of evidence that government officials resisted including new names on the Roll for fear of associated liability. Indian Agents and other government officials were constantly inventing strategies to eliminate names from the legal Roll, a process that continues today. The Double Mother rule was part of the old Indian Act: Individuals whose mother and paternal grandmother were non-Indian could remain on the Roll until they turned twenty-one and then they lost their Indian status. In other cases, if a woman refused to identify the status of her child's father, the automatic assumption by Indian Affairs was that the father was non-Indian.

Historical Context

Some further context is relevant here. We have seen that the term Indian is embedded in the Indian Act and thus has a legal definition. However, there have been several historical versions of the Indian Act. The status criteria became blurred over time and with assimilation. Until the late 1950s, Indian Affairs gave away little information about whose names were included on the Roll. Those living on rural reserves had no idea that they or their children might be removed from it. However, more and more First Nations people began to ask questions, and legal challenges began to emerge.

Until the introduction of Bill C-31 in 1985, the conferment of Indian status followed a patrilineal system. The rules were complex. If an Indian woman married a non-Indian man, she would lose her Indian status, and so would her children. Conversely, if a non-Indian woman married an Indian man, she and her children would automatically become Indians. On the other hand, if a male Indian married a non-Indian female, he retained his status. However, the international courts did not support the Canadian decisions. International pressure as well as pressure by Canadian First Nations women's organizations, were brought to bear on the Canadian government to change the criteria. Specifically the changes were focused on section 12(1)(b). The initial court cases (*Mary Two Axe Early*, *Jeannette Lavell*, and *Yvonne Bedard*) challenged the validity of this section in the 1970s, arguing that it violated the Canadian Bill of Rights' guarantee of gender equality. They lost their cases. However, Sandra Lovelace went on to challenge this section of the Indian Act for violating the International Covenant on Civil and Political Rights. The United Nations Human Rights committee (1978) heard her case and found that the Indian Act did indeed deprive women and their children of the right to enjoy their culture within their communities. Thus, when the Constitution and Charter came into effect in 1982, the federal government began to craft Bill C-31 to rectify those provisions of the Indian Act to bring it into compliance with both the Charter and the international covenant.

In 1985, the government introduced Bill C-31. The goal of the bill was to remove sex discrimination. Bill C-31 introduced a new definition of Status (Cannon 2004). However, First Nations people objected to Bill C-31. When the case went before the Supreme Court of British Columbia, the court ruled that section 12 and 13 of the old Indian Act violated the Charter and as such it was discriminatory. The judge's ruling called for the immediate registration of all descendants of women who had married non-Indians at any time prior to 1985, no matter how far in the past. The federal government appealed the decision and when the Court of Appeal rendered its decision, it found that section 12 and 13 of the Indian Act was indeed discriminatory but in a more limited manner than had the lower court. They ruled that the "forward-looking rules" in Bill C-31 regarding registration were not discriminatory. Sharon McIvor's application for leave to appeal to the Supreme Court of Canada (wanting the court to reinstate all individuals who could prove matrilineal decent from 1867 to 1985 as Indians) was dismissed. The federal government was given one year to make changes to Bill C-31. This was done with the introduction and passing of Bill C-3 (Gender Equity in Indian Registration Act) that substituted sections 6 and 7 for the old sections 12 and 13.

In addition, the court ruled that the rights of those women previously denied Indian status by virtue of the old Indian Act needed to be reinstated. The singular focus was that Bill C-31 was discriminatory in the manner in which it dealt with the transition from the past registration rules to the future non-discriminatory policy. The 2009 ruling by the Appeal Court was accepted by the federal government. First Nations women did not appeal the case as they simply did not have the funds to sustain further court challenges.

The courts' decision provided for the restoration of Indian status and band membership to individuals who had lost it as a result of the discriminatory clause in the old Indian Act. For example those individuals who were denied Indian status under the "Double Mother" clause in the old Indian Act were reinstated. In addition, Bill C-31 allowed for women and the children of women who had been stripped of their status because of section 12(1)(b) to be recognized as status Indians (Canada 1987). The end result of this new bill meant that some people who had lost or were denied status because of the discriminatory sections of the older version of the Indian Act would be reinstated on the

Roll and, perhaps, reinstated on their respective band lists. As of 2013, approximately 125,000 individuals were added to the Indian Roll—approximately 60 percent of all those who applied to be reinstated.

Now a new question emerged as to how Indian status is transmitted from one generation to the next. The new bill (Bill C-3) created two different types of Indians. If an individual was on the Roll prior to 1985, then this individual would continue on the Roll and would be granted "section 6(1) status." If an individual had been removed from the Roll prior to 1985 but was reinstated due to the provisions of Bill C-31, then the individual would be assigned "section 6(2) status." For these individuals, the difference is inconsequential as both types are considered "bona fide" status and fall within the Indian Act. However, under the new rules, when mixing different section types through marriage (including common-law unions), the outcome for offspring can be quite different. For example:

A section 6(1) marries a section 6(1): the children are section 6(1).
A section 6(1) marries a section 6(2): the children are section 6(1).
A section 6(2) marries a section 6(2): the children are section 6(1).
A section 6(1) marries a non-Indian: the children are section 6(2).
A section 6(2) marries a non-Indian: the children are not Indians.

Due to the changes in Bill C-31 and Bill C-3, it is estimated that the number of people with status will grow substantially over the next fifty to sixty years. However, given the new rules for passing on Indian heritage, by the end of the twenty-first century, it is expected that there will be fewer than today.

Bill C-31 Challenge

Bill C-31 ensured that status men, their wives, and their children, would continue to enjoy their status. However, for women and children who had lost status because of section 12(1)(b) (referred to as the "marrying out" rule), they would regain their status but in a "second class" category. Thus, people who had never lost their status could confer status to their children and grandchildren. On the other hand, for those "re-instated," status could be conferred onto their children but not to their grandchildren. Section 6 of the revised Indian Act contains the provisions that determine the eligibility of individuals for Indian status. McIvor argued that section 6 of the Indian Act violated section 15 of the Charter. The Court of Appeal for British Columbia ruled that the Indian Act still discriminated between men and women with respect to having status.

Bill C-31 created three categories of Indians: first, it ensured that any person who held full status (or was entitled to be registered) prior to 1985 would continue to have status. Second, women who were previously removed from the registered list would be reinstated. Finally, a third category created by Bill C-31 would give partial status to persons who have only one parent registered under section 6(1) and would establish a "second generation" cut-off rule through the creation of section 6(2). This last category creates a "two parent rule" in that a child who has only one parent with section 6(2) status is not entitled to any Indian status at all. In short, a second generation of children with only one status parent (6[2]) loses all entitlements to Indian Status.

The federal government was given one year to resolve the issue, at which point it introduced Bill C-3. The main amendment proposed in Bill C-3 was the addition of section 6(1)(c.1) to the Indian Act, providing status to any individual

- whose mother lost Indian status upon marrying a non-Indian man, whose father is a non-Indian,
- who was born after the mother lost Indian status but before April 17, 1985, unless the individual's parents married each other prior to that date, and
- who had a child with a non-Indian on or after September 4, 1951.

Since the introduction of Bill C-31, all people with status have been subject to the "second generation cut-off rule," which occurs as a result of two successive generations of parenting with non-Indians of either sex. However, the act's gender discrimination was not fully remedied by Bill C-31. At the McIvor trial, the judge held that section 6 of the Indian Act violated the equality rights of Sharon McIvor and Jacob Grismer (her

Changes under Bill C-3

Bill C-3 notes that individuals who can answer "yes" to *all* three of the following questions may be eligible for registration:

1. Did your grandmother lose her Indian status as a result of marrying a non-Indian?
2. Is one of your parents registered, or entitled to be registered, under sub-section 6(2) of the Indian Act?
3. Were you, or one of your siblings, born on or after September 4, 1951?

son) under equality guarantees in section 15 of the Charter. The equal benefit of law at issue is the right to transmit Indian status and cultural identity to future generations. Individuals like McIvor and Grismer face the "second generation cut-off" rule one generation sooner than male Indians who married and had children with non-Indians prior to 1985.

Moreover, it is puzzling that under section 6(1)(c.1)(iv), an individual must have a child before being eligible for registration under section 6(1)(c.1). The change in the Indian Act as a result of Bill C-3 also creates administrative inefficiencies, as a person eligible for registration under section 6(1)(c.1) will have to apply not only for registration of his or her child but also to change his or her own registration from section 6(2) to 6(1)(c.1) so the child may be registered (Canadian Bar Association 2010). This is especially true where the section 6(1)(c.1) person has parented a child with a non-Indian. This raises a potential concern for "family status" discrimination, because some people will only be "bumped up" from section 6(2) to 6(1) status if they parent a child (Canadian Bar Association 2010).

The Canadian Bar Association (2010) goes on to state that section 9 of the new Indian Act is problematic given that it removes the right of individuals to sue the federal government for not providing them with status as a result of the gender discrimination addressed by the Bill. If the federal government can be presumed to have been aware that Bill C-31 was not consistent with the Charter as far back as 1985, and did not act for over twenty years until the McIvor decision reached the BC Court of Appeal, the Canadian Bar Association suggests that including such a provision could make Bill C-3 vulnerable to further Charter challenges.

In the end, Bill C-3 will eliminate gender discrimination, but only for some individuals. As demonstrated below, others will continue to experience discrimination by receiving lesser or no status because they had an Indian grandmother, instead of an Indian grandfather. A grandchild born before 1985 descended from an Indian grandfather will be able to transmit status for one generation longer than those descended from an Indian grandmother.

The new Bill C-3 will continue to exclude grandchildren who are descended from status women who had children with non-status men in common-law unions. It will also continue to exclude the female children and grandchildren of status men who partnered with non-status women in common-law unions. Finally, male children and grandchildren of status fathers who co-parented with non-status women in common-law unions will have status. In addition, gender differences are evident in view of "common-law relationships." Bill C-31 grants full section 6(1)(a) status to the male child of a status father who lived in a common-law relationship with a non-status mother of his children. However, children of the status mother who lived in a common-law relationship with the non-status father of her children whom the registrar previously struck from the Roll are assigned to section 6(1)(c).

All of these issues were reviewed and acknowledged by the Standing Committee on Indian Affairs when they reviewed Bill C-3. As a result of their review, they proposed changes (as did the Aboriginal section of the Canadian Bar Association) but the Speaker of the House, informed by the ruling conservatives, found this unacceptable, ruling that the proposed amendments were out of order. Bill C-3 is now law and was challenged by Lynn Gehl, an Algonquin Anishinaabe-kwe woman and Indigenous human rights advocate from Ontario. In the summer of 2015, the Ontario Superior Court of Justice in Toronto ruled that Gehl had not been discriminated against and thus the challenge was dismissed.

A Definitional Hiccup

After thirteen years in the court, the Federal Court of Canada ruled (2013) that Métis and non-status Indians should be considered Indians under the Constitution Act, 1982, thereby placing them under federal jurisdiction. There are many different definitions for Métis. The Métis National Council defines a Métis as a person who self-identifies as a Métis, is distinct from other Aboriginal peoples, is of historic Métis Nation ancestry, and is accepted by the Métis Nation. This definition is similar to that of the Powley Supreme Court of Canada decision that created a "test" to be used to assess whether a claimant is entitled to exercise Métis rights.

In making his decision, Judge Phelan said that he was setting aside the current rules of "blood-lines" or "blood purity" utilized by the federal

The Powley Test

The Powley test includes the following components:

A person claiming to be Métis must be linked to a Métis community that has historical origins;
he or she must self-identify as a member of a Métis Community;
he or she must be accepted by the Métis community;
the Métis community must have historic identification; and
the contemporary Métis community must also be identified.

government because they are antiquated and racist. He posited that criteria based upon geography, cultural location, and membership in an Aboriginal community or organization were more appropriate. He went on to say that the recognition of Métis and non-status Indians as Indian should be accorded a further level of respect and reconciliation by removing the constitutional uncertainty surrounding these two groups. He further noted that the argument that politicians alone should define status was contrary to basic democratic values. Judge Phelan concluded that criteria relating to geographical or cultural location or membership in a First Nations community organization are more civilized ways to define Aboriginality than "blood purity." This ruling is similar to the 1939 Supreme Court decision that included Inuit under federal government legal authority even though they were not Indians and not subject to the Indian Act. What we do not know is how this decision will affect Aboriginal rights under section 35 of the Constitution Act, 1982, or the federal Indian Act. However, the federal government has appealed this decision and it is expected that the case will come before the Supreme Court of Canada for a final resolution. In 2014, the Federal Court of Appeal heard the case and in most instances agreed with Justice Phelan. However, they did not agree that non-status Indians should be regarded as Indians. As a result, the case now will be appealed to the Supreme Court (Bell 2014).

Indian Status versus Band Membership

Bill C-31 gave First Nations communities the opportunity to develop and control their own band membership. Each community was given two years to develop criteria for membership. For the first time, this Bill meant that status alone did not necessarily imply band membership. If First Nations communities did not develop their own criteria for band membership, then Indian Affairs would retain control over membership and use the conditions specified in the new revised Indian Act. Furi and Wherrett (2003) report that after the two-year period, over half the bands went along with the conditions stipulated in the Indian Act. However, the remaining bands developed three major types of band membership rules. Some established criteria that specified that at least one parent had to be an official "Indian" in order to become a band member. Others felt that more stringent rules were needed, and require that both parents have status in order to become a member of a band. Finally, a sizable number of bands introduced "blood quantum" as the criteria. The actual amount of "Indian blood" varies but it is a criterion that is reminiscent of the American rule of descent.

Conclusion

So we return to the question: "Who is Aboriginal?" We know that section 35(2) of the Constitution Act, 1982, recognizes Aboriginal people, but unfortunately we are not told what criteria will be used to identify them. Nevertheless, for "Indians," we have the Indian Act and the Indian Registry, both controlled by Aboriginal Affairs and Northern Development Canada. It is very clear, from this perspective, who has the legal right to be called an "Indian," with criteria identified under the Indian Act. In short, there is a legal definition for Indians, even if the definition itself is not fully accepted by First Nations people.

Chapter 2

Population Profile of First Nations in the Twenty-First Century

Introduction

We saw in Chapter 1 how the First Nations population dropped precipitously following European contact. Thorton (2000) and Wilson and Northcott (2008) suggest that in the sixteenth century between 200,000 and 2 million Aboriginal people lived in Canada. Charbonneau (1984) and Romaniuc (2003) establish that by the end of the nineteenth century, just over 100,000 First Nations people resided in Canada. However, since this time, there has been a major and continuous increase in the First Nations population. By 1951 the First Nations population had increased to 160,000. As a result, the proportion of Aboriginal peoples in Canada continues to increase (4.3 percent of the total population in 2011 compared to 3.8 in 2006). People claiming Aboriginal identity in 2011 made up about 1.5 million Canadians representing an overall 20 percent increase over the past decade compared to a 5 percent increase for the non-Aboriginal population in the same time period. This increase is expected to continue until late in the twenty-first century and will peak at just over 5 percent of the total Canadian population at that time.

Statistical information regarding Aboriginal people is provided by two main sources: the 2011 census and the Department of Aboriginal Affairs and Northern Development. Thus, unless otherwise stated, the statistical data presented in this book are from one of these two sources. It should be noted that these two official sources of information about Aboriginal people use different definitions of who is an Aboriginal and thus there may be some discrepancies if the reader compares the two sources.

Today First Nations people (those who are considered by the federal government to be registered or status Indians) now represent nearly a million people. Between 2006 and 2011, the number of First Nations people increased by nearly 14 percent while the number of Aboriginal people without registered Indian status increased by over 60 percent. The majority of the First Nations population lives in Ontario and the four western provinces. First Nations people represent about 51 percent of the total Aboriginal population and 2.6 percent of the total Canadian population. First Nations people make up the largest share of the total population in NWT and Yukon as well as a significant population in Manitoba and Saskatchewan. About one half of First Nations people in Canada live on a reserve or settlement although this varies across the country. For example, in Ontario, about 37 percent live on Indian lands while in Quebec, 70 percent do so. Given that there are virtually no reserves in the NWT, no First Nations people live on reserves there. Table 2-1 reveals the geographical distribution of the Aboriginal population in Canada.

Table 2-1   Distribution of First Nations People (Indians) across Canadian Provinces and Territories; First Nations People as Percentage of Population by Province and Territory (2011)

Province/Territory	Distribution of total FN population by province/territory (percentage)	Percentage of population that is FN (estimated)
Newfoundland and Labrador	2.3	7.1
Prince Edward Island	0.2	1.6
Nova Scotia	2.6	3.7
New Brunswick	1.9	3.1
Quebec	9.7	1.8
Ontario	23.6	2.4
Manitoba	13.4	16.7
Saskatchewan	12.1	15.6
Alberta	13.7	6.2
British Columbia	18.2	5.4
Yukon	0.8	23.1
Northwest Territories	1.6	51.9
Nunavut	0.01	6.3
Total	100% (851,660)	

Source: Statistics Canada 2011c, *Aboriginal Peoples in Canada: First Nations People, Metis and Inuit, Statistics,* 9

Population Change

The total population of any group of people is affected by three factors: fertility (number of births), mortality (number of deaths), and in- and out-migration. In the case of First Nations people, the extent of "in- and out-migration" is estimated to be as follows: approximately 7,000 First Nations people moved in and out of Canada over the past five years, resulting in little net change in the overall population. First Nations Canadians retain their status regardless of their country of residence while those First Nations people from elsewhere would not be considered status, although they will be considered "First Nations" in the census. In the context of First Nations, the idea of "migration" could also be interpreted as the number of people whose First Nations identity has been either extinguished or added to the government Roll; in other words, the number of people who are considered to have status according to the Canadian government. Recall, however, that the concept of First Nations is a social definition and has no legal basis; as such, an exact identification of people who are or are not First Nations is impossible. As a surrogate measure we use the number of people with status in Canada as defined by AANDC. We now turn to the three factors that make up a population.

Fertility

Since the mid-twentieth century, the fertility rate of First Nations people has declined substantially, although it still remains much higher than the non-Aboriginal population. In the 1950s the fertility rate for First Nations people was 6.4 children per woman, while for non-Aboriginal people it was 4.2. By the end of the twentieth century, First Nations fertility stood at about 2.6 compared to 1.65 for non-Aboriginal people. Since the beginning of the twenty-first century, these levels have continued to decrease for both groups (see Table 2-2). Malefant and Morency (2011) have projected the fertility rates of First Nations people to 2018 and conclude that the current levels of fertility will remain stable over that time. It is estimated that by 2018, 30 percent of the total annual natural population increase in Canada will be accounted for by the Aboriginal population (Lalonde 2006).

Mortality

Tjepkema and Wilkins (2011) as well as Wilkins et al. (2008) have shown that mortality rates for First Nations people are much higher

Table 2-2   Fertility Rates (Children per Woman), 1974–2010

Year	First Nations	Canadian Average
1974	4.42	1.85
1980	3.41	1.69
1985	3.24	1.61
1990	2.83	1.71
1995	2.76	1.67
2000	2.58	1.65
2010	2.56	1.58

Source: Adapted from Loh and George 2003

than for non-Aboriginal people. Consider the infant mortality rate: the average Canadian rate is 8 out of 1,000 births, but it is double that for First Nations people. Boyer (2014) further points out that the infant mortality rate for First Nations on reserve is seven times higher than the national average.

The data reveal a life expectancy of sixty-eight years and seventy-four years for First Nations men and women respectively; this is approximately ten years less than it is for non-Aboriginal people. Projecting into the future, Tjepkema and Wilkins (2011) conclude that the differential between the two groups will decrease, but a significant difference will continue well into 2030. Why is there such a high mortality rate for First Nations people? Evidence suggests that it reflects both geographical location and poverty. Poverty has consistently been linked to poorer health, homelessness, crowded living conditions, and lack of employment, all of which lead to higher rates of mortality.

Suicide

Suicide is the leading cause of death for First Nations people between the ages of ten and forty-four. In fact a third of all deaths among First Nations youth are attributable to suicide. Between the ages of ten and twenty-nine, First Nations youth on reserves are five to six times more likely to die of suicide than their non-Aboriginal peers (Health Canada 2003). These numbers reflect a recent trend: this has not always been the case. Until the mid-1970's, the suicide rate for First Nations and non-Aboriginal people was almost identical. However, in recent years, First Nations people in Canada have suffered from much higher rates of suicide than the general Canadian population. In fact, the data reveal that the overall Canadian suicide rate has declined, while in many First

Nations communities, rates have continued to rise for the past two decades. Although there are enormous variations across communities, bands, and Nations, the overall suicide rate among First Nations communities is about twice that of the total Canadian population. Suicide for First Nations female youth is eight times higher than other female Canadian youth and for adult women the rate is three times the national average.

First Nations males are more likely to die by suicide while First Nations females make attempts more often, although this gender difference is smaller than among the non-Aboriginal population. In a population survey in the Calgary region from 1999 to 2002, First Nations people were three times more likely than the general population in the Calgary Health Region to sustain injuries due to suicide. They also found that nearly 16 percent of the First Nations adult population had attempted suicide in their lifetime. Females were more likely than males to have made an attempt (18 percent compared to 13 percent). More importantly, nearly one third of adult First Nations individuals reported having had suicidal thoughts during their lifetime (Kirmayer 2007).

In 2000, suicide accounted for approximately 1,079.91 potential years of life lost (see Table 2-3). This is nearly three times the 2001 Canadian rate. Potential years of life lost is the number of years of life "lost" when a person dies "prematurely," defined as dying before age seventy-five. For example, a suicide at age twenty-five results in fifty potential years of life lost. Comparing First Nations and non-Aboriginal youth reveals that the First Nations male suicide rate for those aged fifteen to twenty-four is 127 out of 100,000 while for non-Aboriginal males in the same age cohort, the rate is 24. For First Nations females in the same age grouping, the rate is nearly 30 per 100,000 while for non-Aboriginal females of a comparable age it is just over 6 (Chandler 2005).

Table 2-3   Potential Years of Life Lost (PYLL) for Unintentional Injury and Suicide, First Nations On-Reserve, 2000 (Rates per 100,000 People)

	Unintentional Injury	Suicide
Total Population	2,571.7	1,096.2
Males	3,376.2	1,517.9
Females	1,688.7	633.3

Source: Health Canada (First Nations and Inuit Health Branch in-house statistics) 2000

In some communities, suicide is a common form of mortality. However, the data reveal that while suicides are rife in some places, in other communities they are virtually non-existent. Hence researchers have begun to look at specific environmental or structural factors within given First Nations communities that might produce these differences. We must also consider the relationship between cultural continuity and community. Chandler and Lalonde (1998) point out that some First Nations communities are considerably wealthier, better housed, more educated, and more likely to contain working, dual income parents than others. But this does not coincide, as one might expect, with low suicide rates. Suicide rates within First Nations communities are reduced slightly with increased wealth, but the correlation is low. The highest rates of suicide are in those communities that lie on the edge of large urban centers. This dispels another commonly held assumption that isolation and poverty are necessarily linked to suicide. Chandler and Lalonde (1998) find that communities that have built cultural facilities are more than twice as likely to have local control over health care service; however, in these communities high suicide rates persist. Their research in British Columbia shows that in communities where there is a focus on cultural continuity for their young people, suicide rates are low or non-existent.

Ethnic Mobility

Examination of the censuses over the past half century reveals that ethnic mobility is an important factor for estimating growth and composition of the First Nations population (Siggner and Costa 2005). This term refers to the extent to which people enter and leave (defined by themselves or by some external agent) a particular ethnic category. Several factors, such as legislative changes, are involved in an individual's decision to engage in ethnic mobility. In other cases the federal government makes unilateral decisions about who can claim Indian status. In some instances, Métis were given the option of being "First Nations" or "white." This of course, complicates the question of how many people are defined as First Nations each year. Using a conservative definition of First Nations as equal to "registered Indian," the data suggest that we will continue to see the number of people defined by the federal government as First Nations (Indians) increasing for the next several decades. Nevertheless, these projections show that as the federal government redefines who is a First Nations person, people move in and out of this category. For example, as noted previously, until 1985, a woman who married a non-status man would lose her own status.

Conversely, if a non-status woman married a status man, she would automatically be given status. With the passing of Bill C-31 in 1985 this definition changed and well over 125,000 people were redefined as Indian. However, it is estimated that with this new Bill and other recent changes to the definition, the number of First Nations will begin to decrease after 2070 (Clatworthy 2005). Perhaps one of the most startling projections is that of Clatworthy (2013) who confirms the work of Malefant and Morency (2011) that under the current rules about status, there will be a consistent increase in the First Nations population (as defined by AANDC) until 2070 and then there will a massive decrease such that by the end of this century, there will be fewer First Nations people than today. His projections are based upon fertility and mortality rates, the current rules of status, and other various legislative imperatives that have been unilaterally adopted by the federal government, for example, intermarriage rules and paternity rules.

Population Projections

Malefant and Morency (2011) have made projections about the First Nations population. They predict a steady increase in the number of First Nations people, possibly reaching 1.25 million by 2031. As such, the annual growth rate would be just below 2 percent each year—more than double that of the rest of Canada. This increase in population growth will be a result of natural increase (births minus deaths), although if there are legislative changes to the definition, the actual population count may change.

Canada's First Nations peoples are relatively young: 46.2 percent are under twenty-five years old (compared to 29.4 percent of the rest of the population). Only 5.9 percent are over sixty-five (compared to 14.2 percent of the rest of the Canadian population). Table 2-4 reveals the age distribution and median age of the First Nations and non-Aboriginal populations. Closer inspection shows that this holds true across Canada. In Saskatchewan and Manitoba, the median age for First Nations is just over twenty years; this is half the non-Aboriginal population median age in those provinces. Malefant and Morency (2011) project that in 2031 the First Nations population will continue to be "young"; they estimate that the under-fourteen age group will make up between 20 and 30 percent of the First Nations population. Nevertheless, the population will continue to age such that by 2031 it is estimated that the median age for First Nations people will be between thirty-five and thirty-seven while for the rest of Canada the median age will be forty-three or forty-four.

Table 2-4   Age Distribution and Median Age for First Nations and Non-Aboriginal Population, Canada, 2011

Age	First Nations Population	Non-Aboriginal Population
0–4	11%	6%
5–9	10%	5%
10–14	10%	6%
15–24	18%	13%
25–64	46%	56%
65 and over	6%	14%
Median Age	26	41

Source: Statistics Canada 2011c, *Aboriginal Peoples in Canada: First Nations People, Metis and Inuit*, 16

There are both short- and long-term implications for such a demographic profile. For example, the large cohort of young people will soon be at the age when they enter the labour market. However, in Chapter 7, we see that these individuals will not have the requisite skills and education to participate in the primary labour market. This of course will place them in the condition of obtaining social services and not contributing to the tax base—an increasing liability for Canadians. In addition, while the Aboriginal population is young, the rest of Canada is getting older. As such, new programs and policies are being developed that focus on the aging society and neglecting necessary policies and programs that focus on young people. For example, the health system is currently gearing up to deal with the aging population with little thought of how they will deal with the increasing numbers of young Aboriginal people. Finally, it should be noted that given the large number of Aboriginal youth that will not become active participants in the social fabric of Canada, social unrest will increase, a fact that the RCMP have noted.

Clatworthy et al. (2009) show that within the next half century, children who are entitled to have status will be a minority of all the children born to the First Nations population today. Their projections show that the interplay between exogamous parenting and the new inheritance rules will have a significant impact on the number of First Nations people with status, both in the short and long term. For example, they reveal that in the first half decade of the twenty-first century, about 2,000 children annually were born into a cohort that will not be entitled to claim status. Within the next twenty-five years this will increase to over 7,000; within fifty years, well over 110,000 children will be born to that population who will not be entitled to claim status (Clatworthy et al. 2009). This of course does not mean they do not self-identify as First Nations people, but it does reflect how the federal government definitions affect the official numbers.

Migration

Recent evidence of the internal movement of First Nations people in Canada reveals differences from earlier migration patterns and from that of the rest of the population. In the past half century, we have seen a major growth in the First Nations population in urban centres. In 1950, only 7 percent of the First Nations population lived in urban areas. Dion and Coulombe (2008) also show that First Nations people have a much greater mobility rate than non-Aboriginal people. Migration from the reserve to "urban" centres does not mean that they solely move to the large Census Metropolitan Areas but that they also choose to live in rural towns. At any rate, today more than 50 percent of the First Nations population lives in urban areas. However, in the recent past, First Nations communities tended to have positive net internal migration, which contributed to the reserve population growth. This trend is estimated to stop over the next two decades. Overall, First Nations peoples' decision to migrate to the city is declining over time due to an aging population, which is less mobile than younger people (Cooke and Belanger 2006). Within an average First Nations community, just over two thirds of the individuals living on-reserve claimed to have maintained the same residence over a five-year period.

Other Aboriginal People

The other two groups of Aboriginal people in Canada (Métis and Inuit) make up about 450,000 and 60,000 people respectively. Métis represent 8 percent of the total population of the NWT, 7 percent of the Manitoba population, and 5 percent of the Saskatchewan population. Nearly three quarters of Inuit in Canada live in Inuit Nunangat, the northern area that stretches from Labrador to the NWT. This term was introduced in 2009 at the Inuit Tapiriit Kanatami meeting. It replaces the term "Inuit Nunaat," which is a Greenlandic term. The new term is from Canadian Inuktitut and refers to a geographical space that includes land, ice, and water—the homeland of Inuit. The pace of Aboriginal peoples' population growth continues to outstrip that of non-Aboriginal peoples: 20.1 percent versus 5.1 percent between 2006 and 2011. First Nations people who are not registered Indians now make up one quarter of the total Aboriginal population in Canada. In fact, in the Maritimes, about six out of ten people who identify as First Nations are not registered.

Residence and Reserves

In terms of geographic representation, historically First Nations people have been over-represented in western Canada and under-represented in the rest of Canada. As such, the proportion of First Nations people has always been higher in the West and Territories. The projections made by Malenfant and Morency (2011) suggest that this pattern will hold well into 2030. Likewise, it is projected that a majority of First Nations people will continue to live outside major metropolitan areas. Today, there are approximately 2,300 reserves across the country, comprising more than 28,000 square kilometres (about the size of Belgium). In addition, between 1975 and 2002, over 800,000 square kilometres of additional land have come under the direct control of Aboriginal groups through the comprehensive claims process, while specific claims have enabled First Nations to acquire another 861,683 square kilometres of land. Some reserves (originally rural) have gradually been surrounded by major cities such as Montreal, Vancouver, and Calgary and are now part of the urban landscape. Around 50 percent of First Nations people live on reserves, although one in ten residents living on a reserve are not First Nations people.

All together, about 3.5 million hectares are considered First Nations land. This land base has increased since 2006 and will continue to increase as land claims continue to be settled. Since 2006 about 350,000 hectares have been added to reserves, representing a 12 percent increase in their land base. During the same time period only about 500 hectares have been surrendered to the federal government.

Language

The Aboriginal population (status and non-status Indians, Inuit, and Métis) currently living in cities is composed of fifty-two distinct cultural groups speaking more than fifty Aboriginal languages from eleven major linguistic families.

Preserving First Nations culture is a strong priority among First Nations people. An Ekos research study found that 90 percent of those surveyed expressed a strong interest in participating in First Nations heritage activities, including speaking and understanding an Aboriginal language (Jedwab 2006). Today we find that just over 80 percent of the First Nations population speak English or French as a mother tongue.

(Mother tongue is defined as the first language learned at home in childhood and still understood by the individual.) The remainder speak an Aboriginal language as a mother tongue. In terms of home language, just over two thirds use English as the mode of communication at home with the remainder using an Aboriginal language. Nevertheless, almost 70 percent of First Nations people said they could speak or understand an Aboriginal language and this increases with age of the individual (Langlois and Turner 2014). However, current data reveal that only about 17 percent of Aboriginal people can conduct a fluent conversation in an Aboriginal language. Five years ago, 21 percent claimed this ability. In addition, only one in ten First Nations people claimed to speak an Aboriginal language most often at home and even fewer (8 percent) claimed they spoke an aboriginal language regularly at home. These averages would increase when looking at the North, areas with high First Nations population, and isolated reserves (Langlois and Turner 2014). At the same time there is a lower rate of facility in an Aboriginal language at those reserves adjacent to large urban areas. These results demonstrate the rapidity of language loss in First Nations communities.

In terms of Aboriginal languages spoken, Cree, Ojibway, Innu/Montagnais, Dene, and Oji-Cree are the predominant languages spoken across the country. Speakers of these languages live mainly in the western provinces. However, if we look at people reporting an Aboriginal mother tongue in Canada, the highest proportion live in Quebec, Manitoba, and Saskatchewan (Statistics Canada 2011b). We find that a majority of people who report an Aboriginal mother tongue in the languages identified above also speak this language at home. This of course explains both the loss and maintenance of the respective languages.

Overall, less than 1 percent of First Nations people claimed they could not speak in either French or English (Kroskrity and Field 2009). However, it is important to note that there is a mini revival of Aboriginal languages. The fact that there are more Aboriginal people who can converse in an Aboriginal language than there are "mother tongue" speakers is evidence. This reflects the fact that there are nearly 50,000 First Nations people who have acquired an Aboriginal language as a second language and speak it most often at home or speak it on a regular basis in their life activities (Statistics Canada 2011b). To support this concern for maintaining language, a number of First Nations communities have actively participated in Aboriginal language programs for adults who had either lost or never had the ability to speak in their Aboriginal language. This Aboriginal language revitalization is particularly noticeable in Western Canada (O'Donnell and Tait 2004). This trend may be the product of a number of adult language programs now operating in First

Nations communities and a greater interest of youth in learning to speak their Aboriginal language. The question is as follows: to what extent can this mini revival of language maintenance counteract the massive loss of language so evident in Aboriginal languages over the past half century? At present, linguists suggest that only a handful of Aboriginal languages will survive the twenty-first century.

Language Ideologies

Almost all First Nations communities have experienced significant changes as a consequence of their contact with European settlers and their subsequent incorporation into mainstream society. These transformations continue today as First Nations communities affirm the need to express their cultural and political sovereignty (Cook and Flynn 2008). Their beliefs and feelings about language and discourse are now referred to as language ideologies. These language ideologies vary from community to community, with some more explicitly acknowledged or higher on a scale of cultural salience than others. There are ideologies related to language socialization, interpersonal communication, identity construction, and storytelling, to name but a few domains that give rise to language ideologies. Moreover, in many First Nations communities, there is a willingness to give up on the "elder purism" in favour of a certain amount of flexibility such as allowing code-switching (alternating between languages) by imperfect younger speakers (Norris and Snider 2008).

While most First Nations people understand and use English or French in their everyday life, English is seen to be more "reflectionist" in that it emphasizes the denotational and referential function of words for things (Little Bear 2000). First Nations languages are viewed as more "performative," as a more powerful and creative force that embodies the natural and social worlds they inhabit. English names "stuff" but it reveals little about what the "stuff" is doing. Finally, Aboriginal languages are more descriptive than English in precisely those areas most intimately related to the social and personal identities of First Nations communities.

Family Structure

About 60 percent of the First Nations population reports never having legally married. Just over one quarter is legally married and the remainder is separated, divorced, or widowed. A little over 17 percent of the families claimed to be composed of just husband and wife, with another

12 percent living in a "common-law partnership" without children. Only 6 percent of the households consist of single childless adults while parents living on their own (separately from their children or partner) represent an additional 5 percent. However, nearly one third of First Nations families are headed by a single parent compared to just over 10 percent for non-Aboriginal families. In total, more than half of urban First Nations children live in single-parent households versus less than 20 percent for non-Aboriginal children.

The 2006 census found that young First Nations children (age six or under) were more likely than their non-Aboriginal counterparts to live in families consisting of four or more children. Over one quarter of First Nations children live within these large families. At the same time, the 2006 census showed that less than 8 percent of young non-Aboriginal children lived in families with four or more children.

First Nations children under the age of fifteen are more likely than their non-Aboriginal counterparts to live with their grandparents with neither of their parents present. The data showed that 3 percent of First Nations children were living with their grandparents while the proportion of non-Aboriginal children who lived solely with their grandparents was less than 0.5 percent. This information confirms the First Nations cultural tradition of the involvement of many people, including extended family and community members, in raising children. Furthermore, over one quarter of First Nations children received "focused attention" from Elders living in the community at least once a week. Finally, the data reveals that a greater proportion of young First Nations children were living in low-income economic families (57 percent) compared to non-Aboriginal children (21 percent).

Nevertheless, kinship and the belief in the importance of family ties is a crucial component of First Nations culture. In fact, maintaining family linkages was and still is seen as a fundamental component to the preservation of an individual's identity (Innes 2013). This is also tied to the ability of an individual to successfully carry out his or her duties to family. Finally, for many First Nations people, family means a connection to past, present, and future. In a sense, family is an individual's connection to origins and perhaps even future direction. As such, family gatherings are a way to reconnect via family histories and relationships with other family members. As Innes (2013) points out, these family gatherings provide a time and place for people to be socialized about proper etiquette and community responsibilities. For many First Nations people, this component of their culture was truncated with the implementation of the reserve system, the residential school requirements, and the redefinition of Indian with the status system. Family reunions remain important occasions to reacquaint family members. Urban First Nations people have had to make some accommodations in order to maintain family connections; many older women could not live on the reserve (as a result of the old Indian Act). Nevertheless, for urban families, family connections have had an added importance for cementing family bonds. As such, many urban First Nations people have learned the cultural values of kinship and, as best they can, how to carry out their responsibilities (Innes 2013).

Education

Nearly 40 percent of First Nations adults have less than a high school education. However, younger First Nations adults reveal increasing levels of education and in particular, there are growing numbers of post-secondary graduates. About one quarter of First Nations adults living on a reserve were post-secondary graduates compared to 40 percent of the general Canadian population; First Nations women are much more likely to complete post-secondary education than their male counterparts.

Low levels of educational achievement are a result of the historical trauma experienced by many First Nations people through the residential school system. Many individuals do not support the school system or the teachers in the school. Moreover, there is no incentive for Aboriginal people to encourage their children to continue and complete their primary, secondary, and post-secondary education. For example, many remote and isolated First Nations communities have no opportunity to allow industry to emerge and support hunting and fishing activities. As such, academically successful youth relocate to the south to take on jobs. The federal government continues to spend less on Aboriginal schools than the provinces (about $8,000 less per student) and this is regardless of the educational completion rate for any community.

First Nations have set out a broad policy of First Nations control of First Nations education yet the federal government refuses to accept such recommendations. The federal government appears to be unwilling to reconcile provincial laws, programs, and policies with Indigenous rights to education such as ensuring access to education and services by First Nation students; identification of the respective roles of first Nations communities and AANDC, responsibilities and accountabilities of stakeholders; addressing comparability issues; ensuring adequate and predictable funding for First Nations schools and programs; recognition and implementation of First Nations governance over education; strategies to encourage parental engagement; implementation of initiatives to ensure the teaching of First Nations languages; and ensuring the reflection of First Nations cultures and identities throughout the education environment. There is no attempt by the federal government to develop capacity-building educational programs for First Nations. The importance of culturally competent teachers, utilizing First Nations cultural knowledge in the elementary and secondary school experience, needs to be supported for creating optimal learning environments so that students can maximize their learning potential. All these factors have limited the motivation for First Nations communities to commit to the existing educational system.

There also is considerable concern over the content of the current educational curriculum: The absence of various components of Aboriginal culture—including language, history, and cultural issues— in a provincial curriculum has been a major issue with First Nations people for years. The recent National Education Act proposed by the Conservative government now acknowledges the need for these components in the educational system. It will, however, take time and effort for First Nations communities to embrace the current provincial educational systems.

Labour Force Participation

Since 2000 the employment rate for First Nations people has decreased. In 2011 it was just over 50 percent compared to more than two thirds for the rest of Canada compared to 2000 when the employment rate for First Nations people was 58 percent and 61 percent for the rest of Canada. In 2010 the unemployment rate was over 14 percent for First Nations people compared to 6.5 percent for the rest of Canada. As a result of this poor integration into the labour market, we find that nearly one third of all First Nations people depend on social assistance for at least part of the year, compared to only about 8 percent of the general Canadian population. This dependency is a result of structural barriers such as an absence of on-reserve employment, inadequate land and resource base to promote economic development, lack of education and job skills, and discrimination in the labour market. Recent surveys (Howard et al. 2012) have revealed that 38 percent of adults living on reserves had experienced racism in the last year and over one quarter noted that it had an effect on their self-esteem and their perception of labour market opportunity. Discrimination and social exclusion create barriers for First Nations people in terms of their productivity in the national economy.

Many First Nations families are headed by single female parents; these comprise nearly one third of all families, a rate that is five times higher than the non-Aboriginal population. This also affects the labour force participation rate of First Nations people. Satisfactory employment and income are important elements in achieving individual well-being and First Nations people have little of either. Similarly, a healthy economy plays an important part in achieving a strong and healthy community. Unfortunately, these elements are lacking within First Nations communities (FNIGC 2012).

Work and Earnings

Most First Nations people's conceptions of "living in a good way" include not only having access to the means of survival, but also enjoying a useful and productive life, having control over the means of one's livelihood, and living interdependently with the environment and with all of creation (Dumont 2005). Research reveals that imbalance, with respect to poverty and inequalities, strongly contributes to the poor health and well-being observed among First Nations individuals, families, and communities (Loppie-Reading and Wien 2008). Over one quarter of the total adult First Nations population indicated that they are currently not working for pay and are not looking for work. This percentage was higher among females (29.7 percent) compared to males (22.9 percent). The most common sources of income for First Nations people were paid employment, social assistance, and child tax benefits. Two thirds (66.6 percent) of First Nations adults had income from government sources; approximately half (52.5 percent) had income from paid employment; and one sixth (15.8 percent) derived their income from other sources. Over 80 percent of employed First Nations adults reported being employed within their own communities while only about 10 percent work in non-First Nations communities. Those who claimed to receive pay for work also noted part-time rather than full-time work.

Nonetheless, even among those who worked full time for the full year, the most recent census continues to show a disparity in the median earnings between First Nations people ($34,940) and non-Aboriginal people ($41,401). Research shows that although the low-income rate among First Nations peoples in cities dropped between 1995 and 2002, First Nations people remained much more likely to fall into the low-income category (41.6 percent) compared to the general population (17.7 percent).

For the adult First Nations population, those who finish high school are more likely to be employed than those who do not (72 percent versus 47 percent). Data show that the participation rate of First Nations people in attending trade or college post-secondary educational institutions is similar to that of the non-Aboriginal population. Table 2-5

Table 2-5   Income of Aboriginal and Non-Aboriginal Peoples, 2006

	Aboriginal average	First Nations	Métis	Inuit	Non-Aboriginal
Percent of Total Income from Government Transfer Payments	22.2%	27.1%	13.2%	20.5%	16.7%
Average Employment Income	$21,755	$22,771	$22,780	$24,026	$28,931
Incidence of Low Income[1]	20.7%	41.2%	16.3%	16.7%	17.7%
Average Individual Income	$21,845	$16,286	$24,197	$24,646	$29,111

[1] If a family/individual spends 20 percent more of their income than the "average" Canadian family/individual on food, shelter, and clothing, they are considered "low income" or below the "poverty level."

Source: Statistics Canada 2011c

reveals the income of First Nations people compared to other Aboriginal groups and the non-Aboriginal population.

Level of Income

Among employed individuals, one quarter of First Nations workers earn less than $5,000 per year with an additional 15 percent making less than $10,000 per year. Just under half of the First Nations workers earn between $10,000 and $40,000; just over 10 percent make $40,000 or over.

First Nations Bands

Table 2-6 shows the number of bands across Canada. However, it should be noted that the actual number varies by year as some old bands are phased out and in other cases, new ones created. If we look back thirty years, we find that there has been a steady increase in the percentage of First Nations people living off the reserve (increasing from 29 percent in 1985 to nearly half the First Nations population in 2011). Figure 2-1 illustrates the size of the various bands across Canada. What is most noticeable is that most bands are relatively small in size. Over half of the bands have fewer than 1,000 people. Two thirds of these communities are not considered isolated (that is, communities that are accessible by road and are less than ninety kilometres from a physician). The numbers

Table 2-6 Registered Indian Population by Region and Type of Residence, December 31, 2012

Region	Number of Bands	Total a + b + c	On Reserve (a)	On Crown Land (b)	Off Reserve (c)
Atlantic	34	60,928	22,696	43	38,189
Quebec	39	80,785	52,018	2,252	26,515
Ontario *	126	195,139	89,851	1,903	103,385
Manitoba	63	143,758	85,984	850	56,924
Saskatchewan	70	141,379	67,384	1,820	72,175
Alberta *	45	115,436	68,463	2,865	44,108
British Columbia	198	136,478	61,405	328	74,745
Yukon *	16	8,940	526	3,454	4,960
Northwest Territories	26	18,210	363	11,837	6,010
Canada	617	901,053	448,690	25,352	427,011

Note: "On Reserve" and/or "On Crown Land" counts can include individuals living on lands affiliated with First Nations operating under Self-Government Agreements.

Source: Statistics Canada 2011c, *Aboriginal Peoples in Canada: First Nations People, Metis and Inuit*, 7

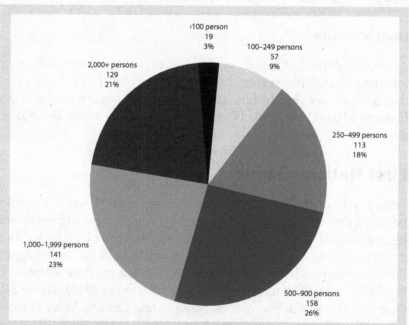

Figure 2-1 Bands in Canada by Size (Total Membership), December 31, 2012

Source: Graph reproduced from Aboriginal Affairs and Northern Development Canada 2013, *Registered Indian Population by Sex and Residence*, xi

of semi-isolated and isolated communities are similar, at roughly 16 per-cent each. Remote-isolated communities (locations where there is no road access and no scheduled flights) represent fewer than 4 percent of communities. Isolated communities are scattered across the country, but most are found in Ontario (27.8 percent) and Manitoba (24.7 percent).

The issue of band membership emerged out of Bill C-31 as the fed-eral government stipulated that each band could develop its own mem-bership codes, but only if it did so within two years after the passage of the bill. If it did not develop its own membership codes, it would have to accept the criteria established by the Indian Act. For nearly 150 years First Nations peoples' concerns were either ignored or rejected by government and this bill was a change. While it did not provide First Nations people with the right to determine status, it did give allow them to determine band membership. Moreover, this move affected not only people who had been reinstated but all First Nations people. The First Nations leaders requested additional time and resources to address the potential increase in band membership, but the federal government rejected the request.

The end result has been considerable dissent among First Nations communities. Some people saw the membership issue as problematic, with further complexities in allocating housing and other services, while others felt that the change finally addressed the issue of sex discrimina-tion. But all agreed that the sudden influx of new members was a prob-lem if no new resources were allocated. While the federal government provided a $7,000 grant to each band to prepare for the new members of the band, and a $15,000 annual increase for bands to help cope with larger membership (Innes 2013), this was insufficient. Bands had to take considerable care in establishing criteria for membership in order to limit the number that would be eligible for band support, such as land and housing.

Conclusion

There is considerable diversity within the First Nations population, and significant differences from mainstream Canadians. First Nations com-munities are small and spread across the country; with the exception of northern Saskatchewan, this leaves them unable to exercise power and influence. Even in areas with high concentrations of First Nations people, their number relative to the overall population is so small that they have little political influence. We also see that the First Nations population is very young, which may influence the increase in pop-ulation over the next generation. Given the overall young age of the

First Nations people, in the next generation, a larger number of young people will be looking to enter the labour market. Unless they are able to fully utilize the educational system, an increasing number will be unemployed, unskilled, and unable to participate in the primary labour resource pool.

We also note that with the changing definition of status, young adults in small bands will be challenged to find suitable mates that allow the band to maintain its population base. If the people on these small reserves engage in intermarriage outside their community, this may hasten the implementation of the section 6(2) rule, producing children and grandchildren no longer considered to be Indians.

The large number of young First Nations people will have implications for Canada as a whole. Given the increasing number of older Canadians, mainstream politicians will begin to develop policies, programs, and services to ensure the well-being of this aging population, as well as maintaining their support for the political parties that look after them. This in turn will mean that younger Canadians (especially significant demographically within the First Nations population) will not be the focus of such policies and programs. In other words, governments may fail to address the issues facing First Nations youth in the new Canadian milieu of the twenty-first century.

Chapter 3

Indian Affairs/Aboriginal Affairs and Northern Development Canada

Introduction

This country has seen a long history of governmental departments designed to "deal" with First Nations people. Until 1830, the military was the responsible organization, given the importance of First Nations allies in territorial battles. However, following the Seven Years War, the military contribution of First Nations was no longer as important. Furthermore, as European settlement increased, First Nations people came to be seen as barriers to development and progress; until the mid-twentieth century, it was the explicit goal of the federal government to assimilate First Nations people. Federal governments have only recently backed away from this policy, acknowledging the legitimacy of multiculturalism in Canada.

The Indian Act

The Indian Act of 1876 was not the first piece of legislation passed by Parliament with regard to First Nations people. Nearly forty different pieces of legislation had already been established prior to the consolidation of these into one act. For example, two acts were passed in 1850: An Act for the Better Protection of the Lands and Property of Indians in Lower Canada, and An Act for the Better Protection of Indians in Upper Canada from Imposition, and the Property Occupied or Enjoyed by Them from Trespass and Injury. Later, in 1857, the Act for the Gradual Civilization of the Indian Tribes in the Canadas was passed, followed ten years later by The Management of Indian Lands and Property Act.

With the consolidation of the Indian Act in 1876, the Department of Interior, then in charge of Indian Affairs, saw First Nations people as "wards of the state." Under the Indian Act, the traditional Aboriginal system of governance—an elected chief and council structure—was changed. Any First Nations people who resisted were offered bribes (or threatened): in 1894 at the Cowessess Reserve in Saskatchewan, for example, the Director of Indian Affairs offered a wagon in exchange for abandoning the traditional manner of selecting a chief. In addition, the Act allowed the federal Crown to appoint an "Indian agent" on each reserve who, over the years, gained increasing power over community operations. For example, the agent had full authority to conduct trials anywhere in the country if a First Nations person was charged with violating a section of the Indian Act. The "pass" system was introduced in 1885 requiring any First Nations person wanting to leave the reserve (for any length of time) to seek approval from the Indian agent before leaving and upon return. While the pass system was not part of the Act, and there was therefore no legislative basis for prosecuting a First Nations person in a court of law if they transgressed it, the Indian agents nevertheless used it in innovative ways with the support of Indian Affairs in Ottawa. Agents regularly withheld rations to those who refused compliance, even prosecuting them for trespass under the Indian Act or for vagrancy under the Criminal Code when they left the reserve (Comack 2012). In other cases Indian agents participated in the community voting on various issues as well as interpreting the Indian Act on behalf of reserve members.

The Indian Act of the day also introduced a "permit" system making it compulsory for First Nations people to obtain permission from the Indian agent before selling or bartering goods that originated on the reserve. This also included the sale of animals, both alive and butchered. In the end, Indian Affairs used its power under the Indian Act to undermine chiefs and band councillors as well as their decisions if they did not like the individuals or the actions of the band council.

The 1876 Act was the first time a single document outlined the duties and responsibilities of the federal Crown with regard to First Nations people. Over the past 125 years, this document has been revised and amended many times. However, even with the many revisions, the basic content of the original 1876 document remains. Only in 1951 did the federal government review the full document in anticipation of revision. However, even when the revisions were made, the "new" document looked remarkably like the 1876 Act.

In 1969 the Liberals under Pierre Trudeau began the process of eradicating the Indian Act. However, groups of activists, religious groups, and non-governmental organizations supported First Nations people and formed an alliance that blocked the implementation of the famous White Paper. Subsequent governments have tried to eliminate the Act but have found that, with little to offer in its place, there has been resistance. As such, today everyone, including First Nations people, agree that the Indian Act is outdated, overly complex, paternalistic in nature, and even includes potentially illegal provisions. Yet there is little appetite for the Crown to change it. First Nations people, fully appreciative of the weaknesses of the Act, also are cautious in recommending changes. While imperfect, any changes must be improvements. There have been several attempts by the National Indian Brotherhood and later by the Assembly of First Nations to craft changes to the Indian Act or to implement changes in the political structure of Canada that would allow the Indian Act to be phased out. However in all cases the federal Crown has rejected these proposals (RCAP 1996b).

Departments of Indian Affairs

Historical Goals of Indian Affairs

Departments of Indian Affairs (or units within Departments) have had several goals over history:

- Military alliances and trade linkages (1500–1700)
- Establishing early treaties with sovereign Indigenous nations (1700–1800)
- Integration and assimilation (1800–1969)
- Denial of Aboriginal rights (1950–1980)
- Acceptance of Aboriginal rights/self-government (1973–1995)
- Abdication of federal responsibility (1970–2000)
- New Comprehensive land claims (1975–2014)
- Increasing federal control for major resource developments on First Nations land (1999–2014)

When the British military was in control of Indian Affairs, their goal was to garner support of various First Nations communities in order to defeat the French, Americans, or other nations that wished to take over what is now Canada. Similarly, the French, in fighting for control over the land, recruited First Nations people to combat the efforts of the English. As such, both the French and the English engaged in numerous strategies to create alliances with First Nations people. However, as noted above, after the Seven Years War (1763) and the defeat of the French, the British no longer needed military support. Colonial settlement became the new focus and the Department in charge of Indian Affairs changed its focus.

At this time the number of British military personnel in British North America decreased. Moreover, the First Nations population was more than three times greater than that of the settlers, so negotiations were needed. The colonial government began to search for new strategies to deal with Aboriginal groups. The Royal Proclamation (1763) outlined in clear terms that the land under First Nations control would remain as such. Furthermore, if lands were to be utilized by settlers, there would have to be a formal offer by the colonial government. Only the government could purchase land from Aboriginal people. An offer would have to be ratified by First Nations people. Moreover, unscrupulous settlers and others who were trying to steal lands covered by the Royal Proclamation would be stopped and prosecuted. Two issues emerged from this proclamation. First, the boundaries of the land covered by the Royal Proclamation have never been delineated and thus considerable conflict has emerged over the years with regard to the placement of the boundaries. This conflict continues today. Second, the federal government failed to honour its promises in the Proclamation. Attempts to redress these failed promises have been disappointing, to say the least.

With the creation of Canada, the Constitution gave the federal government jurisdiction over Indians and lands reserved for the Indians (section 91). At the same time section 92 of the Constitution provides that the provinces have legislative jurisdiction over the other lands and natural resources within their own boundaries. However, at the time of confederation, the four western provinces had not yet been created and the federal government therefore held total control over the land and resources within what was then the North-West Territories. In addition, as we noted above, with the exception of BC, the provinces enjoy what is called the reversionary title to First Nations reserves, even though they do not have jurisdiction over them; this means that if a reserve is no longer needed or is abandoned by First Nations people, the land reverts to the province.

During the nineteenth century, the colonial government encouraged settlers to come to British North America, and as such, new rules regarding the relationship between Aboriginal people and the settlers had to be established. We saw above that First Nations people were no longer a valued ally but rather came to be seen as barriers to progress. The principles of democracy were established in law, but were not fully extended to First Nations people, with the implicit suggestion that they would be unable to understand democracy until they had evolved further. The main federal policies at this time were designed to ensure that land would be available to the increasing number of settlers. This led to many "Peace and Friendship" treaties, which were successful over a short period of time, so long as there was enough land and relatively few settlers.

Over time, the number of settlers increased and the demand for new land placed political and economic pressure on the federal government. The "treaty era" was born in the early 1800s and would last until the early twentieth century. The government established treaties with many of the First Nations communities in Canada. These treaties gave small reserves, annual payments, and other inducements to First Nations in exchange for them relinquishing all their rights to traditional lands. This "extinguishment" process continued over an extended period of time, such that by the early twentieth century, nearly 80 percent of all lands in the country had been "treatied out." Only in areas in BC, the Yukon, NWT, parts of northern Quebec, and some areas in the Atlantic provinces did land issues remain to be negotiated with First Nations people. By the early twentieth century, nearly all of Canada was under the control of the provincial governments. The famous *St. Catherines Milling and Lumber Co.* case (1888) confirmed that land, and its resources, were within provincial jurisdiction. The courts declared that First Nations held usufructuary rights but the provincial government held the land and resource rights. For nearly a century this was the situation, with Indian Affairs operating on this basic assumption. Only lands set aside for reserves would be under the purview of the federal government. Moreover, if land was required by government to fulfill treaty agreements, the province would have to provide the land. But the province held considerable authority as to what land might be turned over to the federal government to be held in trust for First Nations people.

Over the years, it became the goal of Indian Affairs to "take the Indian out of every child" and its assimilation policies were established. The Indian Act itself is a document of control and coercion. It deals with all behaviour of First Nations people—from bedroom to boardroom, from birth to death. The main goal of Indian Affairs for many years was to assimilate First Nations people, recreating them as "white" Canadians who accepted mainstream social, economic, and spiritual institutions as well as mainstream attitudes, values, and norms. From the inception of the comprehensive Indian Act (1876) until 1950, the powers of the Indian Affairs branch and Indian agents located on the reserves grew exponentially. It would not be until after the Second World War that these attitudes began to change.

The change was prompted by First Nations soldiers returning from participating in the war effort. First, they had experienced a sense of "equality" during their time in the military, albeit First Nations soldiers had not enjoyed full equality with non-Aboriginal soldiers. Moreover, upon their return from the war, they discovered that the benefits paid to their dependents while overseas, as well as the benefits they received as veterans on their return, were unequal to what non-Aboriginal soldiers received. Contemporary First Nations activism was born.

Aboriginal Affairs and Northern Development Canada Today

Contemporary Goals

Today Aboriginal Affairs and Northern Development Canada (AANDC) supports Aboriginal people (First Nations, Inuit, and Métis) in their efforts to:

- Improve social well-being and economic prosperity;
- Develop healthier, more sustainable communities; and
- Participate more fully in Canada's political, social, and economic development, to the benefit of all Canadians.

As such, it supports healthy and prosperous First Nations communities through building and supporting strong stable relationships, working to uphold the honour of the Crown and facilitating First Nations participation in economic opportunities. These goals reflect the broader generic policy adopted by the federal government to support economic growth for First Nations people. These goals also reflect the efforts of various other federal and provincial ministries.

While contemporary AANDC policies are admirable, their timing is important. The current goals were not instigated by the federal government. Rather, the development of most of these polices resulted from legal decisions made by the Supreme Court of Canada. For example, the 1990 *Sparrow* court decision forced government to work closely with Aboriginal groups with regards to the management of the Fisheries Act. As such, it introduced several programs that allowed First Nations people access to the management of these resources. It was only after over a century that the government finally addressed this issue, and it was only after the court ruled on the Marshall case in 1999 that policies regarding fisheries access, at-sea mentoring, and fisheries operation management were introduced. The 2004 Supreme Court decision on *Taku/Haida* found that the government had an obligation to consult with First Nations communities who assert (but may have not yet established) Aboriginal title or other Aboriginal rights. Until the courts ruled otherwise, the government had taken no action during the previous century.

Fiduciary Relationships

The department of AANDC is supposed to hold fiduciary obligations toward First Nations people. This means that a relationship exists in which the fiduciary has the right to exercise some discretion or power. It also means that the fiduciary can unilaterally exercise that discretion to affect the beneficiary's legal and practical interests. A fiduciary relationship also implies that the beneficiary is vulnerable to the fiduciary who holds the power. A review of the actions of Indian Affairs over the past century reveals that it failed to live up to its fiduciary responsibility toward First Nations people.

The lesson learned from the above is that government has been unwilling to create new policies and programs that would revise existing policies in order to better support First Nations people and their rights to land and resources. Only when the Supreme Court of Canada makes a definitive decision is the federal government likely to revise its policy. We saw above that even the definition of an Indian remained unclear until the Supreme Court ruled that the then-current Indian Act was discriminatory. The discriminatory aspects of the Indian Act were not changed until the United Nations became involved. And, even after Bill C-31 was passed and First Nations women objected, it once again took the court to force the government to make additional changes to the Indian Act.

Organization of AANDC

Aboriginal Affairs and Northern Development Canada has offices in ten regions across Canada as well as headquarters in Ottawa. The offices identified below (see Figure 3-1) are sub-divided into four broad divisions: Treaties and government, Lands, Economic development, and Education and social development. Northern Development is focused on the Northwest Territories and Nunavut regional offices. AANDC has gone through numerous organizational changes over the past century in an attempt to better serve its major client—First Nations people. Today, the Department has identified a number of strategic outcomes as well as a number of programs that they hope will achieve those strategic outcomes. The following information is drawn from government sources.

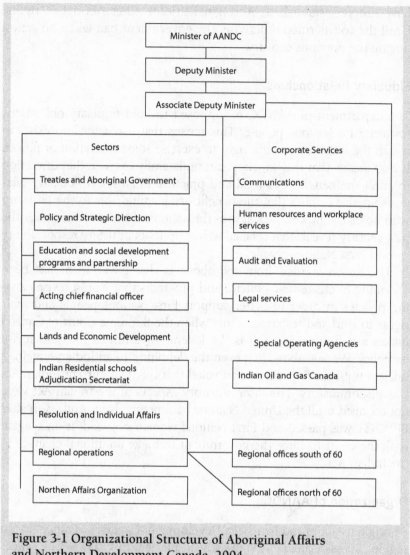

Figure 3-1 Organizational Structure of Aboriginal Affairs and Northern Development Canada, 2004
Source: AANDC

Fiscal Responsibilities of AANDC

It was in 1907 that Canada declared First Nations people to be non-persons, and as such took control of their money, resources, and other financial affairs. This declaration meant that First Nations people were considered non-legal entities. And, as such, they could not be the object of a court's protection. The term emerged out of 1876 British common law that noted that women were not persons and as such had no rights and privileges. This characterization of women as non-persons was actually upheld by the Canadian Supreme Court in 1928: the decision was only overturned when it was appealed to the Privy Council in England two years later.

A similar declaration by the federal government was made for First Nations people. As a result, the federal government unilaterally gave themselves power of attorney over First Nations people. According to the Trust Fund Management System, the Indian Affairs Minister manages First Nations money and the department may collect, receive, hold, manage, and spend this money without the knowledge or consent of First Nations peoples. In addition, this money can only be spent in specific ways and only with the permission of the Minister. Currently the Government of Canada holds some billion dollars in a trust account on behalf of First Nations people. While First Nations people did not have to appeal to the courts for a change in their status as "non-persons," the federal government continues to treat First Nations people as though they are wards of the state.

The department has the primary federal mandate for funding basic services such as education, housing, roads, water and sewage systems, and social and family services to status people living on reserves. These are the funds allocated by Parliament through the annual budget process (see Table 3-2). The department also has specific trust responsibilities for Indian moneys, estates, reserve lands, and band government, and it negotiates the settlement and implementation of specific claims and comprehensive land claims.

Aboriginal Affairs and Northern Development Canada also maintains national models of funding agreements. These methods of transferring funds are used when First Nations communities have not yet entered into their own self-government agreements. These national funding agreement models comply with the Treasury Board of Canada Secretariat Policy and Directive on Transfer Payments. As such, these funding agreements have the following characteristics:

- They accommodate both annual and multi-year funding agreements;
- The policy-related sections are generally found in the main body of the agreements; and
- Program-related sections such as program delivery standards and requirements are found in separate schedules of the agreement.

Table 3-1 shows the costs and revenues associated with the department's activities, as well as the money currently in trust accounts held by AANDC. It also shows payments regarding claims for 2013 and projected

Table 3-1   AANDC Expenditures and Revenues (in Thousands of Dollars) by Priority Area, 2013

People	4,208,786
Land and economy	1,415,570
Government	1,376,299
North	490,664
Internal services	347,919
Office of federal interlocutor	73,781
Expenses incurred on behalf of government	6,960
Total expenses:	7,919,979
Total revenues	2,423
Departmental net debt (2013)	13,662,898
Total trust accounts (including Indian Moneys)	920,104
Payments for 11 outstanding settled claims (2013)	109,000
Liability for outstanding settled claims	432,926

Source: AANDC

liabilities for other specific claims costs, as well as the total revenues for the year as a result of net interest on loans, sale of First Nations land, and resource royalties. In the end, AANDC spends considerably more than they take in. However, under the Constitution Act 1982 and the terms of the treaties, these are expenses that Canada has incurred and pays out annually.

Parliament establishes an annual budget for each federal department. The budgets, as estimates, are reviewed by committee, by the Treasury Board, by the Prime Minister's Office, and finally Parliament approves the yearly expenditures. However, unforeseen events can happen over the year requiring additional funds. As such, departments such as AANDC generally return to Parliament to request "supplementary" funds. Table 3-2 shows the budget estimates for 2012–2013 for AANDC by specific activities but does not include any supplementary funds provided to AANDC by Parliament over the course of a year; e.g., fire fighting, flood compensation.

Strategic Outcomes

To make sense of this bureaucratic structure and to better understand its spending, consider AANDC's current four strategic outcomes. Each of the strategic outcomes is supported by a number of sub-programs

Table 3-2   Budget for 2012–13 for AANDC[1]
(in Millions of Dollars)

Federal interlocutor	75
North	326
Community infrastructure	1,073
Administration of reserve land	112
Economic development	238
Residential school resolution	593
Social development	1,410
Education	1,735
Managing individual affairs	37
Treaty management	718
Cooperative relationships	717
Governance	484
Internal services[2]	319
Total	8,139

[1]The Congress for Aboriginal Peoples (2007) found that an additional 34 separate agencies and departments reported funding programs that focused on Aboriginal people.

[2]Part of the budget for "internal services" is the legal fees paid by AANDC in 2012–13. The bulk of this amount ($106.1M) was spent on legal services provided to the Department of Justice, which includes legal advice and support on negotiations of comprehensive and specific claims and self-government agreements.

Source: AANDC

that determine the action of the government as well as the responsibilities and obligations of both parties. The organizational structure mirrors these proposed outcomes, which are as follows:

Governance
- The governance of government programs is supported by the implementation of sub-programs such as First Nations Governments, and Institutions and Organizations. Through these sub-programs, government programs establish the rules and regulations of their operations.
- The Co-operative Relationships program is supported by four sub-programs that involve consultation and claims (both the negotiation and implementation).
- The Treaty Management program is supported by sub-programs such as the Implementation of Modern-Treaty Obligations, Management of Treaty Relationships, and Management of Other Negotiated Settlements.

People
- The Education program is supported by two sub-programs: Elementary and Secondary Education and Post-Secondary Education.
- The Social Development program is supported by sub-programs such as Income Assistance, National Child Benefit Reinvestment, First Nations Child and Family Services, and Family Violence Prevention.
- The Managing Individual Affairs program is supported by sub-programs such as Registration and Membership, Management of Moneys, and Estate Management. Treaty Annuities is also a sub-program of Managing Individual Affairs.
- The Residential Schools Resolution program is supported by sub-programs such as Common Experience Payments (for residential school survivors), the Independent Assessment Process, and Support to the Truth and Reconciliation Commission. The final report documented six years of hearings and testimony from nearly 10,000 survivors of residential schools. Thus far, the Commission has only published its Interim Report and has identified ninety-four "calls to action" which attempt to redress the legacy of residential schools. The Commission recommended that the government of Canada take action on a number of issues involving two categories: legacy and reconciliation. For example, the report recommends that the government add aboriginal history to all Canadian school curriculums, launch a national inquiry into missing and murdered Aboriginal women, fully adopt and implement the United Nations Declaration on the Rights of Indigenous Peoples, and acknowledge the current state of Aboriginal health and implement programs to deal with it.

Land and Economy
- The Aboriginal Economic Development program is supported by three sub-programs: Aboriginal Entrepreneurship, Activation of Community Assets, and Strategic Federal Investments and Partnerships.
- The Federal Administration of Reserve Land program is supported by sub-programs in the department such as Additions to Reserve, Registration of Rights and Interests in Reserve Lands, Clarity of Reserve Boundaries, and Environmental Management.
- The Community Infrastructure program is supported by sub-programs such as Water and Wastewater Infrastructure, Education Facilities, Housing and Community Infrastructure Assets and Facilities.

Office of the Federal Interlocutor
- This office deals with issues traditionally considered outside the mandate of Indian Affairs. However, given the nature of the court

cases regarding Aboriginal issues, Indian Affairs has chosen to include other Aboriginal groups, such as the Inuit and Métis, as part of their mandate.

• The office of the Federal Interlocutor is supported by the subprograms of Urban Aboriginal Strategy, Métis and Non-Status Indian Organizational Capacity Development, and Métis Rights Management.

Responsibilities of AANDC

The federal Crown derives its mandate from the Constitution, Aboriginal Affairs and Northern Development Canada, the Indian Act, various statutes regarding the treaties (both modern and traditional), as well as from more recent pieces of legislation, such as First Nations Fiscal and Statistical Management Act and First Nations Land Management Act. In addition, its responsibilities emerge from various policy decisions and programs that have been established by Parliament. Finally, court decisions with regard to First Nations weigh heavily in terms of how the federal Crown, through AANDC, carries out its administrative, fiduciary, and fiscal responsibilities for First Nations people.

As such, AANDC carries out its duties as specified by the various pieces of legislation. In addition, it negotiates specific and comprehensive claims and also implements the final decisions of those claims. If self-government is a component of those claims, AANDC is in charge of ensuring that the administration of self-government is carried out. Finally, AANDC provides both administrative and fiscal support for a variety of services provided to First Nations in their communities, such as education, housing, social support, and community infrastructure. Recently the Minister of AANDC has been given additional powers as the government's Interlocutor for Métis, non-status Indians, and urban Aboriginal people. Recent court decisions have forced the federal government to include other Aboriginal groups as specified under the Charter of Rights and Freedoms. Thus, Aboriginal organizations in urban centres—Friendship Centres and Métis Organizations, for example—have now been in negotiations with the Minister of AANDC regarding the government's Urban Aboriginal Strategy policy. Prior to this, the federal government argued that urban Aboriginals were a provincial concern and not a federal one. As such, any Aboriginal organization that focused on urban issues was seen as a provincial responsibility. The newly created Office of the Federal Interlocutor now includes other Aboriginal people as well as organizations that exist outside of the reserves.

The Office of the Federal Interlocutor also attempts to bring together the various parties (municipality governments, provincial governments,

Priorities for Action

Today, the AANDC has identified eleven activities, in three broad areas, that they wish to carry out in order to meet the goals and objectives stated above. Their budget and actions should reflect these as priority areas in dealing with First Nations people:

Transforming for Improved Results

- Reforming Education
- Empowering Citizens
- Enhancing Economic Development and Sustainability
- Continuation of a Northern Strategy

Improving Partnerships and Relationships

- Implementing Reconciliation
- Facilitating Community Development and Capacity
- Developing Partnerships with First Nations Communities
- Negotiating and Implementing Claims and Self-Government Agreements

Managing Resources Effectively

- Implementing the New Policy on Transfer Payments
- Implementing the Results of the Administrative Shared Services Review
- Implementing Public Service Renewal

Aboriginal organizations, and the federal government) with regard to improving the quality of life for Aboriginal people living in the city.

Revenue for First Nations

As noted previously, moneys directed toward First Nations communities are generally controlled by the federal government. Nevertheless, funds are provided to First Nations people in several different ways. First, there are the federal transfer payments through Parliament that are annual allocations managed by AANDC and reflect the priorities set by the federal government. These standard grant and contribution approaches are aided as well by three other contribution funding strategies that departments can use to fund programs. These additional funding strategies are called fixed, flexible, and block contribution approaches (AANDC Annual Report 2010). AANDC uses these various funding strategies to administer transfer payments related to its programs as identified above. As such, the type of funding approach used will depend on a number of factors, such as the design and nature of a program, the program authority, the duration of the program or funding agreement, and the level of risk associated with entering into a funding agreement.

There are other sources of income for First Nations communities. For example, there are "Indian Moneys": here, all moneys collected, received, and held by AANDC for the use and benefit of Indians and bands according to the rules set by the Department. There are two types of Indian moneys: capital and revenue.

Capital moneys are the result of the sale of surrendered lands or from the sale of the non-renewable resources of a band. For example, these moneys include oil and gas royalties, bonus payments, and other proceeds from the sale of timber, oil and gas, or gravel. On the other hand, there are revenue moneys that are Indian moneys other than capital. Revenue moneys include money from the sale of renewable resources, rights-of-way, fines, interest earned on capital, and revenue moneys held in the Consolidated Revenue Fund. AANDC is responsible for the administration of Indian moneys held within the Consolidated Revenue Fund for the use and benefit of Indians and bands. The collection, expenditure, and accounting of these moneys are determined by specific sections of the Indian Act. A recent Supreme Court of Canada decision brought forward by the Hobbema First Nation in Alberta was unsuccessful in having these moneys turned over to the First Nations community for control.

Provinces have increasingly contributed funds to support First Nations communities. While the figures are not directly comparable, Milke (2013) shows there was an increase of provincial funding for First Nations issues from $42 million in 1993 to $711 million in 2012. This reveals the dramatic increase in the provinces' concern with First Nations issues at the same time as a concerted effort by the federal government to download certain costs to the provinces. Milke (2013) reveals that in 1993, provincial program spending per person in the province of Ontario was $7,340 for each non-Aboriginal person and $75 per First Nations person. In 2011, the province was spending $9,205 per non-Aboriginal person and $819 per First Nations person—a dramatic increase in funding over the past two decades by provincial governments.

Finally there are major project grants that the federal government provides First Nations communities. These are contracts signed between the government and the First Nations community for a specific project. For example, these projects may be under the Community Economic Development program, Women's Self-Government Initiative, Aboriginal Language Initiative, or a Community-Based Justice program. There are specific models and templates that are used by AANDC to establish the contract and administer the funds.

Property Rights According to AANDC

From the earliest contact, there has been a belief by ruling officials that private property would help First Nations people better focus their interests and ambitions, as well as ensure their integration into the larger capitalist economy. The belief has been that when First Nations people settled down on their private property with a house, they would establish a proper family life and integrate into the capitalist economic system. Another belief was that private property would reduce violence among the various First Nations groups. In short, government officials believed that private property would solve all the ills besetting First Nations people (Carter 1990). However, this policy of "privatization" was never enacted. Instead, a "location ticket" (or called now a "certificate of possession") system was introduced on the reserves. This was a kind of an individual property right for on-reserve First Nations people. This ticket grants a temporary "title" of the land to a member of the band (almost always a male) who could, subject to band approval, transfer the "title" to another person of the same band, but only with the approval of the Minister of Indian Affairs. This ticket could also be cancelled by band council and re-allocated to another person. However, First Nations people do not own their land "fee simple" as do other Canadians. All land and resources on a reserve are held in trust by the federal government. Today, traditional or customary rights are the most common system of property rights on a reserve. However, it has no statutory basis and its legitimacy comes from the authority of the band under the Indian Act. In short, the band council creates individual interests in a parcel of land. Those who hold a customary land right may build on it, improve it, and transfer it to another member of the band. But, the land can also be removed from that individual's use by the band council for any reason.

There is no way for a First Nations person to obtain "fee simple" title to any land on the reserve. Historically, the only way for First Nations people to obtain fee simple of their land (off the reserve) was to enfranchise: become a non-Indian, move off the reserve, and then purchase a piece of land. In summary, since the original Indian Act, First Nations people do not "own" the land or resources they live on. Rather it is held in trust by AANDC and can only be surrendered to the federal Crown if a First Nations community wants to dispense with its land or make use of its natural resources. Thus, under the Indian Act, First Nations people have quasi property rights. Under the usufruct rule, it means that an individual has the right to use and to enjoy the benefits of property without being able to sell it or give it to someone else. Only when the land is surrendered to the federal government can it then be rented or sold to a third party. And, under the Indian Act, these moneys will be placed in the Consolidated Revenue Fund.

Today, according to AANDC, two different types of land rights exist for First Nations people on reserve. The first is through a "certificate of possession," which is proof of an individual's lawful possession of a parcel of land on the reserve (Flanagan et al. 2010). Only a band member may hold and transfer a certificate of possession. Since their creation in 1955, 140,000 of these certificates have been issued to band members on reserves. This certificate of possession is somewhere between the definition of "fee-simple" and "life-estate interest."

Leasing is a second way in which First Nations people can hold property rights. These can be short-term or long-term leases. Short leases can only be granted for land on the reserve and can only be leased through AANDC. Individuals or bands cannot lease the land themselves but must obtain permission from AANDC to do so; AANDC then does the actual leasing. Long-term leases require that the Band "conditionally surrender" the land to AANDC.

Since 1999, fifty-eight bands have opted into the First Nations Land Management Act that allows a First Nations community to implement land codes that it establishes. A total of twenty-three bands now have their land codes in operation. While this Act allows First Nations communities to develop their own land codes, it still does not allow individuals to own land "fee simple on the reserve." However, if a First Nations person wants to purchase land outside the reserve, he or she is able to but their ownership and responsibilities are outside the parameters of the Indian Act.

Recent Activities of AANDC

Over the past decade, AANDC has taken some very positive steps in its relationship with First Nations people. However, each time these activities are undertaken, the government has undermined its legitimacy with First Nations people. For example, Prime Minister Stephen Harper delivered a Statement of Apology for former students of Indian residential schools in 2008. Before he did so, however, he ensured that the federal government could not be sued for their activities after delivering the apology and accepting wrongdoing on their part. In another example, Canada finally endorsed the United Nations Declaration on the Rights of Indigenous People in 2010. However, for three years prior to this, it had refused to support the document. In the end, Canadian officials stated that the country would sign given that the Declaration did not have any legal standing in Canadian courts. Then, in 2014, Canada sent a representative to the UN General Assembly to vote on the adoption of the document. The document was adopted by all nations by consensus; Canada was the only country to file its objections, flagging as problematic the wording "free, prior and informed consent," a key principle in international law. As such, Canada has stated that it cannot associate itself with the elements contained in the document. Overall, the trust relationship between First Nations people and the federal government is very low. As we have seen, there is a long history fuelling this lack of trust.

The federal government also introduced a new Federal Framework for Aboriginal Economic Development, investing $3 billion between 2006 and 2014 in water and waste water infrastructure for First Nations communities across Canada, signing more than thirty tripartite agreements in the areas of housing, social development, health, education, and child and family services, leveraging nearly $75 million worth of targeted funding specifically for Urban Aboriginal Strategy community-based projects from other federal departments, provinces and municipalities, and the private and not-for-profit organizations. It also worked with the Assembly of First Nations to produce the Outcome Statement from the historic Crown–First Nations Gathering that identified key priorities for First Nations people in the area of education, economic development, and governance.

Nevertheless, it is clear that while these positive actions are applauded by First Nations people, the federal government still refuses to acknowledge the genesis of the structural gap between First Nations people and other Canadians. This is evident in its priorities as well as in the policies and programs that have been implemented to address the marginal existence of First Nations peoples.

Conclusion

As the First Nations Leadership Council (2013) points out, the federal (and the provincial) government's policy toward First Nations people has consistently been both paternalistic and negative. Shifts in government policy have not been the result of good will, but rather in response to conflict and international norms.

In the early twenty-first century, Supreme Court rulings—*Haida* (2004), *Taku* (2004), and *Mikisew* (2005)—represent a major change in government relations with First Nations people. These three cases focused on the court's ruling that the government (federal and provincial) must engage in consultation and accommodation with First Nations people when a policy, program, or development may have an impact on First Nations Aboriginal rights. The year 2008 saw the publication of

Aboriginal Consultation and Accommodation: Interim Guidelines for Federal Officials to Fulfill the Legal Duty to Consult. This document provided general directions to all federal departments and agencies as to how the law required them to engage in consultation with First Nations people. Three years later an updated version of this document was published, setting out governmental approach to meeting the legal obligations with regard to First Nations people. These guidelines are an attempt to coordinate the actions of all departments and agencies. The changes are a result of the more than 200 court cases that have invoked the *Haida* ruling as well as the seven times the Supreme Court of Canada has referred to this decision. In addition, the provincial governments have had to develop their own consultative guidelines.

First Nations people are appreciative of these recent changes. It is clear, however, that the federal government has not taken the lead in developing policies that reflect the "honour of the Crown" and in establishing fiduciary standards in recognition of First Nations' Aboriginal title and rights. For example, under section 91(24) of the Constitution Act, the federal government has exclusive jurisdiction in the areas of fisheries and navigable waters, which are crucial to First Nations Aboriginal rights. However, the recent passing of Bill C-38 and C-45 has seen the federal government abrogate its responsibilities to First Nations people. Overall, it has not exercised its authority under the Constitution to ensure safeguards for First Nations peoples' environment, livelihood, and natural resource development. In summary, the federal government has not taken a lead role with regard to consultation and accommodation. On the contrary, it has taken a minor role, deferring to the provincial governments with no direction as to how the undivided Crown's duty is to be fulfilled or to ensure that First Nations' rights are not violated by provincial or corporate actions. First Nations people point out that the federal government has never sided with First Nations in any court action against a provincial government or a corporation—despite its fiduciary and constitutional relationship with First Nations.

Instead, provincial governments have played a central role in determining the nature and scope of engagement with First Nations people (First Nations Leadership Council 2013). This has resulted in a patchwork of policies across Canada. Moreover, provincial governments operate on the assumption that they have complete provincial Crown title and therefore exclusive jurisdiction of all land and resources within the provincial boundaries. As the First Nations Leadership Council (2013) points out, the provinces should not benefit from the lands, minerals, and royalties as a source of revenue until the burden of Aboriginal title has been addressed as expressed in section 109 of the Constitution Act, 1867.

Chapter 4

Economic Growth and Development

Introduction

Historically the "deficit and dependence" paradigm has been the model used by all levels of government as well as the private sector in dealings with First Nations people (Ponting and Voyageur 2001). This model, however, has perpetuated colonialist outlooks with respect to the economic development of First Nations communities in Canada.

History shows that First Nations people had sophisticated systems of trade and administration in place prior to European contact. However, as treaties were established, the autonomy of First Nations people was undermined. Colonial powers (and later the federal government) began to mould new institutions to "manage" First Nations' communities. This began with the control of lands inhabited by First Nations' groups, particularly the creation of reserves and legislation that specified all Indian lands be held "in trust" for First Nations communities and not owned by First Nations people.

Since that time, many different approaches have been taken to improve the economic position of First Nations people in Canadian society. These approaches can be roughly categorized into two groups. The first is called the "Jobs and Income" approach; here money is seen as being the solution to the problem of First Nations' marginal involvement in Canadian economics. The band council (or other groups in the community) respond to potential funders. The focus is on the creation of a business that will provide jobs or bring capital into the community. In this model, little attention is given to the issue of long-term impacts and sustainability of the new business. Until recently, this has been the primary approach to address the issue of economic development.

Today, Aboriginal communities have moved beyond this perspective and are focusing their economic efforts on the second category, a new strategy that we may call "Nation building." Advocated by the Harvard Project on American Indian Economic Development, Nation building takes a more holistic approach. First, money is not seen as the only solution, but rather a component to the wider strategy of economic development. The community seeks to create a social, political, and economic environment that will be able to sustain business in the long term. The community also deals with economic development as a political problem that requires sound institutional structures and long-term business plans. It is the role of the band council and other community leaders to set policy and long-term visions that others then implement. In this way there is a "firewall" in place between the politics of the community and the implementation of business programs.

Economic Development versus Economic Growth

The concept of *economic development* has changed over time. Today we understand this term to encompass a web of interconnected elements including economic indicators, human rights, preservation of culture, and environmental sustainability.

Economic growth is different from economic development. Economic growth describes a country or a region's gross domestic product (GDP). Federal governments have by and large used economic growth as the sole "gold standard" for determining policy in Canada. However, a single-minded focus on economic growth has many shortfalls. It fails to take into account all goods and services, such as childcare provided by family members, whereas a daycare centre would be included. Economic growth as the sole means of measurement also fails to account for the range of costs associated with certain economic activities in which industrial and environmental pollution are not part of the calculus. A notable example here is tar sands development. The benefits of a healthy environment are generally not measured in indicators of economic growth.

Economic development takes into consideration not just the growth of the economy of a people but also sustainability, equitable income distribution, social justice, environmental responsibility, and empowerment. In Canada, community economic development includes local actions that create economic opportunities and improve social conditions. This conceptualization views the economic, social, and environmental aspects of life as interdependent (Canadian Community Economic

Development Network 2013). In this view of economic development, the focus should be on building the organizational capacities of the community (Lotz 1999).

Three Perspectives of Development

First Nations leaders fully recognize that any development project should embody participation by the entire community. As such, three frameworks have shaped First Nations' perspective on appropriate economic development of their homelands. First, the activity must produce freedom. As Ali and Crain (2002) point out, there is a clear connection between economic freedom and the economic development of a people. This means that First Nations communities must be free from the unilateral decisions by AANDC, both economically and politically. History has shown that federal governments have continually forced First Nations communities to embark only on government-funded economic projects that the government deems acceptable and therefore worthy of funding.

There are a number of factors that have limited the freedom of First Nations people in their economic development efforts. First, there is a gap between the needs and culture of First Nations communities and the policy developed by the federal government. Second, the lack of trust between the two parties has continued to grow, and the federal government continues to act in a manner that reinforces this mistrust. For example, the recent passage of the First Nations Financial Transparency Act was imposed on all First Nations to disclose all their financial dealings. If they fail to do so, AANDC will withhold funding for both non-essential and essential programs and services. In addition, the federal government has recently approached the courts to force those First Nation communities who have not submitted their financial statements. First Nations people argue that the federal government does not act in a transparent and accountable manner so why should there be this double standard? Nor do other private sector organizations that receive government funding have to publically disclose all their finances. For example, Pratt and Whitney and Bombardier Inc. have received over four billion dollars in federal government subsidies over the past decade with no requirement that they open their books to the public (Milke 2013). Others have gone to court to quash the Act, arguing that it violates both human rights and the content of treaties. While some government decisions may not deliberately engender mistrust, the end result is the same.

Finally, First Nations communities have experienced the impact of colonization over the years. They are now moving toward decolonization, with a final goal of being in control of the development cycle and improved economic freedom. For example, the Fort McKay First Nation of the Athabasca Wood Buffalo area have pulled out of a joint federal–provincial oil-sands monitoring program (a program begun in 2012) because their concerns and input were being largely ignored. Moreover, the Fort McKay band won a judgment allowing them to appeal a ruling by Alberta Energy Regulator. The Alberta Energy Regulator had approved a bid by Brion Energy Corp. to extract 50,000 barrels of bitumen per day using steam-assisted gravity drainage technology. The band argued that a buffer zone between the mine and the community was required; they also voiced concern for the drainage process that would change the ecology of the area. The Regulator's decision was based on the fact that providing a buffer zone would restrict the removal of approximately five billion barrels of oil and the environmental impact of gravity drainage would be minimal.

In another case, the controversial Taseko Mines Ltd Proposal near Williams Lake, BC failed its second environmental assessment. It was to be the tenth-largest copper and gold mine in the world. The province approved the mine plans but the federal reviewers rejected them. The Conservative federal government then allowed a revised proposal to be resubmitted a year later, in 2011. Already, however, the federal government is planning to challenge the ruling of the Canadian Environmental Assessment Agency; the Agency maintains that this project would cause significant environmental degradation on Tezan Biny and the First Nations culture in the region. After the second rejection by the Canadian Environmental Assessment Agency, the company filed a lawsuit against the Western Canada Wilderness Committee last year (2012) for stating that the mine would create a "tailings pond." This is part of a strategy—often used by big corporations—of filing nuisance lawsuits to intimidate groups that oppose development projects. The Western Canada Wilderness Committee is a non-profit NGO that aims to protect the environment and wildlife. It originated in BC and its headquarters remain there but it has field offices in Manitoba and Toronto. Today it has about twenty paid employees and hundreds of volunteers who promote the mandate of the organization. Most of the funding (approximately $2 million per year) comes from individual donations and membership fees. It should be noted that under new legislation passed by the Harper government, the federal government cabinet can now overrule environmental review decisions (although no such ruling has yet occurred). A second factor that has limited the freedom of First Nations people in their economic development efforts focuses on the hope of First Nations communities to transform themselves, rather than depending on others to carry out transformations. First Nations communities want to embark on development activities that increase their capacity while also reducing their vulnerability. First Nations communities want to preserve their local culture while also strengthening it through economic activities. This means that development activities should lead to sustainable business activities. The creation of the Kitasoo Aqua Farms and Seafoods Ltd is a good example of how economic activities can link with local culture. Salmon fishing has always been part of the Kitasoo community's traditional lifestyle. However, with access to less than 5 percent of the rich salmon fish stocks in the community's traditional territory, local people could not develop a sustainable economy on fishing. Instead, community members sold their fishing fleet and invested in a salmon farm; they built their own farm and processing plant, and now successfully market their own salmon. Working with environmental partners and salmon farm research groups, they have developed a sustainable economic activity that has inspired others to engage in the labour force (Sisco and Stewart 2009).

A third factor that has limited the freedom of First Nations people in their economic development efforts is the lack of an asset-based community development. Traditionally, economic projects are proposed and developed by external stakeholders rather than from within a First Nations community. As such, each First Nations community must assess its assets, strengths, and capabilities—these include natural resources, human capital, and infrastructure—before moving toward economic development. The case of Arctic Adventures is a good example. Aboriginal communities in Nunavik realized that they were heavily reliant on external suppliers for basic necessities. The community also found that the products supplied from outside did not meet their needs. Moreover, community members found that they could not sell their products at a fair price at existing venues. The community began to assess its assets, strengths, and capabilities. Community members observed the increasing growth of sustainable eco-tourism. Over time they have built up a steady clientele interested in hunting and fishing as well as related activities such as dog sledding, hiking, and the opportunity to observe and experience Inuit culture first-hand. Today in Nunavik eco-tourism is a thriving business that has been featured on television, including on the Sportsman Channel and Wild TV, as well as in *American Hunter* and *Fly Fisherman* magazines. It has been endorsed by the Safari Club International and other environmental organizations across North America.

Government Policy and First Nations Economic Development

The Supreme Court has ruled that First Nations people have a set of rights that include the following: the right to use and occupy their land exclusively, and the right to choose how the land will be utilized. The courts also have clarified that all First Nations land has an inescapable economic dimension: this means that First Nations people have the right to enjoy the economic benefits of their land (First Nations Leadership Council 2013). There are two categories of Aboriginal economic rights in Canada, as established in law. These are:

(1) food: social and ceremonial rights ensure they have the right to raise and sell food. This includes the right to fish for salmon, for example, and the right to sell cultural/ceremonial icons such as totems and masks that are related to food.
(2) sale or trade for livelihood to support a modest lifestyle, as long as the goods or services are not prohibited by law. This means that products produced by First Nations people can be entered into the marketplace. For example, wood can be harvested to create furniture that in turn can be sold to support community members.

Both these rights allow First Nations to engage in commercial trade of various goods that may be produced on or off reserves. These rights had, in the past, been denied by the federal government (*Van der Peet* 1996; *Delgamuukw* 1997).

The federal government has taken a proactive stance with regard to economic development for First Nations such that development should support healthy and prosperous Aboriginal communities with the following policy guidelines:

- building and supporting strong stable relationships,
- upholding the honour of the Crown, and
- facilitating Aboriginal participation in a variety of economic opportunities.

This policy reflects the broader generic policy that has been adopted by the federal government in order to support economic growth for Aboriginal people. It also reflects the efforts of various other departments that work with First Nations people. Finally, it is worth noting that regardless of the numerous programs that have been established to address the objectives and goals of the new policies, all of them are short-term projects, lasting between one and four years. The assumption is that the "problems" will be solved within a four-year span. What's more, the federal government has by and large only addressed real economic development for First Nations people when forced to by court decisions.

Access to Capital

Prejudice and discrimination, in addition to some of the provisions of the Indian Act, have prevented many individual First Nations people from acquiring financial help in establishing a new business. The economic development of First Nations communities also is too often thwarted by similar restrictions. Inadequate access to business capital for First Nations individuals from established financial institutions is a common problem. The reluctance to lend money arises partly from mainstream stereotypes. Many First Nations communities also have been unable to develop the necessary business infrastructure to accommodate the purchasing needs of their populations. In other words, when a band does manage to increase its per capita income, the money is not easily reinvested in the reserve or the band; residents do not find what they need on the reserve, and the money flows out of the community.

Federal government policy has failed to evolve over the years. For example, although the federal government holds money for First Nations economic development initiatives, accumulated finances for any First Nations community are placed in a trust fund and invested in government bonds. This money, estimated to be over $100 million annually, is not within the control of First Nations communities. It is held by the federal government "in trust," restricting many First Nations business ventures' ability to obtain financial support. When a First Nations community requests funds from the federal government, there are many bureaucratic procedures involved. A first step involves obtaining approval from the federal government for a given project. The Indian Act and AANDC policies and administrative procedures often either stop or delay economic projects for First Nations communities (National Aboriginal Economic Development Board [NAEDB] 2013). The NAEDB points out that non-workable legislation and processes hinder development. For example, AANDC has both a fiduciary relationship with First Nations people as well as a requirement to carefully account for the Crown's liability. This is, of course, a conflict of interest; most of the time the liability issue takes precedence in approving a project. Several other reports note that bureaucratic oversight and complexity creates undue delays and blocks the growth of reserve economies—the difference between the speed of business and that of AANDC. These reports also demonstrate that AANDC internal business practices are inefficient. Moreover, there is little "client focus": as such, too many projects are rejected or delayed (NAEDB 2011; AANDC 2012). Finally it should be noted that the cost and complexity of designation votes, lack of flexibility when circumstances change, and the time and complexity in securing a registered lease from AANDC all contribute to stunted economic growth on reserves. For example, under the Indian Act, lands on the reserve are designated for specific purposes. If a community wants to change the land designation, they have to engage in a long and complex voting process by which the community (and then AANDC) approve the change. The current funding approach by AANDC is primarily a "cash-based" financing model with a prevailing "one size fits all" approach. In the end, AANDC largely takes the role of "gatekeeper" rather than actually giving proactive support for First Nations' economic development. Many First Nations communities have seen, and continue to see, the actions of AANDC as barriers to economic development. The federal government must move toward a modern relationship with First Nations based on stable, long-term, and predictable fiscal arrangements.

First Nations people have limited equity, although there are some moneys held in trust in the Consolidated Revenue Fund that do have potential (Shanks 2005). However, the federal government refuses to review its policies and procedures. First Nations leaders attempting to develop business opportunities on-reserve face significant barriers in accessing financial resources (Shanks 2005). For example, the role of Aboriginal Credit Corporations (ACCs) is well established amongst the First Nations business community. There appears to be solid support for the work they are doing in providing capital to on-reserve businesses. They fill a niche that the major financial institutions do not and will not fill. However, ACCs could do much more if they had more capital at their disposal.

Other potential sources of money emerge from natural resource development that takes place on First Nations land. For example, the Indian Oil and Gas Act, 1974, and Indian Oil and Gas Regulations, 1995, are other examples of how legislative and regulatory instruments for the government create barriers for First Nations communities attempting to access money. The federal government manages all oil and gas exploration and development on Indian reserve lands. This regime has remained virtually unchanged for the last thirty-five years. Recently, however, First Nations people are seeking change. On some reserves, particularly those in Alberta, oil and gas activity is a significant source of potential capital that could provide access to economic development opportunities for approximately two hundred First Nations. In 2010–11 alone, over $300 million in oil and gas revenues were collected on behalf of First Nations communities with active petroleum agreements. For these communities, this revenue and increased access to oil- and gas-based economic development opportunities have the potential to improve well-being and self-reliance. Unfortunately, in most cases, the infrastructure to engage in new economic developments is insufficient. The development of the Osoyoos Band in BC is a perfect example where development projects were held up nearly a decade by AANDC before the band was able to accumulate enough funds to begin development—in this case, a winery. As pointed out by the NAEDB (2012), the current need for on-reserve infrastructure is nearly $5 billion for all reserves across the country and that does not include the operations or maintenance of the facilities. This has a direct impact on the ability of First Nations to realize their economic potential (Perrin, Thorau, and Associates 2009).

Proposed Economic Programs

A number of different strategies have been undertaken to enhance the economic development of First Nations communities. The ultimate goal of these strategies is to move toward self-determination and sovereignty. The belief is that economic self-sufficiency will help First Nations communities move toward economic and political independence. Several strategies have been implemented to increase revenues for First Nations communities in their quest to achieve self-sufficiency.

Taxation

The first of these strategies relates to taxation. In the 1980s, the federal government passed an amendment to the Indian Act that allowed First Nations communities to collect taxes from residents (Flanagan et al. 2010). This amendment gave the Band the right to collect property tax from lease-holders living on the reserve. At the same time, under current law, the province has the right to tax a user of federal land if it has been designated as "lease land." This means that if a non-First Nations business establishes itself on a reserve, the province can tax this business even though they are on federal land. British Columbia and Quebec do this. Other provinces, finding that there are few non-First Nations businesses on the reserve, have chosen not to enforce this taxation process. However for those provinces not initiating a tax on businesses on reserves, they have publicly noted they will begin to implement taxation as soon as the number of non-Aboriginal businesses increases on the reserves, making tax collection financially viable. In the meantime, both First Nations and non-Aboriginal people operating a business on a reserve are potentially subject to double taxation: two taxes—provincial and band. As a result, many non-First Nations businesses choose not to establish themselves on a reserve unless the province formally vacates its right to tax the business on the reserve. At the same time the Supreme Court has ruled against the First Nations community with regard to some types of taxation and thus the extent of the taxation powers of a band are unclear (Canadian Council for Aboriginal Business 2012).

We also find that the revenue gains from such taxes—such as the First Nations Sales Tax on selected products and the First Nations Goods and Services Tax—have been limited. This is because First Nations people are poor, and given this poverty, additional taxes simply decrease the amount of disposable income available for basic needs.

Others have argued that under section 87 of the Indian Act First Nations people should be exempt from taxation. Currently for First Nations people, income from personal property, inheritance, and pensions is exempt. It also used to be the case that if an employer was located on the reserve, then anyone who worked for that employer was not liable to pay income tax on their salary. However, much of this was changed in 1993 when Revenue Canada unilaterally changed the tax exemption rules for First Nations people. Today, tax exemption for employment income is applied only when job duties are performed entirely on the reserve. Employment income for work performed entirely off the reserve but where both the employer and individual reside on the reserve is similarly exempt. Employment income for work carried out mostly on reserve in cases where either the employer or the individual reside on reserve is (along with other exemptions) pro-rated by Revenue Canada for taxation purposes. All other income, including investment income, is fully taxable. First Nations people also are subject to GST when purchasing goods off-reserve. In the end, Revenue Canada has dramatically revised First Nations tax exemptions and substantially reduced the number and types of tax exemptions for First Nations individuals as well as First Nations corporations and other types of First Nations organizations. Nevertheless, the data reveal that at the end of the day, little revenue has been generated by these changes on the part of Revenue Canada.

Long-term leasing

Another way in which First Nations communities can develop economic projects is through long-term leasing arrangements. In the case of "long-term leases," the First Nations community must "conditionally surrender" the land or designate the land to the federal government for the purpose of leasing. The request must also be approved by the band through a public vote. This means that if a First Nations community wants to initiate mineral activity on its reserve, it must first surrender its mineral interests to the federal Crown. Then mineral rights can be negotiated for sale to third parties for the purposes of mineral exploration or development. Sometimes a community will create a private corporation, sell the mineral rights to the corporation, and then disperse the profit (or not) to community members once the project generates a profit. But the interest on that money remains with the federal minister. In addition, up to ten other federal departments have some say in the economic development of a project. Finally, in addition to the federal agencies, there are also many provincial agencies that become involved in economic development activities by First Nations people.

Casinos
Following the lead in the United States, Canadian First Nations leaders have entered the business of casinos. Using "up front" money from international corporations and signing long-term contacts with these corporations, First Nations leaders have established numerous casinos across Canada. However, the nature of the contracts and the flow of money have not provided meaningful long-term financial support for many First Nations communities. For example, a corporation helping a First Nations community establish a casino generally agrees to help with the following: financing the casino and linked hotel, training local members of the band to participate in the casino operations, and arranging to train additional personnel as required. In return, it takes a percentage of the profits for the first twenty-five years and then slowly relinquishes its rights so that thirty years after the opening, the entire infrastructure and operation are controlled by the band—along with all the liabilities. Unlike the $28 billion annual business generated in the United States on Indian reserves, Canadian casinos have not generated anywhere near that amount. Canada lacks the large traffic generated in the United States, where casinos can be established near major cities or tourist centres.

Alternative land use
Other researchers (Flanagan et al. 2010) suggest that with land reserves totaling 2.7 million hectares, First Nations are wealthy land owners. However, the majority of the land provides very little potential for agriculture, forestry, and trapping. Less than 10 percent of all First Nations land suitable for cultivation is of sufficient quality to grow crops. This situation was created through decisions by successive federal governments

as to where reserves were located. Under current conditions, just over 300 additional farms could be operating; such a miniscule addition would not bring about significant change to the economic status of First Nations people. Although First Nations land contains over 11,000 square kilometres of forest and commercial yield potential, only a small amount of this is at present being harvested by First Nations people. This is largely a result of limitations imposed by provincial governments through licensing procedures. Sixty reserves (out of more than 2,000) in Canada have oil and gas wealth. There are just a few that have other types of natural resources like gravel and coal that could be developed for the benefit of the First Nations people.

First Nations Perspective on Economic Development

The predominant questions traditionally posed to a given community in assessing a development project have been as follows: How much land does the community possess? What is the quality of this land? Does it contain any mineral resources? New understandings of limited First Nations' participation in the labour market take into account the institutional environment in which resource allocation decisions are made (Anderson and Parker 2006).

A modern vision of First Nations economic development is grounded in the needs of the community and linked to the assets of the community. It allows for freedom and transformation, and is also supported by a majority of the residents of the community. The development has to fit into the culture of the community and may challenge the myth of "globalization," which dictates that we no longer need to be connected to a place (Norberg-Hodge 2010). As noted elsewhere, land is of utmost importance to First Nations people, a fact that is an essential component of any successful economic development endeavor. For example, the Taku River Tlingit First Nation in northern British Columbia has invested in green technology to generate electricity that produces electricity for the remote community. The micro-hydro project is efficient, cost-effective, and environmentally sensitive.

Any development should enhance and support First Nations culture (Newhouse 2005). As such, there should be an increase in the community well-being—improved housing, employment, or social health, for example—as the development becomes sustainable. Moreover, it is expected that capacity-building will result from the economic development taking place in the community (Taylor and Kalt 2005). Finally, economic development of First Nations communities must be shown to

Five Principles of Development

Economic development, from a First Nations perspective, encompasses five principles:

1. it should create self-sufficiency or self-sustainability,
2. it should promote self-determination,
3. it should ensure long-term stability,
4. it should produce integration with environmental outcomes, and
5. it should be based on social determinants of health.

First Nations communities also believe in the "Four-Directional Model": the vision here is of an interconnected structure of social, economic, spiritual, and environmental dimensions pervading all elements of life for both individuals and their community (Orr 2013). First Nations communities also see economic development through the lens of social justice. This reflects their concern with the existing inequality between First Nations and non-Aboriginal communities in many aspects of life, such as health, income, and education. It also reflects the goal of achieving self-determination over issues such as economic development, land, and education.

link to sovereignty and First Nations organizations in the community. As Lewis and Lockhart (2002) point out, there has to be a cultural match between governing and other institutional structures that are linked with individual First Nations' cultural standards of legitimacy and feasibility. The T'Sou-ke First Nation undertook a solar panel installation for the generation of clean energy, producing enough power to sell surplus back to BC Hydro. The community first embarked upon a "visioning process" that included the entire community. All community members provided input into the plan. The community "drives" the project to help keep it sustainable. The project is environmentally sustainable, designed to end the community's dependence on fossil fuels. It will also help move toward a goal of sustainability while at the same time making a profit. Consistent with the First Nations tradition of "sharing information," the community is giving away the technology and information gathered to anyone who wants it.

First Nations leaders argue that a successful "nation-building" outlook in economic development must encompass three fundamental building blocks. First, as I discuss elsewhere, there must be some recognition of First Nations sovereignty. This does not mean that First Nations communities have sovereignty in the legal, international sense of the word but it does mean that the community has the right to make decisions that reflect its vision of economic development. As Cornell and Kalt

(2000) note, government bearing the full responsibility for improving the economic position of First Nations people may be good rhetoric, but it is a bad business model. First Nations leaders agree, arguing that there must be local responsibility for the actions of their community.

First Nations communities must build stable and transparent organizations and policies that enable both the community members and outside investors to have a clear understanding of all the rules relevant to a given organization's operation. This also engenders fairness and accountability by First Nations organizations. For example, the Millbrook First Nation in Nova Scotia has created an online training program to assist non-Aboriginal people to better understand Aboriginal culture. All employees working on the Truro Power Centre participate in an Aboriginal culture and sensitivity training and awareness program. This has facilitated the hiring of First Nations people. The major development of the Millbrook First Nation is the Truro Power Centre that is developed, managed, and owned by the Millbrook Mi'kmaw First Nation. To ensure openness and transparency for non-Aboriginal people who wish to situate their business at the Centre, the band has established the Millbrook Economic Development Council, which has created bylaws and policies that are organized and designated for private sector development. The Millbrook First Nation's organizational structure includes a financial management team to ensure sound financial practices and processes used in performance measurement, decision making, and for establishing accountability by the band.

A second condition is the notion of a clearly articulated dispute resolution process for all interested parties. We saw above that development must be separate from daily politics. Band councils and other community leaders must set policy and strategic plans for economic development; only then may others implement those policies. The community must hire and retain competent individuals to operate the projects. Initially these may be "outsiders," but through the process of mentoring and capacity-building, over time these jobs will be transferred to First Nations people.

A third condition identified by First Nations leaders is that the community must develop a vision of economic development as well as a strategic plan by which that vision will be achieved. Each community must first assess its capacity to engage in specific economic development activities. For example, the community may need start-up funds to engage in pre-development actions; alternatively, the community may require a partner or business leader who has relevant experience or an in-house expert with management skills. When these capacities are present, the community can then begin the process of mapping out its vision and strategic plans. On the other hand, if they are lacking, the community must then develop strategies for enhancing those capacities—such as skills and education—that are necessary to achieve the goals of the community. Finally, there must be a sufficient useable land base as part of the community's physical assets. These lands may include land appropriate for economic development, land suitable for traditional pursuits, and land for community purposes such as housing and recreation (AANDC 2013a). For example, the Whitecap Dakota First Nation (Saskatchewan) first established its economic vision and mission as well as its economic goals before embarking upon any economic development projects. The community's analysis of its capacity identified a need to upgrade the education, training, and work experience of its members before a successful economic project could be launched. When these upgrades were underway or achieved, the band then embarked upon a series of development projects, including Dakota Technologies, Whitecap commercial real estate, and hotel management. The interrelationship of the factors in this vision of development is depicted in Figure 4-1.

In the end, First Nations leaders agree that economic development in their communities requires meaningful control over decisions at the community level. It is unclear whether or not AANDC agrees.

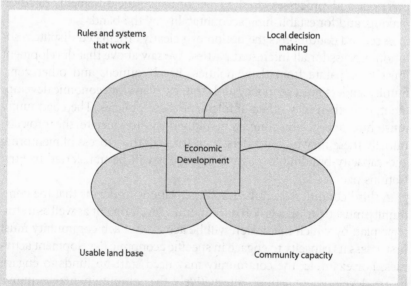

Figure 4-1 Interconnectedness of Factors to Enhance Sustainable Economic Development

Nevertheless, extensive research has shown that First Nations communities achieve better economic outcomes when they have genuine decision-making power; such power leads to improved accountability. First Nations communities must also have organizations that create a stable business environment (Jorgensen and Cornell 2007). For example, the community must develop depoliticized effective management of resources through skilled administration. Finally, each economic project requires legitimacy. When there is a match between the institutions of governance and cultural beliefs within the First Nations community, economic development is more likely to be successful (Cornell and Kalt 2000). See, for example, other reports that support this position: *The Report of the Royal Commission on Aboriginal Peoples* (1996); *A Hand Up, Not A Handout* (Senate Standing Committee on Aboriginal Peoples. 2007); *Status report of the Auditor General of Canada to the House of Commons—Chapter 4: Programs for First Nations on Reserves* (Office of the Auditor General 2011); *Expanding Commercial Activity on Reserve Lands* (Fiscal Realities 1999); and the various reports of the Harvard Project on American Indian Economic Development.

Private Sector

A report by the Fraser Institute pointed out that there are more than six hundred major resource projects in Canada that are expected to generate an estimated $650 billion for Western Canada during the next decade. Each of these projects will affect at least one First Nations community. As such, there is considerable opportunity for First Nations people to become involved in private sector development projects. At the same time, the private sector has argued that it can be difficult to attract qualified First Nations job applicants. When hires are made, there are further challenges with regard to work performance and retention. Cultural differences and differences in socialization make it difficult for First Nations people to adjust to the formal administrative structure of the private sector as well as the conditions of employment. However, some 38 percent of the First Nations adults living on reserves reported experiencing racism in the last year (both in and out of the employment arena), and over one quarter noted that it had an effect on their self-esteem (Howard et al. 2012). Discrimination and social exclusion create barriers for the productivity of First Nations people (Allan and Smylie 2015). Even though the private sector is subject to Employment Equity provisions, there has been little enforcement on the part of the federal government such that less than 0.01 percent of workers in large companies are First Nations people (Bakan and Kobayashi 2000; Burleton and Gulati 2012).

There is general consensus that a strong anti-reserve bias exists within the mainstream business and banking community. This bias seems to be a result of financial officers and legal consultants, as well as government officials, who are involved in the capacity as fiduciaries for First Nations bands. These same individuals also are used as advisors by the business and banking community and are unfamiliar with First Nations culture and organizations. They appear to confuse legal and business risks when they make recommendations to their employers. The solution to this problem is to ensure that these consultants and business advisors are knowledgeable about First Nations culture and their community organization.

First Nations Businesses

As early as 1977, First Nations leaders like Harold Cardinal argued that the creation and sustainability of First Nations businesses was one way First Nations people could become independent from government and corporate control. He argued that in cases where external agents, such as government or private sector interests, controlled the programs or funding for the program, First Nations communities should not participate. Cardinal argued that if economic projects were to take place in a First Nations community, the community should ensure that it had its own expertise, organizational structure, and resources to support the development. This of course could take time. Cardinal however argues that the principle was paramount if First Nations were to become self-sufficient and economically independent. Nevertheless, some First Nations communities such as the Secwepemc and Skeetchestn Bands of interior BC (west of Kamloops) have chosen to work with multi-national corporations in an attempt to become economically self-sufficient. They have an agreement with New Gold Inc., a mining company, in which the First Nations obtain 2 percent of the profits of the company in its first year; this ultimately amounts to $750,000. Other provisions in the agreement provide for additional income over the life of the mine. In another example, the Ermineskin Cree Nation and the Goodfish Lake First Nation have signed an agreement with Coalspur Vista (a thermal coal mine) near Hinton, Alberta. The agreements cover opportunities for community development, infrastructure, and business ventures as well as ensuring First Nations participation in ongoing environmental monitoring of Coalspur's operations.

Aboriginal people today have become a positive economic force—both as a market and as business development. For example, TD Economics (2011) estimates that the combined total income of

Aboriginal households, businesses, and government sectors reached $24 billion in 2011, double the $12 billion tally recorded in 2001. Estimates show that by 2016 the figure could exceed $32 billion. If this were achieved, the total Aboriginal income would be greater than the GDP of Newfoundland and Labrador and Prince Edward Island combined. While individual households and community governments have contributed to this growth, the most significant expansion of the Aboriginal market is in the business sector. Over the past decade, the personal income of Aboriginal people has grown from $6.9 billion in 2001 to $14.2 billion in 2011. This reveals a gain of more than 7 percent each year (TD Economics 2011). Part of this increase is the growing employment and labour force participation rates of First Nations people as they enter the labour market. Both on- and off-reserve, they drive up their personal and community income growth. Consider the context of the Canadian business world. There are more than 2.2 million businesses in Canada today; half of these employ one or more people other than the business owner(s). Of those, 0.3 percent have more than 500 employees. The vast majority of businesses (98 percent) have fewer than 100 employees; 74 percent have fewer than ten employees, and 57 percent have only one to four employees. In short, small firms employing less than 100 people make up 97 percent of goods-producing businesses and 98 percent of all service-providing employer businesses. Today we also find that there are over 12,000 self-employed First Nations individuals in Canada, representing about 3 percent of the total First Nations population (TD Economics 2011).

Weir (2007) demonstrates that there has been a tremendous increase in Aboriginal for-profit organizations, particularly small businesses and entrepreneurs. Of the 6,000 First Nations organizations listed in the early 1990s, it was estimated that approximately 50 percent were not-for-profit or governmental, while the other 50 percent were private businesses. Today, approximately 3,000 organizations continue to provide not-for-profit and governmental services to First Nations peoples and communities, while the number of small businesses now stands at over 27,000. For example, between 1998 and 2009 in Alberta, First Nations companies earned more than $3.7 billion while working with industry in the oil sands. According to TD Economics (2011), estimates of Aboriginal-owned entities across the country collectively brought in about one billion dollars in earnings in 2011.

One of the most active areas of economic development today is taking place in northern Alberta. Currently, about 100 majority Aboriginal and First Nations–owned companies operate in the Wood Buffalo municipality. For example, the Fort McKay group of companies emerged in 1980.

Beginning with 300 employees, they now have over 1,000 employees. They built their business by getting rid of low-profit ventures, taking on smaller projects, and diversifying its client base. At the same time, they began working with major transnationals such as Royal Dutch Shell and Suncor. Suncor, for example, has invested $2 billion in contracts with First Nations and Aboriginal business in the past decade; half of this investment has taken place since 2009. Suncor claims that it makes sense to work with local companies who know the area, the customers, and the environment. They argue there is real value in local suppliers providing services; but this change largely came about because of Supreme Court decisions regarding consultation and accommodation of First Nations people in respect of development projects. Nevertheless, revenue projections for the group revealed a combined total of nearly $200 million in 2014. A second example is the Mikisew Group of Companies that employs 500 individuals, about one third of whom are Aboriginal. Their 2014 revenue was in excess of $100 million (*Financial Post* July 4, 2014, B6).The provincial governments also have partnered with First Nations in the economic sector. For example, in BC, the Taku River Tlingit have signed a "revenue sharing" agreement with the province. This is the twenty-second non-treaty agreement that the province has signed with various First Nations groups and is based on the First Nations Clean Energy Business Fund.

At the same time, federal funding spent on First Nations people has increased from $6.8 billion in 2001 to over $10.3 billion in 2011. On average, this represents an annual income growth of 4.1 percent per year over this period. Nevertheless, federal contributions have shrunk over the past decade, such that the government share of total income has decreased from 38 percent in 2001 to just over 30 percent in 2011. As First Nations businesses continue to grow, the federal government's contribution is expected to result in additional decreases. Table 4-1 summarizes Aboriginal business incomes and projections. It identifies the increasing income generated by Aboriginal businesses as well as their rate of increase. In addition, it identifies the increase in per capita income for Aboriginal individuals compared to those of all Canadians. It also shows that in 2001, Aboriginal per capita income was about 30 percent of the average Canadian but by 2016 it is projected that it will rise to 40 percent.

There are two approaches to economic development being pursued by First Nations. One is creation of an economy through support for local entrepreneurs and the development of individual enterprises, such as Westbank First Nation. The other is the creation of an economy through the development of First Nations community-owned and

Table 4-1   First Nations Business Income, 2001–16

	Business income (in millions of dollars)				Average annual % change	
	2001	2006	2011	2016	2001–11	2011–16
Small Business Earnings	443	590	974	1,255	8.2	5.2
Economic Development Corporation Revenues Realized	3,679	5,836	8,122	11,767	8.2	7.7
Total Business Income	4,122	6,426	9,096	13,022	8.2	7.4
Total Income Per Capita (Aboriginal)	10,950	16,204	19,217	23,412	5.8	4.0
Total Nominal GDP Per Capita (Canada)	35,722	44,524	50,224	58,691	3.5	3.2

Source: Canadian Council for Aboriginal Business 2011, 2012; INAC 2009; Wilson and Macdonald 2010; Bakan and Kobayashi 2000.

operated business enterprises that, in turn, provide for the training and capacity-building of individual First Nations members. For example, the mining company BHP has signed an agreement with the Kawacatoose, Day Star, and Muskowekwan First Nations that provides for employment, business, and community development opportunities involving the Jansen Potash project (located approximately 140 kilometres east of Saskatoon).

In 2010 there were about 250 active Aboriginal Economic Development Corporations across Canada. TD Economics (2012) estimates that today there are close to 300. Regardless of the approach, First Nations leaders have identified three key areas of revenue generation: the development of lands, resources, and water; benefit and revenue sharing agreements; and partnerships.

Researchers have demonstrated that private enterprise with band-member ownership is an important economic development model in use by First Nations communities. However, they also show that the success of an economic enterprise depends on "political institutions capable of protecting investors and entrepreneurs and capable of enforcing workable business codes and the law of contract" (Weir 2007: 11). Others note that there is a critical connection between self-governance and economic development. However, they point out that achieving self-governance in and of itself is no guarantee of economic development. Business sustainability depends on a match between self-governing institutions and culture, as well as a separation of politics from business.

First Nations Business Profiles

Of First Nations people who are self-employed, over 14 percent were based on a reserve. On-reserve businesses were more likely to be sole proprietors and hire Aboriginal employees, while businesses off-reserve were more likely to operate as a partnership and less likely to hire Aboriginal employees (Burleton and Gulati 2012). The Canadian Council for Aboriginal Business found that one third were female entrepreneurs, but less than 10 percent were young, under the age of 29. Moreover, just over half of the entrepreneurs resided in urban and off-reserve communities. According to Statistics Canada, First Nations entrepreneurship grew 150 percent faster than the Canadian average between 1991 and 1996, and 800 percent faster than the Canadian average between 1996 and 2006. Despite this rapid growth of entrepreneurship in First Nations communities, fewer than 4 percent of First Nations adults owned a business in 2006 compared to the Canadian average of 8 percent (Industry Canada 2002). However, of the businesses surveyed in the Aboriginal Entrepreneurs Survey (2002), approximately 72 percent reported increased profits and approximately two thirds had operated for more than five years.

Government Support of First Nations Businesses

Aboriginal Business Canada (ABC) is an AANDC program that supports First Nations people's participation in the economy through business development. ABC works with First Nations entrepreneurs and businesses in a range of ways that include the following: partnering with First Nations financial institutions; working with the national Aboriginal Economic Development Board; and creating linkages with other partners in the private sector. Other federally based programs help First Nations entrepreneurs in a variety of ways. For example, the Aboriginal Business Service Network has been established to provide First Nations entrepreneurs with the governmental information and resources needed for business start-up and operations. It uses the organizational experience of Business Canada service centres located across Canada. The federal government also continues to play an important role in the development of First Nations small businesses through its Procurement Strategy for Aboriginal Business. This strategy, launched in 1996, was initiated to stimulate Aboriginal business development, and to increase the number of Aboriginal firms competing for federal contracts. In 2010, well over 6,000 federal contracts were awarded to Aboriginal-owned firms for a total of over $334 million.

In addition to government business programs, there are two First Nations banks that specialize in supporting small- and medium-sized First Nations businesses and non-Aboriginal businesses. Peace Hills Trust was created in 1985 and is owned by the Samson Cree Nation of Hobbema, Alberta. It employs over 120 people, serving more than 20,000 customers through a network of eight regional offices. The First Nations Bank of Canada (an affiliate of the Toronto-Dominion Bank) was launched a decade after Peace Hills Trust was established. It is a federally chartered bank serving Aboriginal and non-Aboriginal people throughout Canada. It provides banking services to First Nations and non-Aboriginal customers through its offices located in Saskatchewan, Manitoba, Quebec, Ontario, and the Yukon.

Employment

Two of the most important challenges for First Nations economic development are finding and retaining qualified employees and financing. The employment rates for First Nations peoples have decreased steadily since the beginning of the twenty-first century—from 58 percent to less than 54 percent. While there was a commensurate decline for non-Aboriginal people (from 66 to 62 percent), the employment rate for non-Aboriginal people still remains nearly 10 percent above the First Nations rate. Similar statistics are revealed when we look at the participation rate in the labour force for those fifteen years and older. The non-Aboriginal group reveals a participation rate of 68 percent while for First Nations it is less than 50 percent. Finally, in 2010, the unemployment rate for non-Aboriginal people was 6.5 compared to nearly double that for First Nations people.

In recent years, we find that the effect of the market downturn in 2008 has lasted much longer for First Nations people than for non-Aboriginal people. For most non-Aboriginal people, the losses were recouped by 2011, while by 2014 First Nations people are still struggling to achieve pre-2008 employment levels (Usalcas 2011). Moreover, the employment losses for First Nations workers were primarily in full-time work and in private sector jobs in the trades, transport and equipment operation, sales, and services. These are all common occupational categories for First Nations people. As a result of this decline, the gaps in employment, unemployment, and participation rates widened between

First Nations and non-Aboriginal people. Today, nearly 60 percent of on- and off-reserve First Nations people are absent from the labour force. This number is more than five times the rate for non-Aboriginal people in Canada. Barriers to employment are social, not geographical. Most First Nations people entering the labour market lack the benefit of a network of mentors, connections to whom they can go for advice on a number of employment and business issues.

Usalcas (2011) found that for those First Nations people who are employed, there are substantial differences in the type of employment. For First Nations people, over half are employed in sales, services, or the trades. This compares to just over one third of the non-Aboriginal population. Both First Nations and non-Aboriginal people are almost identical in their involvement in the business and finance sectors, as well as health care–related and government jobs. An additional 17 percent of the First Nations population is involved in the area of farming, forestry, hunting, and agriculture. This comprises nearly three times that of the non-Aboriginal population. Nearly twice as many First Nations as non-Aboriginal workers are in "primary industries" such as logging, farming, and mining, while the reverse is true for those engaged in scientific or related employment. We also find that well over half of First Nations people are employed in the secondary labour resource pool. Finally, we should note that First Nations people are clustered in jobs that are temporary or part time; research shows that only 18 percent of First Nations people worked full time compared to over 50 percent for non-Aboriginal people.

Going Forward: Tripartite Economic Activities

In early 2013, the federal government appointed Douglas Eyford as a special federal representative for west coast energy infrastructure. His job was to draft a report about better participation of First Nations people in expanding energy markets. First Nations people argued that Eyford was also the federal government's chief negotiator on comprehensive land claims; as such, the federal ethics commissioner should have declared him to be ineligible for such a role. This request was rejected, underscoring once again the reasons behind First Nations people's distrust of federal government and why they are often suspicious of such reports. Nevertheless, Eyford's report was designed to provide the federal government insights into development of the Northern Gateway pipeline that would move Alberta crude oil to the west coast and link with foreign markets. Eyford (2013) points to energy exports of about $110 billion in 2012 (representing one quarter of Canada's total exports); nearly all of our energy exports go to the United States. Aboriginal communities have noted that while this report has some value, they also observed that it is biased, mainly serving the federal government and the private sector's interests in the desire to build a pipeline through First Nations traditional territory. Eyford notes that there has been a history of distrust by Aboriginal people and provides some general recommendations as to how the federal government and the private sector might undertake steps to ensure the building of the pipeline. However, in the end, given First Nations' anti-pipeline bias and their distrust of Eyford, the report did little to assuage their concerns.

First Nations people accept that energy development is necessary if Canada is to build a national strategy for economic development. But they demand that energy projects be environmentally sound and sustainable, and that these projects involve First Nations people in the short- and long-term economic activities. At the same time, First Nations people and their communities have constitutionally protected rights, requiring that impacts on those rights be taken into consideration. To date very little concern has been given to the long-term impact of energy projects on First Nations people. First Nations people know that economic development cannot be separated from broader issues, such as education, employment, domestic violence, and language. Poverty and lack of participation in the labour market are major contributors to a host of social problems that are now so evident in First Nations communities. Lack of economic development reduces the ability of a First Nations community to enhance its quality of life and well-being.

Until recently, the proponents of major resource development projects generally focused on short-term benefits for First Nations' communities. The argument has been made that many First Nations' concerns transcend project-specific proposals and regulatory reviews. For example, the regulatory boards that are charged with oversight of proposals rarely give much consideration to the cumulative impacts of development projects. This is true even though such impacts are written into most environmental impact legislation. Thus, when First Nations communities attend a hearing and raise issues about a proposed project, the regulators are unlikely to take into consideration issues such as "cumulative impact," land rights, or issues that might involve a treaty. The regulators argue that they are only allowed to focus on the immediate impact of the proposed project. In other cases, First Nations concerns about building capacity or resolving treaty or Aboriginal rights with regard to any given development project is considered by industry and regulators as "not their problem."

In preparing for his report, Eyford (2013) visited and discussed energy development projects with many different First Nations communities in Alberta and British Columbia. He made four major recommendations about how these projects should involve First Nations people.

First, he noted that "building trust" was an important issue. He argues there must be a constructive dialogue between industry, government, and First Nations communities although he is not specific as to how this might take place. A recent study by the School of Public Policy at the University of Calgary supported Eyford's findings: Aboriginal people have a deep distrust of the oil and gas industry and also retain a substantial distrust of government. One third of the Aboriginal respondents had zero trust in the oil and gas companies as well as the Canadian Association of Petroleum Producers. This study also found that land and the environment was the number one concern among Aboriginal participants. At the same time about half of the respondents felt that the development of energy projects should continue, and were supportive of energy development projects (*Financial Post*, July 4, 2014, B6).

Second, Eyford argued that all development projects must "foster inclusion" of First Nations people. This means that a requirement of these projects is the creation of business opportunities for First Nations people. He also suggested that the private sector engage in collaborative efforts with First Nations communities who would be affected by the development project. Finally, he pointed out that government should support First Nations financial involvement in these projects.

Third, Eyford noted that industry and government must rethink their efforts to build relationships with First Nations communities, particularly in the definition of consultation and engagement. In short, he argued that both the government and the private sector must engage in reconciliation with First Nations communities when negotiations take place. In some cases this might mean that the government would be prepared to resolve land claims or other specific claims the First Nations community might have as part of the negotiations.

Finally, Eyford proposed that the Crown establish a First Nation–Crown–industry tripartite structure that would create an open and sustained dialogue with regard to any energy project being considered. In the end, while Eyford's recommendations may have struck a sympathetic note, First Nations people are reticent to believe that the report is serious in providing guidance for either the federal or provincial/territorial governments in implementing the recommendations. Thus far the Harper government has not publicly responded to the report nor has it shown any evidence that concrete steps have been taken to implement the recommendations.

As such, First Nations people tend to view the report as "window dressing" rather than a catalyst for substantive policy changes.

In *Canada's Economic Action Plan 2012*, the Government of Canada committed to improving the incentives of the on-reserve Income Assistance Program while encouraging those who can work to access training that would improve their prospects for employment. In the period 2012–13, AANDC invested more than $14 million for the implementation of thirty-six pilot projects in 134 First Nations communities to enhance the delivery of active measures. However, at the same time the government began to cut support to various programs. For example, the Aboriginal Skills and Employment Partnership (ASEP) program to support Mine Training Organizations was discontinued. Given the importance of mining in northern Canada, this program had been of key importance. The Assembly of First Nations pointed out that First Nations Canadians received just $6,500 per person compared to other Canadians who received more than $15,000 in services from their combined federal, provincial, and municipal governments (Milke 2013).

Conclusion

The Aboriginal Task Force (2008) identified a number of critical factors necessary for the success of First Nations businesses. The Task Force observes that First Nations communities must consider the following question with regard to any new proposed business plan: is it based on political or pragmatic business model? If the answer is yes to the first alternative, the Task Force suggests that this is not the appropriate model. If it is the latter, the community and leaders should proceed carefully, considering the viability of such a project. The community must also ensure that members and leaders alike can commit to long-term involvement. The old process involved continuous turnover on the boards that oversee an economic project; this invariably increases the likelihood of failure. Next, the leadership and the community must fully understand both the short- and long-term objectives of the project. In addition, the community must assemble a board that establishes effective, clear, and continuous communication links with the community. This means that leaders must be prepared to engage in discussions with the community in an open and transparent information-sharing process.

Once an agreement is in place, there should be a clear understanding of the values and expectations of the community, how the project fits into the holistic environment of the community in terms of its socioeconomic, environmental, and cultural goals. This should also be clear to other partners, particularly the government and the private sector.

As the project proposal is being reviewed, the community should ensure it has sufficient capacity, such as skills, funding, infrastructure, and governance structures; or the community should at least ensure that capacity-building will be completed when required by the project. Also, members of the community must be involved in the process of capacity-building, given that they will have to support this process as the project unfolds.

All members of the community and other stakeholders should be prepared to use an adaptive and flexible approach in moving a project forward. The manner in which the community is engaged in the process of supporting a business project should be open, transparent, and flexible. Moreover, a consistent economic approach to the project should be presented that is responsive to the needs and issues of the community.

In addition, all stakeholders should be clear as to what the next steps will be as the project is approved and undertaken. Finally, all the stakeholders need to make a long-term commitment to the project. During this process, the community and other stakeholders should develop appropriate agreements (like Impacts and Benefits Agreements and Memoranda of Understanding) and these must be clear about the long-term benefit to the community. In the end, the success of this process is built upon mutual respect and trust by all parties. This may take some time but once it is established, the enactment of further business projects will move forward.

Cornell and Kalt (2000) have studied over a thousand First Nations communities in the United States, by evaluating the number, type, and inter-linkage of various institutions. Their research revealed that institutional structure, type, and linkage did indeed matter in economic success, as did natural, human, and financial capital. In addition, they also found that the institutional order structure of a First Nations community is important (Jorgensen 2000).

Overall Cornell and Kalt (2006) found that there are two approaches to Aboriginal economic development, as discussed earlier in this chapter: the historically unsuccessful "standard" approach and the "nation-building" approach. This latter strategy has seen success in many Aboriginal communities across North America. The following discussion must by necessity simplify the complex information contained in Cornell and Kalt's report, but it does reveal insights into how First Nations' business can be better managed. The so-called "standard" approach is short term and non-strategic. It allows outsiders to set the agenda regarding economic development, views development as an economic problem, defines Aboriginal culture as an obstacle to development, and focuses on how elected leadership in the community distributes resources. Cornell and Kalt (2006) found that this approach to economic development was characterized by decision-making power residing with the federal government or some other outside agent. It is no surprise that it generally led to failure and continued poverty despite the influx of substantial financial inputs.

Cornell and Kalt (2006) have shown that many Aboriginal communities have proposed a very different approach to economic development on reserves. They have identified five attributes of this new "nation-building" approach. The central core of this strategy is that First Nations assert their sovereignty; this might also be called "self-rule" or self-governance. Self-rule is supported with appropriate governing institutions in the community. These institutions are established as being compatible with Aboriginal political and social culture. In this approach, the leadership develops a strategic orientation to development and reveals a leadership (chief and band council) focused on "nation building."

While the "nation-building" approach has not yet resulted in major policy changes in the United States, the Bureau of Indian Affairs has supported this model in pilot projects. Based upon the success of these projects, the Bureau is currently in the process of proposing substantive changes in policy. For example, the Bureau has shifted from program funding to block grants, developed evaluation criteria that meets the needs of Aboriginal people as well as the funder, and has moved to a partnership relationship with Aboriginal communities, in which joint decisions are made regarding the development of economic projects on the reserve. Finally, the Bureau has acknowledged that self-governing Aboriginal communities will make mistakes regarding economic development activities but such mistakes must be accepted as learning experiences (Jorgensen and Cornell 2007).

In Canada, AANDC has not recognized any of the principles of the "nation-building" model and continues to punish those communities that make mistakes. Such mistakes are used as examples of why the federal government must continue to control economic activities on the reserve. Leading Aboriginal thinkers argue that if economic success is to be achieved by First Nations communities, policy development must encompass the perspectives of First Nations people, including their self-determination goals, the process of transformation, healing, decolonization, and mobilization that have affected their communities for years (Orr 2013).

Public policy solutions need to recognize the strength of the First Nations desire to be full participants in directing the course of their own destiny. Governments at all levels must resist long-standing urges to impose paternalistic solutions. Further, governments must find ways to break the "fiduciary grid-lock" to constructively engage and share risks with First Nations as partners.

First Nations find that economic development is a complex process linked to the maintenance of cultural and territorial integrity, self-determination, creation of community wealth, internal governance that embodies accountability, self-government, and the establishment of government-to-government relations with municipal, provincial, and federal governments (Shanks 2005).

As Shanks (2005) points out, many First Nations leaders find themselves in a quagmire of non-existent economies as a result of a mixture of historic events precipitated by non-Aboriginal stakeholders, outdated public policy, and the social dynamics of the First Nations community. The question today is whether or not stakeholders are prepared to make substantive changes to allow for economic development on First Nations lands.

Chapter 5

Crime, Justice, and Victims

Introduction

Historians have shown that pre-contact First Nations societies were relatively peaceful, characterized by low levels of crime. The community's response to the occasional crime was to support the victim and bring balance to both the community and to the individuals involved in the crime (Hylton 2010). No discussion of crime, justice, or victimization would be complete without a clear understanding of the impact of colonization on these aspects of First Nations lives. Discussion of First Nations crime or justice issues needs to take place alongside discussion of historical trauma. The impact of colonization, according to the Royal Commission on Aboriginal Peoples (1996b), is the root cause of much of the social disorder in First Nations communities and among First Nations individuals.

First Nations people have been victims not only as individuals but also as communities. First Nations communities lost control over their lives, their families, their land, and their resource base through the creation of such legislation as the Manitoba Act, Dominion Lands Act, and the Indian Act. First Nations people have found their culture sapped of its traditions and its autonomy. As Brown (1994) argues, First Nations people have internalized rage and shame on three levels, within the individual, the family, and the community. As such, symptoms of depression, family violence, suicide, and addiction are rife. All of these are closely related to crime and justice issues.

The colonial process devalued Aboriginal people and culture. The so-called extinguishment policy was enacted through the social, economic, spiritual, and educational institutions of Canada, and ultimately touched every aspect of First Nations culture. As a result, social bonds were broken and the fabric of society that intertwined relationships and helped to regulate behaviour was unraveled. The end result was social disorganization, family breakdown, poverty, and economic marginalization. This resulted in a loss of hope as well as a loss of self-respect. Patterns of self-defeating and self-destructive behaviour took hold and are often passed on from one generation to another. The residential school experience is another example of intergenerational trauma, perpetrated for more than five generations.

Colonialism was the process by which settlers assumed cultural superiority over First Nations people, destroying traditional culture. First Nations people have effectively been subject to a foreign legal system (Lane et al. 2002). This process began with the insistence of the colonial government and the settlers that only "one rule of law" could exist. These actions created a major rupture of traditional control mechanisms in First Nations communities, sparking a condition of anomie, a breakdown of social bonds between individuals and their communities. This breakdown of norms has led to a lack of interpersonal relations that are necessary for regulating individual behaviour. Today, it is generally accepted that trauma theory, emerging out of colonization, explains the disproportionate rates of crime and victimization of First Nations people.

The Justice System

The legal system is perhaps one of the most central institutions in Canadian society. It transcends economic and social systems, even at times trumping religious institutions. The legal system clarifies the values and attitudes that underpin the behaviour of individuals who are able to participate actively in the institutions of a society. It also allows individuals to achieve civility and justice as they interact with each other. Individuals who do not reflect these attitudes and values are considered to be deviant; if they break these rules, they suffer the consequences.

The justice system is composed of police, lawyers (defense and prosecutors), judges, and correctional institutions along with a number of secondary actors such as parole officers, social service providers, and court workers. These representatives of the justice system enforce a strict protocol of behaviour. The orientation of most of these representatives is adversarial as they bring forward evidence and argue cases against perceived offenders.

Significant changes are needed to improve the organization and delivery of justice for First Nations people. It is widely agreed that the conventional justice system has failed First Nations people and that alternative, innovative practices, rooted in First Nations traditions and experiences, should be introduced. There is also agreement that changes must address the legacy of over-representation of First Nations people (as both victims and offenders), the lack of First Nations participation in the justice system, and the high level of estrangement.

For example, Environics (2010) reveals that more than half of First Nations peoples have little or no confidence in the criminal justice system. The Department of Justice Canada found that by contrast 75 percent of Canadians expressed high confidence in the criminal justice system. First Nations people are more than twice as likely to have low confidence in the justice system compared to non-Aboriginal people. The National Justice Survey found that people who were more confident in our public institutions were also more likely to have a greater sense of belonging to Canada (Department of Justice Canada 2007; Public Safety Canada 2004).

It is worth noting that some First Nations people have found that the courts have helped them achieve legal recognition in the face of government intransigence. They also have found the courts to be effective in advancing their interests, such as addressing discrimination in the Indian Act. The courts also have helped convey to the rest of Canada that there are Aboriginal rights. However, at the same time, the process of using the courts is slow and costly. Moreover, the final disposition of the courts is unknown when litigation is undertaken (Peach 2011). Many times First Nations communities have had to drop their litigation because of the high cost or they have had to divert money from programs to support their legal case. For example, in a case involving a First Nations community in Western Canada against the federal government, the legal wrangling lasted seven years, and cost approximately $32 million. In the end the case was lost.

The Evolution of Justice for First Nations Peoples

The federal government's approach to dealing with First Nations people and the criminal justice system can be summarized into four major policy eras. In the first phase (pre-1973, which we may call the Status Quo Era) the federal government saw little reason to involve First Nations people in the justice system. A majority of First Nations people lived in rural enclaves, so their involvement in the justice system was limited. Deviant behaviour on the reserve was to an extent an internal matter. Unless it was a serious crime, it would be dealt with by the local authorities. Thus, no programs or special arrangements aimed at First Nations people were seen to be necessary (Clairmont and Linden 1998). However, the famous *Calder* decision (1973) by the Supreme Court of Canada acknowledging Aboriginal rights forced the government to rethink its position. This decision was followed by *Guerin* (1984) and *Sparrow* (1990), two decisions confirming Aboriginal rights. Thus during this era, many Aboriginal rights issues came before the courts.

The second era (1974–90, which we may call the Reform Era) saw more than twenty government reports on the need for specialized programs and services for First Nations people. These reports called for better access to all facets of the justice system, greater control over service delivery by First Nations people, and more equitable treatment in the justice system. These reports also recommended more recruitment of First Nations people into the justice system, cross-cultural training for non-Aboriginal personnel, and the development of alternatives to incarceration such as community service. While these reports were made public and widely discussed, the end result was that very little changed.

The third era (1991–2003, known as the New Agenda) was the result of the Law Reform Commission's report and the Aboriginal Justice Inquiry of Manitoba. Moreover, in 1999, the Supreme Court's *Gladue* decision ruled that for serious crimes, the background and context must be taken into consideration before rendering a decision and punishment against a First Nations defendant. The reports set the stage for the development of a new policy format that would emphasize the establishment of an improved justice system in which First Nations people would exercise some control. During this period, the federal government reorganized the structure and delivery of First Nations justice. For example, policing for First Nations communities was moved from Indian Affairs to the Solicitor General of Canada (Clairmont and Linden 1998). An Aboriginal Corrections Policy unit was formed and Justice Canada created the Aboriginal Justice Directorate. The overall mandate of these programs was to address Aboriginal justice interests, improve relationships, and provide greater control over justice issues in First Nations communities. This was re-emphasized in the 1996 Royal Commission on Aboriginal Peoples. In addition, "tripartite agreements" among the federal, provincial/territorial, and First Nations communities were established. In the realm of corrections, new Aboriginal-based jails were constructed to facilitate the delivery of culturally appropriate services for First Nations male and female offenders, such as First Nations substance abuse programs, inmate liaison worker programs, and the National Parole Board's introduction of elder-assisted parole hearings.

During this period the Native Legal Studies program was established; the University of Saskatchewan has been a leader for the past quarter-century in training Aboriginal lawyers. The Native Court Worker program also was established during this era to address the unique challenges faced by Aboriginal people when involved with the criminal justice system. Both of these programs are still in operation. The Native Court Worker program is implemented by providing first-contact assistance—whether it is navigational or informational—in an effective and efficient manner for any First Nation person accused requiring it. Court workers essentially act as a bridge, liaising with accused and legal professionals to ensure cultural and linguistic issues with the justice system are mitigated. In some cases these programs are still funded by Justice Canada, while in other cases, provincial institutions have taken over (Clairmont and Linden 1998).

The fourth period of 2004 to the present represents the downsizing era in which the Conservative government embarked upon a "get tough on crime" policy. Here, justice programs for First Nations are deemed unnecessary or unaffordable. During this period, many of the earlier programs and services available to First Nations people have been cancelled or their funding has been reduced. As a result, special services for First Nations people in the community, in policing, or in the court system have been diminished or discontinued

The diversion, mediation, and other restorative justice programs that were initiated in the late twentieth century have long since been phased out. Attempts to implement restorative justice have been rejected by the government (Frideres and Gadacz 2010) and other innovative strategies also have been phased out. A number of alternative justice programs such as community mediation services, sentencing circles, and community peacemaking circles, implemented in the late twentieth century in an attempt to provide First Nations involvement in the justice system, are now either defunct or seldom used. Many of these programs were funded as "pilot" projects and operated for short periods of time. When the funding was withdrawn, the program ended. First Nations communities want to strengthen their community involvement in the process of justice. However, today the federal government is approaching crime and justice for First Nations as though they are no different than mainstream Canadians.

Over the past two decades, there have been many more commissions and justice inquires conducted in every province and territory throughout Canada. The resulting research reports almost unanimously conclude that the justice system is both unfair and oppressive for First Nations people, given cultural differences, the impact of colonization, and various discriminatory components in the legal system. The result of this is a dramatic over-representation of First Nations people in the justice system, with disproportionately high rates of crime as well as victimization. Furthermore, they have noted that First Nations people have a deep alienation from a foreign justice system that they see as inaccessible, incomprehensive, and biased against them.

At the same time, research reveals that many First Nations people do not have a "fear of crime" in their community in spite of high levels of crime on reserves and in areas of urban centres where First Nations people live. First Nations people living in these high crime areas may well have "normalized" high levels of violence.

Justice and Law: A Tale of Two Societies

First Nations individuals experience high rates of violence and crime in their communities although the evidence reveals that most First Nations crime is committed against other First Nations victims. Numerous studies (Brzozowski et al. 2006; Charron 2010) show that First Nations people are over-represented as victims and offenders, as well as among incarcerated persons. There have been two major explanations for the high levels of First Nations people coming into contact with the judicial and correctional system in Canada. Some argue that the conflict between First Nations and non-Aboriginal culture propels them into the legal system either as victims or as offenders. While not disagreeing with this explanation, others suggest that the over-representation in the legal and correctional system is a result of discriminatory processes within the criminal justice system.

Today, researchers argue that we must examine First Nations crime in the broader socio-economic context, investigating the link between an individual's life experiences as well as the social milieu in which he or she operates. In addition we also must understand the operation of the legal system. This position was echoed in *R. v. Ipeelee* (2012), where the Supreme Court cited the *Gladue* ruling, again calling on the judicial system to use a different method of analysis in determining a proper sentence for First Nations offenders by paying attention to the unique circumstances of First Nations offenders. The Supreme Court also called for culturally appropriate sentences.

Cultural Differences

The differences between the two cultures is wide, and there has been little attempt by the legal profession or the justice system to address those differences. For example, the deeply held values of First Nations people include harmony, generosity and sharing, and preservation of relationships; there is a general avoidance of confrontation and emotional behaviour. First Nations culture also maintains considerable respect for others as well as a firm belief in non-interference and teaching through example. While some of these values are also embedded in non-First Nations culture, they do not hold the same salience or priority. Finally, it should be noted that the concept of "innocence or guilt" is not afforded the importance in First Nations culture in the same way as it is in mainstream Canadian justice system. In First Nations communities, the establishment of guilt by someone who breaks a norm is not the primary consideration in dealing with the individual. For First Nations people, deviant behaviour is evidence that "something is wrong and needs to be fixed." Thus, the primary focus is on a restoration of "balance" for individuals who are breaking community norms. In short, the deviant behaviour of an individual suggests that there is some "imbalance" between the individual and his or her linkage with the land, the creator, or spirits. As such, this imbalance must be addressed to bring the individual back into balance.

The court system in Canada reflects major differences between western justice and traditional First Nations justice. For example, as noted above, in First Nations culture, the idea of "guilty or not guilty" is foreign. It would be considered dishonest for a First Nations person to plead "not guilty" if he or she had broken a law. Contrast this to the Canadian concept that allows individuals to plead "not guilty" even though the individual has committed the offence. As part of the legal court process, witnesses testify in front of the accused, and are expected to tell the "whole truth." Moreover, only certain people are called to testify in relation to specific subjects. In First Nations culture, there is a reluctance to testify given that it is a confrontational position. Moreover, the witness cannot tell the "whole truth" as it is impossible to know the whole truth in any situation. In First Nations culture, all are free to speak and thus there is no selectivity as to who may testify for or against the offender.

The western model of justice involves conformity, punishment, and social protection; by contrast, First Nations culture understands justice as a process of healing the offender, restoring peace and harmony in the community, and reconciliation. Punishment is not the final objective.

Discrimination

A number of inquiries and commissions have studied the systemic discrimination of the justice system and the impact of this on First Nations people. These include the Royal Commission on Aboriginal Peoples (1996), the Aboriginal Justice Inquiry of Manitoba (1991), the Reform Commission of Canada: Aboriginal Peoples and Criminal Justice (1991), and the Commission on First Nations and Métis Peoples and Justice

Reform (2004). Their findings confirm systematic discrimination in the justice system at both the provincial and federal levels toward First Nations people. Despite the many recommendations offered by these studies, there has been little change in the legal system. The Canadian Human Rights Commission (2004) concluded that while the Correctional Services of Canada has made some progress, systemic human rights problems remain, and systemic discrimination may in part be contributing to the escalating numbers of First Nations people incarcerated.

Researchers also show that First Nations inmates are more likely to be defined as "security" risks, and thus ineligible for various social programs to prepare them for discharge. Furthermore, a First Nations inmate is less likely to receive parole after serving the same time as a non-Aboriginal inmate, and the process of "over charging" is much more likely with First Nations offenders. Subsequently, First Nations people are less likely to be able to negotiate their release after charges are laid. We also see that First Nations people are less likely to serve their sentence in some form of conditional release, an option that is often extended to non-Aboriginal offenders. Adding to all this, the Office of the Correctional Investigator (2006) noted that the jails fail to manage First Nations inmates in a culturally responsive and non-discriminatory manner.

Amendments to the Criminal Code in 1992 recognized the over-representation of First Nations people in the justice system and the systemically discriminative aspects that produced such over-representation. It identified alternative measures and diversion programs that the court might use to deal with offenders. It specifically noted that judges should consider sanctions other than imprisonment for all offenders. However an analysis of judicial decisions since this time reveals that many judges do not take this into consideration when sentencing First Nations offenders. As a result, in 1999 the Supreme Court of Canada (*R. v. Gladue*) gave explicit instructions to sentencing judges with regard to handling systemic discrimination. The court introduced a two-part test for evaluating the circumstances of all First Nations offenders. First, sentencing judges should be aware of the contextual factors that brought the Aboriginal offender before the courts. Second, judges must review the types of sentencing procedures and sanctions that would be appropriate in the context of First Nations heritage. In short, the court acknowledged that the criminal justice system needed to take into account the quality of life of a First Nations person prior to the commission of the crime. In addition, the judge needs to more fully understand how justice and reconciliation might be best exercised as well as how the offender is connected to his or her family and community.

Criminal Behaviour

Individuals living in marginal cultural and socio-economic environments find themselves dealing with the legal system much more frequently than those in the middle class or part of the elite. Some of the more commonly recognized factors are youth, low educational achievement, unemployment and low income, overcrowded housing, and high residential mobility—all characteristic attributes of First Nations people. These factors can alone or in combination increase individual probabilities of becoming an offender or a victim of crime (Brzozowski et al. 2006).

Crimes committed by First Nations offenders reveal a high proportion of violent and social disorder offences compared to non-First Nations offenders. At the same time, property offences and crimes of fraud, armed robberies, and drug trafficking were much higher for the non-First Nations population. In the end, petty offences constitute the majority of crimes committed by First Nations offenders. Nearly half of violent crimes were directed toward family members. Roughly half of the crimes committed by First Nations offenders were related to substance abuse. Only 10 percent of the crimes committed by First Nations offenders were against persons; a majority of those were committed against other First Nations people.

Since 2005–06, there has been a 43.5 percent increase in the federal Aboriginal inmate population, compared to a 9.6 percent increase in non-Aboriginal inmates. First Nations offenders generally serve their sentence in jails rather than in community service. For example, about one third of non-Aboriginal offenders were serving their sentence in some form of conditional release while only about 20 percent of First Nations offenders were in the community. We also find that First Nations people represented nearly one quarter of those charged with a homicide. As Brzozowski et al. (2006) point out, First Nations people were ten times more likely to be charged with homicide than were non-Aboriginal people, with second-degree murder the most common homicide charge. This indicates that the murder was unplanned and usually the result of either an impulse or a context involving intoxication or substance abuse. However, we also find that well over four fifths of those First Nations individuals charged with murder have previously been convicted of a crime.

First Nations Communities

First Nations people come into contact with the criminal justice system on a regular basis. It is estimated that nine out of ten First Nations individuals have had some contact with the criminal justice system before the age of twenty-four, be it as a victim, offender, or witness. Most claim to have a negative experience due to cultural and language gaps, lack of knowledge, and lack of appropriate counsel. Moreover, they point out that the number of First Nations people working within the justice system is virtually non-existent. Generally, crime seems to be more prevalent on-reserve. We find a rate of 7.1 violent crimes per 1,000 population on-reserve, while off-reserve it is 1.2 per 1,000. Property crimes on reserve were slightly higher than off-reserve, at 5.9 compared to 4.2. All other crimes revealed a rate of 15 per 1,000 population for on-reserve compared to 3.2 for all other Canadians (Brzozowski et al. 2006; Boyce, 2013). Overall, many First Nations communities reveal a pattern of crime and social disorder characterized by personal assault and public disorder (Clairmont and Linden 1998). These patterns suggest a general lack of community cohesion, and therefore the need for a different type of justice. However, the legal system continues to argue for one rule of law. Others point out that there is a cohort of recidivists in these communities who commit most of the crimes; it is these individuals who require innovative rehabilitative strategies. However, the government now argues that given the small size of First Nations communities, major service delivery programs are uneconomical. What rehabilitative programs are available in each First Nations community represent a patchwork of services that are a result of "funding dependency."

Overall, Aboriginal people make up about 4 percent of the Canadian population while accounting for over 20 percent of people in custody. This is even more skewed in western Canada where Aboriginal people are 8 percent of the total population while comprising over 80 percent of those in custody. While the R. vs. *Gladue* (1999) case reformed the Criminal Code of Canada and requires judges who sentence Aboriginal offenders to avoid imposing a sentence of incarceration whenever possible, most judges have not exercised this duty.

Prevalence of First Nations Victimization

We saw above that not only are First Nations over-represented as offenders, they are also over-represented as victims of crime. Victimization is not only common in First Nations communities but also prevalent in urban centres (Quann and Trevethan 2000; Hanselmann 2001; Chartrand and McKay 2006). The results from research show that First Nations people experience high rates of victimization; nearly 40 percent claim to have been victimized over the past year compared to less than 25 percent of non-Aboriginal Canadians. Violent crimes against First Nations people generally are carried out by someone the victim knew, such as a family member, relative, or friend. Only 25 percent of the First Nations victims claimed to be victimized by a stranger.

Nearly two thirds of First Nations people living on reserves or urban centres claimed to have been personally victimized in the past five years. However, this victimization predominantly involves women and children. The most important lesson here is that the experience of family victimization is associated with subsequent victimization and criminal behaviour carried on later in life. Research shows that the more severe the child abuse, the more likely the abused individual will be involved in criminal activities, both as a juvenile and later as an adult. Exposure to violence victimizes and traumatizes First Nations children as if they were the targets themselves. The Aboriginal Nurses Association of Canada (2001) has found that many behavioural problems of First Nations children are linked to exposure to violence in the home. As such, childhood victimization and the perpetuation of a cycle of violence is the outcome for many First Nations people (Chartrand and McKay 2006).

One of the major issues regarding First Nations victimization is that a large number of First Nations victims do not use the justice system (Brzozowski et al. 2006). Issues such as isolation, police indifference, community norms, kinship networks, and band politics have a chilling effect on the decision to use the justice system. There is also a fear that the involvement of police will implicate other family members (for crimes unrelated to the charge). There also is fear of exposure to outsiders who may not be trusted, as well as a general fear of the legal system with its unfamiliar adversarial ways and apparently unlimited punitive powers. Finally, there is a "conspiracy of silence" that surrounds domestic and sexual abuse. Studies have found that nearly three quarters of the First Nations people who experienced family violence did not report such incidents to the police in both reserve and urban settings (McKay 2001).

Nearly 40 percent of First Nations people have reported victimization compared to just over one quarter of non-Aboriginal people. Sexual assaults made up more than one third of all violent incidents with a First Nations victim. First Nations young people (ages fifteen to twenty-four) are the victims of nearly half of all incidents reported by First Nations people, even though they only make up about 20 percent of the First Nations population (Brzozowski et al. 2006). Not only are First Nations people at high risk of being victims of violent crimes such as sexual assault, assault, and robbery, they also are over-represented as victims of the most serious forms of violence—homicide. Nearly 20 percent of homicide victims in Canada are First Nations people. The First Nations homicide rate is about 9 per 100,000, nearly eight times higher than for non-Aboriginal people (Correctional Services of Canada 1999; Statistics Canada 2006c).

First Nations people make up 17 percent of all the victims of crime in Canada and nearly one quarter of all individuals accused of committing a homicide. Put another way, First Nations people were ten times more likely to be accused of homicide than non-Aboriginal people. However, at the same time, First Nations people were less likely to be charged with the most serious type of homicide offence—first-degree murder. Only 20 percent of First Nations people charged with homicide were indicted on first-degree murder charges compared with nearly half of the non-Aboriginal population charged with homicide (Wood and Griffiths 2000). Overall, most of the criminal charges against First Nations offenders were of a minor charge, such as mischief or disturbing the peace. However, on-reserve, the incidence of violent crimes—such as assaults, sexual assaults, and homicides—is eight times higher than elsewhere. By contrast, the rate of robbery charges against First Nations defendants living on reserve was about half of the rate for the rest of Canada.

Nearly 40 percent of First Nations people over the age of fifteen reported victimization at least once in the preceding year. This is much higher than the proportion of non-Aboriginal people, at 28 percent. In addition, First Nations people reported being victimized more than once over the same time period. Nearly one quarter of the First Nations individuals reported victimization more than twice in the past year, compared to just over 10 percent for non-Aboriginals (Brzozowski et al. 2006). These data are consistent with the same data collection a decade earlier. In terms of violent crimes against First Nations individuals, the data reveal that violent victimization is about three times greater than for non-Aboriginal people. For example, physical assault was 3.5 times greater for First Nations victims than for non-Aboriginal victims; these rates are unchanged from a decade earlier. Violence against First Nations females and males was 3.5 times higher than for non-Aboriginal males and females. However, violence against young First Nations youth is more than six times greater than for non-Aboriginal youth (Munch 2012).

Women as Victims

In Canada, numerous programs and policies have been developed to address violence against women (Johnson and Dawson 2010; Status of Women Canada 2002; Dauvergne 2012). Despite these programs, research has shown that violence against women continues to be a serious problem in Canada (Brzozowski et al. 2006). To understand this problem, we must first differentiate between Aboriginal and non-Aboriginal women's experiences of victimization.

In 2009, close to 67,000 Aboriginal women aged fifteen or older reported being the victim of violence in the previous year. Overall, self-reported violent victimization among Aboriginal women was almost three times higher than the rate of violent victimization reported by non-Aboriginal women (Wesley 2012). Police records reveal nearly 1,200 homicides and unresolved missing person reports of Aboriginal women over the past three decades, meaning First Nations are significantly over-represented in Canada's violence against women statistics (RCMP 2014b). However, the data indicate that police solve almost 90 percent of the female homicides for both First Nations and non-First Nations cases.

In terms of female victimization, there are some similarities between First Nations people and non-Aboriginal people. For example, research shows that close to two thirds of Aboriginal female victims were between the ages of fifteen and thirty-four, a pattern that is also representative of non-Aboriginal female victims (RCMP 2014b, 2015). An overwhelming majority of violent incidents against First Nations women committed outside of a spousal relationship did not result in injury and did not involve the use of a weapon. Similar findings were seen among non-Aboriginal women. Other research shows that three quarters of non-spousal incidents involving both First Nations and non-Aboriginal women were not reported to the police. Finally, both First Nations women and non-Aboriginal women claim that they were satisfied with their personal safety from crime. One major difference between First Nations women victims and their non-Aboriginal counterparts was that First Nations women often reported that they had been injured due to spousal violence while non-Aboriginal women rarely report this (Amnesty International 2004; RCMP 2015).

Incarceration

We saw above that the criminal justice system of Canada is based upon punishment, either in the form of fines or incarceration. Overall, Canada has one of the highest rates of incarceration in the world. Even though crime rates have plummeted over the past three decades, Stephen Harper's Conservative government continues to promote harsh punishment and incarceration. Recent legislation has forced judges to impose minimum sentences for some crimes, even when the circumstances do not warrant it. First Nations people find that the justice system is unresponsive to the circumstances of their everyday life, such as poverty and marginalization. In the end, First Nations people today experience even higher incarceration rates than in the past.

While Corrections Service Canada has implemented innovative provisions for the delivery of Aboriginal correctional programs and services, the funding of these programs has been reduced to the point where they are no longer viable. Some provinces such as Alberta and British Columbia have created designated justice branches to deal with Aboriginal issues and to develop appropriate policies. The resulting programs for incarcerated Aboriginal offenders include Native Liaison Services, Cultural Skills, and Community Reintegration. However, these are not pan-Canadian programs. While there is a high level of recognition that First Nations offenders have specific needs in prison, the implementation of programs to deal with those needs has faltered as funding has been reduced or eliminated over the past five years.

Until the mid-twentieth century, the First Nations prison population was proportionate to their numbers in the overall Canadian population. However, more recently we have seen a steep increase in the number of First Nations people incarcerated, and this increase continues. Today, the overall incarceration rate for non-Aboriginal people (for both provincial and federal jails) in Canada is 130 per 100,000 population and has stabilized at that number for some time. However, for First Nations it is 1,024 per 100,000 and increasing (Correctional Services Program 2015). Some researchers suggest that these numbers are low since inmates are not required to identify their First Nations status in either a federal or provincial jail. Thus the true number of First Nations people in the jails could be more than one fifth of the prison population. The highest percent of federal First Nations offenders are in the prairie region, with the Pacific region following next. From 1998–2008, Aboriginal adults, as a proportion of adults admitted to provincial and territorial sentenced custody, grew steadily from 13 to 18 percent. One positive recent outcome over the past five years is that overall the number of admissions to sentenced custody has decreased over time for both Aboriginal and non-Aboriginal adults, declines have been larger for non-Aboriginal adults. Nevertheless, First Nations people are still nearly nine times more likely to be sent to jail than non-Aboriginal people (Perreault 2014).

In 2012 it was reported that nearly one third of the women in federal correctional facilities were First Nations (Wesley 2012). Looking at the increasing rate of incarceration reveals that between 1996 and 2002, the number of federally sentenced First Nations women increased by 37 percent, even higher than the 6 percent for

First Nations men (Solicitor General of Canada 2002). First Nations adult women accounted for nearly half of all admissions to provincial/territorial jails, and over one third of all women admitted to remand. Jails for women are rarely near the offenders' homes; this means that First Nations women are often placed in facilities that cannot be easily accessed by their families and friends. Moreover, women's prisons are not funded equally with those that are for men. In some cases, First Nations women are housed in men's federal prisons or psychiatric wards; these women are unable to access programs and services that men receive (Perreault 2014; Sapers 2014).

Nearly a quarter of all admissions to provincial/territorial jails were First Nations people. For federal prisons, 18 percent of those admitted were First Nations people. First Nations people in jail are highest for Saskatchewan, Alberta, and Manitoba—80 percent, 68 percent, and 39 percent of the prison population respectively. This rate needs to be compared to their relative contribution to the overall provincial population of 10 percent, 11 percent, and 4 percent respectively (Sawchuck 2015). (See Table 5-1.) When we look at the proportion of First Nations offenders with regard to provincial facilities, First Nations offenders make up 25 percent of all those offenders currently serving their sentence; 20 percent of offenders in remand awaiting trial or sentencing, 21 percent serving a conditional sentence, and 20 percent of offenders on probation (Perreault 2009). We find that the incarceration rate for the Aboriginal population in Saskatchewan is nearly 30 times higher than the rate for the non-Aboriginal population for those who are twenty to twenty-four years of age. For those aged twenty-five to thirty-four, this ratio is lower, at 19. In Alberta, the incarceration rate of First Nations offenders is 11.4 times higher than among the non-Aboriginal population. We find similar patterns in the other provincial/territorial jurisdictions (Perreault 2014).

Nearly one quarter of all youth admissions to remand—the temporary detention of a person while awaiting trial, sentencing, or the commencement of a custodial disposition—were First Nations; they accounted also for about one third of admissions to sentenced custody, similar to the situation for First Nations adults (Porter and Calverley 2011). Data reveals that while Aboriginal youth make up 5 percent of the total youth population, they account for over one fifth of admissions to open custody, 20 percent of admissions to secure custody, 19 percent of admissions to remand, and 12 percent of admissions to probation. Latimer and Foss (2004) found that Aboriginal youth were eight times more likely to be incarcerated than their non-Aboriginal counterparts.

In western Canada and Ontario, the proportion of First Nations adults admitted to sentenced custody was six to nine times higher than

Table 5-1 Percentage of Adult Admissions to Provincial/ Territorial Jails, by Aboriginal Identity, 2009

Province/Territory	Aboriginal as percentage of prison population	Aboriginal as percentage of general population
PEI	2	0.8
Nova Scotia	9.0	1.5
New Brunswick	10.0	2.0
Newfoundland and Labrador	17	1.0
Quebec	3.0	0.9
Ontario	9.0	1.5
Manitoba	71	11
Saskatchewan	79	10
Alberta	40	4
British Columbia	25	4
Yukon	80	20
Northwest Territories	88	45
Nunavut	98	79

Source: Calverley 2010

their proportion in the population. This over-representation was less pronounced in the Atlantic provinces and Quebec, although the proportion sentenced to jail was still two to three times higher than the proportion in the population. First Nations youth accounted for nearly 40 percent of young people admitted to the corrections system in 2011–12. This over-representation of First Nations youth was more disproportionate among females, who accounted for nearly half of all female youth admitted to corrections system (Perreault 2014).

Upon entry into the jails, First Nations offenders are much more likely to be classified as "high risk" for re-offense, between 68 and 85 percent. For example, First Nations offenders were more likely than the non-Aboriginal population to be identified as gang members (23 percent compared to 14 percent) (Auditor General of Canada 2014).

The data in Table 5-2 shows the substantial gap between Aboriginal and non-Aboriginal offenders in terms of violent offences. The results show that a greater percentage of Aboriginal offenders are charged with violent crimes. Schedules I and II identify specific behaviours of a "violent" nature that can be prosecuted under the Criminal Code. The data show that Aboriginal people are less likely to be charged with murder I or II but they are more likely to be charged with other criminal violent

Table 5-2   Percentage of Federal Offenders by Type of Offence, 2005

Type of Offence	Aboriginal (%)	Non-Aboriginal (%)
Violent offences (murder or schedule I)	82.0	67.4
Murder I or II	17.4	18.6
Schedule I offence	64.8	48.9
Schedule II drug offences	4.5	16.0

Source: Correctional Service Canada 2009, *Strategic Plan for Aboriginal Corrections*

offences listed in schedule I of the Criminal Code, such as assault, break and enter, or theft. The data in Table 5-2 shows significant differences between Aboriginal and non-Aboriginal offenders with regard to drug offenses (also listed in Schedule II). The data also reveal that federally sentenced Aboriginal offenders continue to be more likely to be imprisoned (19 percent) rather than to be in the community on a supervised release (14 percent) (Correctional Services of Canada 2009). Moreover, they serve a greater proportion of their sentences in jail, and have a higher rate of re-incarceration during periods of conditional release. In addition, Aboriginal offenders are more likely to be under supervision in the community and have a restrictive form of release rather than full parole like non-Aboriginal offenders (Auditor General of Canada 2014).

Recidivism Rates

Data collected by Correctional Services Canada show that the rate of re-offending while on supervision for First Nations offenders is about one third higher than for non-Aboriginal offenders. These results are further supported by the data in Table 5-3. It shows the rate of recidivism for both Aboriginal and non-Aboriginal offenders after two and five years following custodial sentences. In both cases, Aboriginal and non-Aboriginal return to custody show increases from 2001 to 2006 (Sapers 2014).

When we look at the five-year period, we see that the rate of return for both groups is stable, even though the rate for Aboriginal people is about 20 percent higher than for non-Aboriginal peoples. One of the main reasons for recidivism is the lack of community and family support upon release from jail. Community engagement programs in jails have focused on "healing-based" approaches as well as citizen engagement strategies to prepare the offender for release into the community. While a number of initiatives have been introduced, not all federal prisons have such programs. Nevertheless, research has shown that the role of elders, Aboriginal Liaison officers, community representatives, and Aboriginal organizations have helped in the successful reintegration of offenders (Rudin 2010).

Research reveals that those inmates who are given statutory releases or have to serve their full time are more likely to be recidivists than those who are given parole early and reintegrate slowly into their community. As such, the new legislation passed by the Conservative government will ensure that more First Nations inmates will return to prison.

The new "continuum of care" approach introduced into some prisons in 2003 focused on attempts to incorporate First Nations values, culture, and traditions into prisons. Correctional Services Canada is taking a major step forward, compared to only three decades ago when sweetgrass was routinely banned in federal institutions and Elders were given little respect. Sweetgrass is considered a sacred plant; many First Nations people use it in smudging or purifying ceremonies. In addition, one of the properties of sweetgrass is that it bends under the weight of a human, but does not break. As such, it is also considered a symbolically virtuous plant, reminding us that an unjust act can be responded to by a kind behaviour, reflecting the plant's ability to bend but not break. Hence rather than terminate the relationship with the other, the relationship between the two parties can continue. The continuum of care model provides specific approaches to address the needs of Aboriginal offenders. It integrates culturally appropriate and spiritually significant interventions when the offender is in jail. It begins at intake, followed by paths of healing while in jail, and ends with programs to enhance the reintegration of First Nations offenders back into their community. Correctional Services Canada calculated that the cost per year for each offender was $71,004 in 2005. This figure is now approaching $100,000 per year and as such, many cultural programs are now being phased out (Sapers 2014).

Table 5-3   Rate of Return to Federal Custody for Any Conviction after 2 and 5 Years, 2001, 2004, and 2006

	2001		2004		2006	
	2 years	5 years	2 years	5 years	2 years	5 years
Aboriginal	11.8	23.2	12.7	20.5	14.2	20.5
Non-Aboriginal	8.9	16.8	9.4	16.4	10.1	16.3

Source: Correctional Services Canada, http://www.tbs-sct.gc.ca/dpr-rmr/2006-2007/inst/pen/pen04-eng.asp

First Nations individuals who are currently in correctional facilities are young, less educated, and more likely unemployed compared to their non-Aboriginal counterparts. We also find that in many cases, those First Nations people serving time in correctional facilities have substance abuse needs upon entry that are not being met by the correctional facility programs.

Corrections Review Panel Recommendations

The Corrections Review Panel report was released in 2007 and focused on five issues: offender accountability, removing drugs from prisons, enhancing employability upon release, earning parole, and modernizing the jails. Until there are relevant cultural programs, and restorative justice principles are established through the involvement of the First Nations community, there will be limited First Nations participation. As Mann (2010) points out, at the very least, there would need to be a great expansion of existing First Nations specific corrections programs if the goal of accountability for First Nations offenders is reached.

It is a well-known fact that incarcerated First Nations people are at a high risk of substance abuse. Most First Nations offenders have drug and alcohol dependency when they enter jail: nearly 80 percent of First Nations offenders in jail are high needs for addiction issues. Hence when the "drug free prison" recommendations were made, the Panel also noted that the correctional system has little to offer the First Nations offenders to help them reduce their reliance on drugs and alcohol. The third focus of the Review panel was to develop employability skills and experience for inmates. However, given that First Nations prisoners have low levels of education and little employment history, existing programs rarely meet the full needs of First Nations offenders, who do not meet the minimal standards necessary. We saw above that a higher proportion of First Nations prisoners are defined as "security risks," and are therefore unable to participate in many programs. As such, until new programs are implemented that reflect a holistic perspective and deal with the deficiencies of education, work, and language skills, the existing programs are of limited use for Aboriginal inmates.

The panel recommended that major new mega-institutions be created in each region of Canada. However, the distance between First Nations offenders and their families and communities has been shown to be a major factor in the lack of successful reintegration to Canadian society (Task Force on Federally Sentenced Women 1990). Also, given that a higher proportion of First Nations offenders are "over classified" upon entering the correctional facility, it means that they will be sent to major regional jails that are farther away from their home communities.

Finally the Panel recommended changes in the "earned" parole process. In short, the offender should convince the National Parole Board that he or she has changed, and one way to do this is to accept responsibility. The data reveal that First Nations offenders are less likely to be granted parole and more likely to serve more of their sentence before receiving parole (Mann 2010). In short, First Nations offenders rarely leave the prison until their statutory release.

Alternative Forms of Justice

Under the terms of the Corrections and Conditional Release Act, First Nations communities are able to provide alternative means for First Nations offenders to deal with their punishment. However the use of these alternative forms of justice, such as sentencing circles, remain highly underutilized and do not provide a forum of First Nations justice. This is due to the condition that alternative methods of justice can only be implemented if the Canadian justice system so agrees. In the case of First Nations women, we see the justice system has not allowed for any appropriate community alternative correction service.

However, there have been some new developments in recent times. In 2000, there was the creation of three Canadian courts for First Nations people. Specifically, the Saskatchewan Cree court, the Tsuu T'ina Nation Peacemaking, and the Gladue court in Toronto. These Aboriginal courts believe in diverting offenders to programs that reflect restorative justice and healing within the community. These restorative justice programs are voluntary and must have the consent of the Crown prosecutor. However, their goal is to have the offender admit to the harm they have caused, accept responsibility, and restore the relationships in the community. Unfortunately, we have little data to provide us with the impact of these courts in terms of recidivism rates compared to western courts (Canadian Criminal Justice Association 2000).

A majority of First Nations peoples support the concept of a justice system that incorporates alternate approaches to justice. First Nations peoples believe alternate approaches would help reduce First Nations crime rates, improve community safety, and increase confidence in the justice system in Canada. However, given the resistance of this idea by most Canadians and the tight grip of the legal profession on criminal law, this seems unlikely to happen in the near future.

Conclusion

Research reveals that First Nations offenders are incarcerated—specifically in provincial jails—for minor infractions that reflect social, rather than criminal, problems. However, once in jail, recidivism is likely. Moreover, the passage of the Conservative government's Violent Crime Act in 2008 has had major implications for the future incarceration of First Nations people. First of all, this act created minimum sentences for violent crimes, such that conditional sentencing is not available. Given that nearly two thirds of those First Nations people in jail are serving sentences for violent offences, increased mandatory minimums will mean longer periods of incarceration and an increase to the proportion of First Nations people in jails. This new act runs counter to the *Gladue* court case that provides for judges to look at all available sanctions other than imprisonment that are reasonable, with particular attention to First Nations offenders.

Prior to the passage of the Violent Crime Act, when a person was detained following an arrest, in principle the judge had to release the charged individual at the bail hearing. However, this does not happen under the new regulations. In turn, the person charged must convince the judge that he or she should be released. When the new Act was passed it stipulated that anyone who has been convicted three times for a serious crime is presumed to be a dangerous offender, and must remain in jail for an indeterminate period of time. Already today more than 23 percent of all dangerous offenders are First Nations people. Since the act was implemented, the number of people defined as "dangerous offenders" has escalated from an average of 14 per year to now over 22 offenders per year. It has increased each year.

Recently there has been some recognition of the high levels of First Nations incarceration. Both the Criminal Code and the Youth Criminal Justice Act were revised to deal with this issue. However, the data since these revisions reveal that the over-representation of First Nations people in the correctional system continues to grow, suggesting that judges are not taking the *Gladue* (1999) recommendations into account in their sentencing.

Chapter 6

The Well-Being of First Nations People

Introduction

Boyer (2014) shows that historically First Nations people had a relatively disease-free society and they practiced medical and health ceremonies with a knowledgeable base of pharmacopeia of medicines and treatments. However, with large-scale European settlement, a change in lifestyle, epidemics of new diseases, and poorer quality nutrition following the result of a loss of traditional food sources (as well as confinement to reserves), population health began to decline. Settlers coming to Canada had been exposed to a range of diseases for centuries and had developed some immunity. First Nations people had no historical exposure and as such, the introduction of smallpox, measles, tuberculosis, and other communicable diseases was devastating (Daschuk 2013). It is estimated that over the first 500 years of European settlement in North America, nearly 90 percent of the First Nations population died of various diseases introduced by the settlers (Dobyns 1966). Smallpox was by far the most infectious of diseases, leading to the greatest decline in the First Nations population. Smallpox, along with certain other diseases, tends to cycle every seven to fourteen years. As such, the existing First Nations population could never reproduce a fully immune generation (Boyer 2014). Meanwhile, other diseases such as cholera, chicken pox, diphtheria, and whooping cough added to the decimation of the population. Between the sixteenth and the nineteenth centuries, any health policies established by the colonial government were aimed at protecting the health of non-Aboriginal people, not First Nations people.

By the beginning of the twentieth century, Canada had virtually no coordinated effort to address the First Nations health crisis.

Wealth equals health. The Canadian Medical Association has observed that in the years between 2009 and 2012, the gap between those earning less than $30,000 and those earning more than $60,000 widened by 29 percent. This gap is reflective of the decreasing number of people self-reporting good health. Poorer people such as First Nations people are much less likely to say they have excellent health (Kondro 2012). Today, First Nations people are more likely than non-Aboriginal people to be obese, smoke daily, and have infrequent physical activity. They also are more likely to report a number of chronic health conditions (Lix et al. 2010). Compared with non-Aboriginal people, the profile of health is changing more rapidly for First Nations people; it appears to be worsening.

First Nations people argue that most health care providers have little understanding of their historic experiences or the practical realities of their everyday life. Consequently, health care providers make inaccurate assumptions about the ability of First Nations people to care for themselves and about their access to services and resources. The health systems now in place all too often fail to provide First Nations people with opportunities to communicate in their own languages, participate in ceremonies, and eat traditional foods (Health Council of Canada 2013). For example, rural First Nations people, particularly the elderly, must often travel to the city for anything beyond primary health care. This travel creates considerable disruption to their lives, as well as for those who must accompany them to the city. In addition, because many First Nations people lack the same level of care in their communities as non-Aboriginal Canadians, their health conditions become more severe; this in turn increases the amount of care they need.

The issue of health care also is made more complex by jurisdictional conflicts as to responsibility for service provision. First Nations people continue to face gaps in health care and other health supports because of poor coordination and communication among the federal government, provincial/territorial governments, health authorities, and First Nations communities (Health Council of Canada 2013). In 2007, the Assembly of First Nations lodged a human rights complaint regarding the poor funding for home and community health care for First Nations children. After numerous appeals and other forms of Government resistance, finally in 2013 the federal government had to appear before the Canadian Human Rights Tribunal. We await the final decision of the Tribunal.

This chapter begins with a brief history of health care provisions for First Nations people, followed by an overview of current health trends.

History

The first recognition of any rights of First Nations people originated with the 1763 Royal Proclamation. This document focused on land issues, with little mention of other dimensions of First Nations life. A similar outlook is found in other treaties as well as the implementation of the first general Indian Act in 1876. In short, health may have been discussed by First Nations and government officials but with the exception of Treaty 6, it is left unwritten in formal documents. As such, the federal government has taken the position that the provision of health care for First Nations people is a matter of policy and not a legal obligation. In 1974 the Policy of the Federal Government Concerning Indian Health Services reiterated that there are no statutory or treaty obligations to provide health services to First Nations people (Boyer 2014). This is again restated in the Romanow Report, *The Future of Health Care in Canada* (2002). The governments' provision of health care emerges from its continuing interest in how First Nations health can affect the rest of Canada's population.

First Nations health was first addressed in the Indian Act (section 73[1]) in the late nineteenth century when it specifically dealt with government intervention to prevent the spread of infectious diseases. However, the Office of the General Medical Superintendent would not be created until 1905 to look after health issues for First Nations people. It was followed by the Mobile Nurse Visitor Program, implemented in 1922. In the early days, health care provisions for First Nations people, as for other Canadians, depended upon family, friends, and voluntary organizations. The federal government was unable or unwilling to engage in large-scale preventive health initiatives until the mid-twentieth century.

The Department of National Health and Welfare, which incorporated the Indian Health Program, would not be formed until 1945. The program included on-reserve health centres, nursing stations, and hospitals across the country. At this time, the Department of Indian Affairs was the centralized and sole provider of health care for First Nations people living on reserve. Five years later the administration of First Nations health services was decentralized, spread out to regional offices across the country. At the same time, the government also established the Aboriginal Health Policy for First Nations people; this, however, was undertaken with the understanding that it was not a legislative mandate. Then, in 1957, the Hospital Insurance Act was passed and its provisions applied to First Nations people. The Medical Services Branch (Indian Health Services unit) was created, resulting in the merging of Indian Health and Northern Health services with other independent federal field services in 1962. The Medical Services Branch was composed of all federally mandated health services such as Indian health, emergency health services, the Department of Immigration, and civil-aviation medicine. By mid-1960, the medical insurance program was created, covering half the costs of medical services for First Nations people.

Since the 1970s, the federal government has argued that all its policies (including health) are built upon three pillars, a commitment that has not changed since. The first of the three pillars is the promotion of community development. Put another way, social and economic development must occur in First Nations communities. This pillar is based on the assumption that the conditions of poverty prevent members of the community from achieving a state of physical, mental, and social well-being. The second pillar is for the federal government to play the role of advocate for First Nations people, with the goal of helping them achieve their aspirations. This takes place through the development of the First Nations community capacity, ideally with First Nations leaders involved in the planning, budgeting, and delivery of programs in First Nations communities. Finally, the third pillar specifically focuses on the Canadian health system. The system is complex, involving federal, provincial, territorial, and First Nations interests. The federal government agrees to coordinate this system so that health promotion, the detection and mitigation of hazards to health, and other public health activities in First Nations communities will be seamlessly provided.

By 1980, the government created the Strategic Policy Planning and Analysis Directorate to enhance the implementation of the three pillars. In addition, this move would transfer the Medical Services Branch management of health services to First Nations and Inuit communities and organizations. Subsequently the Canadian Health Act was passed; by 1986, the government presented its Health Transfer Policy that would be enacted at the end of the decade. This policy identified twenty-seven different programs that were funded and managed by the Department of Indian Affairs. It decided that fourteen of these programs—such as Tobacco Control, Dental, and HIV/AIDS—would never be transferred to First Nations organizations for management or control. However, the remainder would be slowly transferred to First Nations communities. In 1990 the First Nations and Inuit Health Branch was created. Between 1990 and 2004, seven programs were transferred to First Nations control. However, by 2005 the federal government established a moratorium on transfers, and this has not since been removed.

In 1996, two years after the completion of the Royal Commission on Aboriginal Peoples, the Federal government published *Gathering Strength: Canada's Aboriginal Action Plan*. In this document, the government focused on two health issues. First, it established additional programs and funding to deal with diabetes and tuberculosis initiatives for First Nations people. Second, it established the Aboriginal Healing Foundation in 1998 with an eleven-year commitment.

The Foundation's mission was to provide resources to First Nations communities to promote reconciliation with Canadians of non-Aboriginal heritage and to encourage and support Aboriginal people and their communities in the area of mental health. The Foundation took a holistic approach in dealing with mental health issues incurred through the intergenerational trauma experienced by First Nations people, particularly the residential school trauma. A secondary goal of the Foundation was to provide resources to promote reconciliation between Aboriginal people and non-Aboriginal Canadians. An initial commitment of $350 million was set aside for the Foundation, although in 2005 an additional $40 million and in 2007 another $125 million was provided. At that time the mandate was extended to 2012, and by 2014 the final audit was completed and the Foundation ceased to exist.

The Complexity of Delivery

Health Care Bureaucracy

The federal government assists provinces and territories in funding health care for all their residents (including First Nations) through an annual transfer of funds under the Canada Health Transfer program. This transfer is based on a per capita calculation using population estimates that include First Nations. However, the provinces and territories argue that this per capita calculation is based on outdated population estimates. Furthermore, it does not take into account the actual cost of delivering health care services to remote communities or to First Nations people with complex care needs (Health Council of Canada 2013).

The complexity of health care provision for First Nations people can be more fully appreciated when the mandate of the various stakeholders is identified. For example, the provinces support hospitals, doctors, and public health programs for all Canadians, but do not operate direct health services for First Nations people living on reserves. On the other hand, Health Canada funds primary care in remote First Nations communities. It also provides funds for public health nursing, health promotion, and disease prevention, as well as environmental health services. Health Canada also provides some home and community care in all First Nations communities. Health Canada administers the National Insured Health Benefits program that provides supplementary health benefits for certain medical services. AANDC funds assisted living programs that provide non-medical social support and an income assistance program. At the same time, First Nations communities have taken on the role of designing and delivering a wide range of community health services by signing agreements with the federal government. This complexity has been addressed in a landmark shift in health delivery for First Nations people in British Columbia, where authority for health care in the province has been transferred to a provincial First Nations Health Authority. This new approach has been touted as a model of health care delivery that other governments need to consider.

First Nations and Inuit Health Branch

In 2000, the First Nations and Inuit Health Branch was created. This provides for and supports the delivery of community-based health programs on reserves. It also deals with the non-insured health benefits program that provides a range of services to First Nations that includes dental, vision, prescription drugs, medical supplies, transportation to medical services, and mental health counselling.

Today the Strategic Policy, Planning, and Analysis Directorate within AANDC provides long-term policy and planning advice for the management of health-related issues and initiatives. There also are four divisions within Health Canada that focus solely on Aboriginal issues regarding health: Health Information and Analysis Division, Office of Inuit Health, Policy Development, and Strategic Policy and Planning. These offices analyze health information about First Nations people, carry out research on health issues, develop strategic policy and planning, and prepare the First Nations and Inuit Health system to respond to long-term challenges. They also deal with community programs such as healthy child development, youth suicide prevention, addiction prevention and treatment, disease and injury risk factor prevention, and community capacity-building initiatives. In the end, all of these divisions examine health issues related to First Nations and propose solutions. As a result of these efforts, the health care infrastructure employs nurses and physicians to operate alcohol and drug treatment centres, nursing stations, home and community care, primary health care in remote communities, and health centres across the country.

Social Determinants of Health

How is it that some people have longer, healthier lives and a greater sense of wellness than other groups of people? One explanation is genetics.

However, epidemiologists and social scientists have observed that the health of an individual is a complex result of the interaction of social, economic, genetic, environmental, and individual behaviour. These are known as the "determinants of health." While each one of the above factors has its own impact on health, as a group they all interact. An individual can, for example, eat a healthy diet, exercise, and have a good job; but if he or she lives in an area that is heavily polluted, his or her health will be affected. In the end, epidemiologists agree that it is a combination of factors that determines the overall health status of an individual or community. Some actions by individuals, such as smoking and alcohol use, precipitate these interactions. We know, for example, that nearly 60 percent of First Nations individuals smoke, compared to 24 percent in the general Canadian population. On the other hand, Health Canada (2003) has shown that the proportion of First Nations consuming alcohol is considerably less than the general Canadian population. However, the small proportion of those reporting "heavy drinking" amongst First Nations people is nearly double that of the general Canadian population. Moreover, the excessive use of drugs or alcohol can have a number of effects on both the physiology and social aspects of an individual and her/his community. The surrounding environment also has considerable impact on health. Finally, changes in nutrition (from traditional foods to processed store-bought foods) for First Nations people have resulted in high levels of obesity that have contributed to diseases such as hypertension, coronary heart disease, diabetes, and certain cancers (Chansonneuve 2007).

Self-Rated Health

Over the years, a number of surveys have been carried out with regard to First Nations people's view of their own health. Self-rated health is an individual's perception of his or her global health, rated on a scale from excellent to poor. The information obtained from a number of these surveys reveals that a lower proportion of First Nations people report "excellent" compared to the general Canadian population. For example, about three quarters of First Nations people report "good to excellent" health compared to nearly 90 percent of the general Canadian population in 2006. Moreover, we find that there has been an 8 percent drop in First Nations people reporting "good to excellent" health between 2006 and 2012 (Aboriginal Peoples Survey 2012). This measure is clearly subjective, and does not indicate what might be called an objective condition, but it does give us a good summary of overall health of the population. It could be argued the differences in self-reported health between the two groups are not that significant. And, if the two populations were comparable in age structure, perhaps that would be true. However, as we noted in Chapter 2, the First Nations population is much younger than the general population. Thus, while we know that for the general population the last thirteen years are generally associated with declining health, for First Nations people, we find that their health is continuously poor from birth and throughout the lifespan. Second, we know that poor self-rated health is correlated with subsequent hospitalization and mortality (Kennedy et al. 2001).

Nevertheless, a surprisingly high percentage (70 percent) of First Nations people feel they are in "balance" with regard to their physical, mental, emotional, and spiritual well-being. Nevertheless, nearly a fifth of First Nations respondents to health surveys reported contemplating suicide compared with just over 3 percent for the general Canadian population. In fact, the actual suicide rate for First Nations is double that of the general population; in some areas, it is six times higher. If we look at the prevalence of disability for First Nations, we find that the rates are almost the same for males and females and comparable with the general Canadian population. And, like the general population, First Nations people tend to have more disabilities as they age.

Currently, First Nations peoples have the poorest health, in terms of both objective and subjective measures, in Canada. They have shorter life expectancies and higher infant mortality rates than other Canadians. In addition, they are more likely to have inadequate nutrition, insufficient housing, unsafe water and sanitation, high levels of unemployment, and high rates of poverty. Despite the negative impact of colonization and a variety of poorly conceived government policies, many First Nations communities have made improvements in their overall well-being (Saini and Quinn 2013). However, when compared to the general Canadian population, their level of well-being remains much lower.

First Nations Epistemology and Health Care Services

The concept of health—or, as it is more commonly called among First Nations people, "well-being"—is composed of physical, emotional, and spiritual components. For this reason, many First Nations people use the medicine wheel to symbolize their holistic well-being. In addition, the natural world is a core component of well-being, given that humans are inextricably linked to other entities, living and non-living, and to their environment (O'Donnell and Tait 2004). To achieve well-being,

Table 6-1   Differences in World View between Aboriginal and Non-Aboriginal Canadians

Aboriginal (holistic)	Mainstream culture (biomedical)
Relational, circular	Linear, point A to B
Mind, body, spirit/One	Psyche is the focus
Mystical/acceptance	Scientific/verification
Ceremonials/rituals	Psychotherapy
Tribal connectedness	Individualism
Spirituality and balance	Organized religions
Co-operation/sharing	Competition/winning
Patience/respectful	Assertive/forceful
Present-oriented	Future-oriented
Herbs, plants, nature	Psychopharmacology

First Nations people require balance and harmony among all these components. The different ontological perspectives held by First Nations people and mainstream Canadians have led to significant failures in health care provision.

In summary, the world views and belief systems of First Nations people may create conflicts in accessing and utilizing health care facilities. First Nations people are strong believers in the idea that each person is composed of mind, body, and spirit as a single entity. Moreover, their perspective is that all physical things, animate and inanimate, are part of the spirit world. Cajete (2004) relates that the first First Nations cosmologies were based on the idea that the spirit of the universe was within the earth and that included humans. A person's understanding of the behaviour of animals and plants as well as the interconnectedness of all things in nature results in the development of a culture that includes ethical, moral, political, and social aspects. Through this, First Nations people came to know of the "natural democracy" that underscores the relations and interconnectedness of humans with all other objects on the earth such as plants, animals, rocks, water, and spirits. The spirit world existed prior to its embodiment and will exist after death. First Nations people feel that health (wellness) is harmony and that illness (both natural and unnatural) is disharmony of mind, body, and spirit. Health, then, embraces a holistic approach encompassing the physical, emotional, intellectual, and spiritual well-being of people living in harmony with well-functioning social systems in a healthful environment. Health is also grounded in traditional beliefs.

Cultural Competence

The Canadian health care system is based on a biomedical western model, and is considered universal for all Canadians. Its basic assumptions include germ theory, individual responsibility to cure, and voluntary decisions. In addition, the Canadian health care system is based upon a middle-class liberal perspective that underlies its provisions and sustainability. Think of liberalism at one end of the continuum and First Nations communitarianism at the other end. For liberals, what matters are things such as individuality, individual rights, personal autonomy, and freedom of choice.

At the other end of the spectrum, First Nations people think that what matters are things like membership of communities (families, neighbourhoods, and associations), being similar to others, sharing interests, and accepting responsibility for one another. First Nations people aim to focus on the social nature of life, identify relationships and institutions, and restore the notion of community to proper prominence. In summary, within the First Nations holistic world view, a moral breech in the cosmic alliances and social relations can cause disharmony or imbalance that can cause poor health. As such, traditional medical systems in First Nations communities contain causal explanations that locate the genesis of illness within the social realm in relations among people, animals, animated objects, and the cosmos (Waldram 2004; Waldram et al. 2006).

As one can see, the liberal, biomedical model is in many ways a poor fit for First Nations people, who have a different world view. Western medicine focuses on the individual in the treatment of the illness and the individual has the responsibility to cure. Embodied in this perspective is the acceptance of a biomedical model of health that permeates Canadian thinking. This view draws upon a bio-chemical explanation of illness as the basis for health care. It is concerned with categorizing and manipulating the biological mechanisms of the body. The body is understood as a kind of machine; broken parts need fixing. This model focuses primarily on biological factors to the exclusion of psychological, environmental, and social influences. There is little discussion as to how other sources of knowledge could help the patient, such as elders with traditional medicine, or how the community fits into the curative process. However, the health care system in Canada has recently recognized that health practitioners should have some competence in service provision that is free from discrimination and stereotypes. Moreover, the health care system has come a long way in recognizing the need to treat First Nations people with empathy, dignity, and respect. Health care managers have a responsibility to address the needs of minority populations suffering from poor health, when these populations do not access services in the same manner as other groups. Nevertheless, there is considerable evidence that Aboriginal people do not fully utilize the mainstream health care system.

Health Care Usage

Many First Nations people do not use the mainstream health system because they have experienced discrimination and contempt. As a result, most First Nations people do not have a general practitioner they see regularly or have regular physical check-ups. Randall et al. (2012) found, perhaps as a result of this situation, that of the over 13,000 emergency department visits by individuals in Alberta, nearly half were by First Nations individuals. Respiratory issues and injuries were predominant reasons for the visit. First Nations people used inpatient care much less than non-Aboriginals. The study also found that First Nations populations had significantly lower rates of recorded physician visits than the non-Aboriginal population.

The values and attitudes of health care professionals have alienated First Nations people, thereby reducing opportunities for early intervention and prevention of disease and injury. Just over a third of First Nations adults reported difficulties accessing health services. For example, staff at a major hospital invented "code words" among themselves to describe First Nations peoples' issues. This allowed them to dismiss complaints by First Nations people and to postpone any treatment sought by the individual. In other cases, health care professionals have excluded First Nations families in the planning process for a patient's care because they "would not understand" the proposed treatment. First Nations people see this as stemming from a lack of education about Aboriginal history and issues. At the same time, a considerable number (40 percent) of First Nations adults reported that they make use of traditional medicine (Health Council of Canada 2012).

The mistrust of health care professionals is based on a history of discrimination and stereotyping. Other reasons for refusing mainstream health care services include the western focus on disease rather than on the whole person, the life circumstances that may be affecting overall health and subsequent treatment, and the lack of respect for traditional First Nations approaches to healing. Many First Nations people take a more holistic approach, focusing on the integration of spiritual, physical, and emotional well-being—an approach that has by and large been rejected in mainstream health care provisions.

  Traditional medicines are not viewed by the medical profession as being useful, although it is worth noting that some change is taking place. Recently, researchers have examined plants used by contemporary healers and elders to treat various illnesses. For example, research has shown that several plants used by Cree Elders can be used to prevent and treat type 2 diabetes; these plants, such as Balsam fir, the inner bark of the tamarack, jack pine cones, the pitcher plant, and the leaves of the Labrador tea plant, are high in phenolic antioxidants and help regulate blood glucose levels as well as influence fat metabolism (National

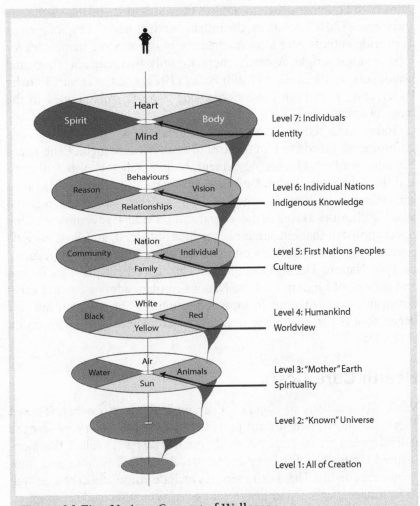

Figure 6-1 First Nations Concept of Wellness

Source: First Nations Information Governance Centre 2012b, *First Nations Regional Health Survey: 2008–10*, 6

Aboriginal Health Organization 2012). Other research has confirmed that traditional medicines exhibit chemical properties that can effectively and safely treat illness.

In summary, the health care system available for First Nations people has its origins in a piecemeal of legislation, policies, and funding. In some cases the linkages of each of these components are seamless, and it works well. However, for the most part, as Marchildon (2005) points out, there are gaps and failures. In short, it is a fragmented system that has spanned a patchwork of policies and programs for First Nations people across Canada (Lavoie and Gervais 2010).

Provincial and territorial governments are also responsible for the delivery of a number of health services to First Nations people. As Lavoie and Gervais (2010) point out, the Indian Act does not outline obligations or provide authority for a comprehensive health services framework for First Nations people. As such, there are only two national Aboriginal health policies: The Indian Health Policy (1979) and the Health Transfer Policy (1989). In both these documents there is ambiguity as to the range of applications.

Today, some self-government agreements have created First Nations government's jurisdiction in the area of health. These include the James Bay and Northern Quebec Agreement, Nisga'a Valley Health Authority, and the Athabasca Health Authority. More recently, cross-jurisdictional agreements have brought together First Nations, Métis, and regional health authorities as well as the federal and provincial governments. One novel approach that encompasses provincial, federal, and First Nations governments is the British Columbia Tripartite Framework Agreement on First Nations Health Governance. This agreement provides federal and provincial funding for First Nations to plan, administer, and carry out health care programs in local communities. The program has just begun so it is not possible to evaluate the efficacy of such an approach at this time.

Health Care Costs

While all Canadians are eligible for certain health care benefits, as noted above, additional benefits are provided to First Nations people by the federal government. Health Canada operates what is called the Non-Insured Health Benefits Program, for which all First Nations and Inuit people are eligible. These extra services include vision and dental, as well as pharmaceuticals. Other health care services include medical supplies, short-term crisis intervention, and mental health counselling, which are available at no charge for First Nations and Inuit peoples. The total bill for these services was in excess of $2.4 billion in 2012. As a result of this high cost, Aboriginal health organizations have become a target for major funding cuts. While many of these cuts involve services that are not a legal obligation or constitutional requirement, the overall lack of services has placed First Nations peoples' health in jeopardy.

Figure 6-2 illustrates the rising cost of health services for First Nations and Inuit people, until recently when it has been reduced. Figure 6-3

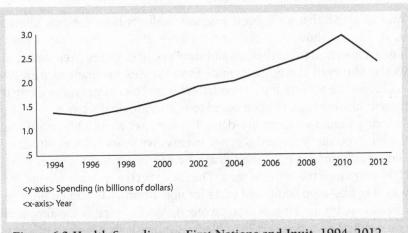

<y-axis> Spending (in billions of dollars)

<x-axis> Year

Figure 6-2 Health Spending on First Nations and Inuit, 1994–2012
Source: Milke 2013, 23

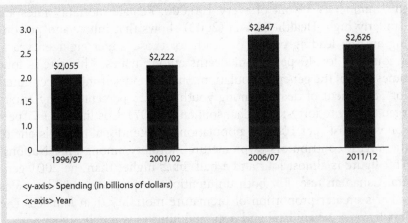

<y-axis> Spending (in billions of dollars)

<x-axis> Year

Figure 6-3 Health Canada First Nations/Inuit Spending per Eligible Person
Source: Milke 2013, 23

reveals the per-capita expenditures for First Nations health. It shows that, in 2012, the amount spent by Health Canada was $2,626 per capita, a marginal increase since 1996 and a decrease since 2006. Put another way, there has been an annual increase of just over 1 percent per year over the past fourteen years for health care of First Nations people. This stands in stark contrast with the annual increase of just over 4 percent each year for all other Canadians' health care.

Health and Well-Being

We saw above that socio-economic status affects health status. Kliewer et al. (2002) show that people who have attained less than a grade nine education double their risk of developing diabetes. Wenman et al. (2004) surveyed the proportion of First Nations pregnant women living below the poverty line. Their babies were three times more likely to present low birth weight compared to non-Aboriginal women.

Using Canadian mortality data, Tjepkema et al. (2009) found that the life expectancy for males at age twenty-five years old was fifty-three additional years for non-Aboriginals; by contrast it was just over forty-eight years for First Nations men. The life expectancy at age twenty-five was over fifty-nine additional years for non-Aboriginal women but only fifty-two years for First Nations women. Mortality rates for almost all types of disease reveal that First Nations individuals have nearly a two-to-one ratio when compared with non-Aboriginal people.

Standardized mortality rates of death due to external causes for First Nations males are 189 out of every 100,000; for non-Aboriginals this number is 54 out of every 100,000. Female mortality rates are similarly high. Health Canada (2003) shows that injury and poisoning are the leading causes of death for those under eighteen years, accounting for 40 percent of deaths among males. This rate is four times that of the general population. Suicide and self-injury accounted for 38 percent of deaths among youth and 23 percent among adults aged twenty to forty-four (Chansonneuve 2007). Costing 2571.7 "person years lost" per 100,000 population, unintentional injury is one of the largest contributors to premature mortality among First Nations. This figure is almost four and a half times higher than the 2001 general Canadian rate. For both unintentional injury and suicide, males suffer a greater proportion of premature mortality than females. The incidence of severe fatal and non-fatal injuries is much higher among Aboriginal Canadians than non-Aboriginal Canadians (Bougie et al. 2014). The data further show that the high rates of hospitalization and death from injury, poisoning, and suicide are all closely related to impairment from alcohol and other psychoactive drugs (National Native Addictions Partnership Foundation Inc. 2000).

Overall, injuries are the leading cause of death for First Nations (both external and self-inflicted); this is more than double the number of other causes of death. Circulatory disease follow closely behind, and then different types of cancer. AIDS represents a major health issue for First Nations people. They are especially vulnerable to HIV infection given their poor access to health services, high rates of poverty, substance abuse, intravenous drug use, and tattooing. Janz et al. (2009) found that chronic conditions such as allergies, asthma, arthritis, hypertension, and high blood pressure reported by First Nations males and females showed higher rates than their non-Aboriginal comparison group. Bruce (2000) found that the prevalence of diabetes is more than double that of non-Aboriginal people. Yip et al. (2007) found that of the ninety-seven cases of pediatric tuberculosis occurring between 1990 and 2004, over half were First Nations children. Overall, research shows that First Nations people have the poorest health of almost any ethno-cultural group in Canada.

Health and Disease

We now turn to a comparison of rates of specific diseases between First Nations people and the general Canadian population. Table 6-2 identifies the incidence and comparison of various diseases. It shows that

Table 6-2 Chronic Diseases (Age-Adjusted Prevalence) 2011

Condition	Incidence in the Canadian Population (%)	Ratio of Prevalence (Aboriginal to Canadian Average)
Heart problems		
Male	4	3.3
Female	4	2.5
Hypertension		
Male	8	2.8
Female	10	2.5
Diabetes		
Male	3	3.7
Female	3	5.3
Arthritis/Rheumatism		
Male	10	1.8
Female	18	1.5

Source: Earle 2011; First Nations Information Governance Centre 2012

with a few exceptions, First Nations adults have a higher incidence of disease than non-First Nations adults. While there are small differences for such diseases as asthma and high blood pressure (not shown in the table), the differences are substantial for other diseases such as diabetes, heart problems, and hypertension. The rate of diabetes increases with age for First Nations people. For example, nearly one quarter of the women over sixty-five have diabetes, compared to 11 percent for non-Aboriginal women in the same age group. Moreover, in most cases, the diabetes suffered by First Nations people is type 2, "adult onset." As Boyer (2014) points out, type 2 diabetes reflects the social conditions—poverty, lack of education, stress, and so on—that characterize the lives of First Nations people.

Type 2 diabetes and circulatory conditions such as stroke and heart disease are of particular concern. In terms of mental illness morbidity, there is a high rate of alcohol and drug abuse, depression, and neurotic disorders among First Nations populations. Finally, it should be noted that nearly half of all positive HIV test reports between 1998 and 2010 were from Aboriginal women. In summary, First Nations people reveal high rates of many diseases; combined with limited participation in mainstream health care service, it is no surprise that this results in a lower life expectancy.

Compared to the general Canadian population, rates of heart disease among the First Nations population is more than three times higher; type 2 diabetes is four to five times higher and increasing. Tuberculosis infection rates are eight to ten times higher than the general Canadian population. We also find that a greater number of young First Nations' people are being diagnosed with type 1 diabetes (Nettleton 2007; Public Health Agency of Canada 2009). While type 1 diabetes is most often diagnosed in young people and has traditionally been viewed as genetic, recent research reveals that both types of diabetes have origins in lifestyle and poor nutrition (leading to obesity), along with smoking and alcohol use (Oster et al. 2011). However, it also has been hypothesized that First Nations people may have a predisposition to diabetes given a "hefty fetal phenotype." This argument suggests that newborns who are "overweight"—normally a good thing, helping to ensure the baby's survival—are actually at risk for developing type 1 or 2 diabetes (Dyck et al. 2001). When these children are exposed to unhealthy eating patterns in addition to poverty, they are at an even higher risk.

Tuberculosis first appeared as a First Nations health issue in residential schools. Between 1884 and 1890, the TB mortality rate was 90 out of 1,000 children in residential schools. The 1922 publication by Peter

Bryce of *The Story of a National Crime: An Appeal for Justice to the Indians in Canada* demonstrated that one quarter of all pupils that had been in residential schools had died—mostly from TB. The response of both the federal governments and church institutions involved was that the cost of implementing certain health care interventions was too high; as such they refused to act on the recommendations of Dr. Bryce. In turn, Dr. Bryce lost his job with the federal government.

Today, some 16 percent of all tuberculosis cases identified in Canada are found in First Nations communities. It had been believed that tuberculosis was defeated in the 1940s with antibiotics and improved hygiene. Improvements in socio-economic conditions, improved lifestyles, and greater knowledge and vigilance by primary health care workers should have successfully eradicated this disease. However, over the past several decades, while the incidence of tuberculosis has been reduced for non-Aboriginal people, First Nations people have experienced significant increases. In 2009, the tuberculosis incidence rate for First Nations people was 28 out of 100,000, which was six times higher than that of the non-Aboriginal population. It is also thirty-one times greater than the rate of Canadian-born non-Aboriginal people.

A third major disease, unknown thirty years ago, is that of HIV and AIDS. Today, First Nations make up over 8 percent of all the HIV cases in Canada. The HIV rate is nearly four times higher than it is for other Canadians. First Nations women are almost three times more likely to contract AIDS than non-Aboriginal women (23 percent versus 7 percent) (Boyer 2014). Health Canada also claims that nearly 10 percent of all new cases emerge from the First Nations population. This suggests that while the overall rate of HIV in Canada is stabilizing, in First Nations communities, the incidence continues to grow (Masching 2009). Well over half of the HIV cases for First Nations individuals came about through the use of infected needles for drug injections. For non-First Nations HIV-infected individuals, most of the infections were due to men having sex with infected men. The rate of HIV infection in federal prisons is fifteen times greater than that in the community as a whole; given the high proportion of First Nations men in jail, they are disproportionately infected with HIV. We also find that about 20 percent of all sexually transmitted infections (chlamydia, gonorrhea, syphilis) are from individuals who are members of First Nations communities. While antibiotics have been developed to deal with these transmitted infections, in many cases, the diagnosis comes too late. As a result, sexually transmitted infections are responsible for a significant number of deaths in First Nations communities.

Environmental Concerns

For decades, First Nations people have raised concerns about ongoing and escalating impacts of major development projects, including potential effects on human health, water quality, water diversions, wildlife populations, and air quality. First Nations communities are both surrounded and affected by development projects all over Canada. In many cases, these communities rely on the land, water, and wildlife for hunting, fishing, trapping, gathering, ceremonial, recreational, and domestic uses such as bathing, cooking, and drinking. Communities, especially those living downstream from these projects, have argued for effective and strong watershed protection. More recently the concerns of First Nations people with regard to the impact of development projects have focused on their constitutionally protected rights (Droitsch and Simieritsch 2010).

Aboriginal Affairs and Northern Development Canada is charged with protecting First Nations' environment, but has singularly failed to do so. Boyer (2014) points out that many landfill sites, sewage treatments, and other polluting activities on the reserve operate without permits. These issues are usually addressed by provincial and municipal laws, which are not applicable to reserves; meanwhile, there are few federal regulations that do apply to environmental protection on reserves. Boyer (2014) goes on to note that while the federal government wants First Nations people to look after their land, preventing pollution, AANDC accomplishes next to nothing. Today, nearly 800 sites in Canada have been identified as contaminated, for which AANDC is legally responsible. The related costs represent a liability of about $2.5 billion.

Water

Over the past half-century, surface water and ground water have been increasingly polluted by many different anthropogenic (human-made) contaminants, such as dissolved metals and non-metals and synthetic organic materials. These contaminants are introduced to surface and subsurface water resources through such activities as untreated sewage, agricultural fertilizer runoff, solid waste disposal, industrial operations, and mining operations. As a result of these actions, many First Nations peoples find themselves without clean water.

During the 2013 year, 110 First Nations communities in Canada were under drinking water advisories, including some communities where drinking water advisories have lasted several years. This has affected nearly 200,000 First Nations people. While AANDC provides funding for water services and infrastructures such as the construction, upgrading, operation, and maintenance of water treatment facilities on First Nations communities, it has invested very little over the past three decades ($5 million per annum). The department also provides financial support for the training and certification of operators. However, it is only prepared to train one person per community. In addition, Health Canada helps to ensure that drinking water quality monitoring programs are in place in First Nations communities. Over the past three years there have been sizeable increases in the budget to deal with water issues, but the backlog is so great that even these increased resources are doing little to solve the water crisis in many First Nations communities. In 2009 the federal government invested $2.5 billion in water and waste water infrastructure. A year later legislation was introduced to develop federal regulations for drinking water that are comparable to provincial regulations (Canada 2013). The National Assessment of Water and Wastewater report showed that it will take an additional $5 billion over the next decade to make water safe for First Nations people.

In a recent assessment of nearly 600 First Nations community water systems, about 40 percent posed a high risk of negative impact on water quality. Only one quarter was in the low- or no-risk category. It is estimated that the capital cost to address these water and waste water systems would be approximately $800 million. Today, one quarter of First Nations housing units under AANDC management have inadequate or no water services and an equal percentage have inadequate or no sewage services. The capital investment to provide basic water and waste water services to about 5,300 homes that currently do not have basic water and waste water services would be an additional $300 million (AANDC 2011).

Inadequate water and sanitation services present a threat to human health and the environment in these communities. For example, research has shown that safe water and sanitation services are important factors in preventing the outbreak of communicable diseases. Beyond the safety of water quality in First Nations communities, many lack easy access to water. As a result, only a little over half of the reserves have fire departments; this places these communities at substantial risk for injury or death due to fire.

In other communities, there is concern about water quality as a result of fracking (Linnitt 2012). Those living near major resource development projects like the oil sands developments argue that their water has become contaminated (Kelly et al. 2010; Royal Society of Canada Expert Panel 2010). First Nations people also are concerned about both water quality as well as the quantity of water removed from the rivers for commercial purposes; this has a substantial impact on the ecology of the environs of First Nations people (Davidson and Hurley 2007). For example, in the oil sands region, the companies currently have water licences to draw enough water to supply a city of three million annually. As the development increases, additional waters will be drawn from the rivers in the area to support the increased development. This siphoning of water has lowered the water table, affected the caribou in the region with the consequent reduced sustainability of hunting, fishing, and trapping. In short, local ecology has undergone major transformations.

Housing

The health of First Nations people and their communities must be considered in the context of their housing and living conditions. "Home" is a term associated with feelings of safety, security, and privacy. However, for many living in First Nations communities, housing and living conditions are substandard, with little improvement since the 1996 Royal Commission on Aboriginal Peoples (First Nations Information Governance Centre 2012). Inadequate, unsuitable, and unaffordable housing has been linked to chronic health conditions such as asthma and poor mental health (Health Council of Canada 2005). Poor housing has also been linked to the spread and chronic occurrence of viruses and bacterial infections (Public Health Agency of Canada 2010), and the increased prevalence of unintentional injuries.

There has been a general downward trend in Canadian household size over time, holding steady at 2.5 residents per household since 1996 (Roberts, et al. 2005). In contrast, First Nations adults reported 4.2 household occupants. Approximately one quarter of First Nations adults lived in overcrowded housing. This represents a substantial increase in overcrowding since a previous survey was carried out in 2002–03. In the general Canadian population, 7 percent of adults live in overcrowded housing. Half of First Nations adults are living in homes with mould or mildew, representing an increase since the previous survey.

Many First Nations people live in overcrowded conditions which produces stress for all family members and, along with poor nutrition, puts everyone at higher risk for diseases such as tuberculosis. Inferior housing conditions also make it difficult to receive many different kinds of homecare services. Finally, many First Nations people are not able to afford to cover the cost of adapting their homes to accommodate disabilities.

Nearly a quarter of First Nations housing units have a water supply that is inadequate in terms of volume or health requirements or both.

The proportion of Aboriginal on-reserve households that are below the Canada Mortgage and Housing Corporation adequacy standard is over ten times that of households in the general population (22.4 percent compared to 2.0 percent). The quality of life of any population is related to the proportion of the people living in crowded housing. People living on the reserve are sixteen times more likely than the average Canadian family to house more than one person per room. This overcrowding is particularly important in view of the rates of infectious diseases as well as non-infectious respiratory diseases such as asthma. In addition to inadequate housing, the sub-standard water and sanitation systems on the reserve all add to the poor quality of life and high rates of illness in the First Nations population.

Addiction and Substance Abuse among First Nations People

Health Canada (2003) reports that alcohol and drug abuse are major problems in First Nations communities. For example, one in five Aboriginal youth reported having abused solvents; of these, one third was under the age of fifteen. Over half of those surveyed has started using solvents before age 11. Overall, the cause of death due to alcohol use is estimated to be 44 per 100,000 in the First Nations population, almost twice the rate of the general population. The rate of death from illicit drug use is approximately three times that of the general population (National Native Addictions Partnership Foundation Inc. 2000).

The Royal Canadian Mounted Police serve nearly all the First Nations communities in Canada, and point out that the top three issues—violence, poverty, and crime—facing First Nations people are related to drug and alcohol use. When looking just at First Nations youth, we find that they are at a two to six times greater risk for alcohol-related problems than their non-Aboriginal counterparts. Moreover, they are more likely to use a variety of drugs, and they begin to use substances (tobacco, solvents, alcohol, and cannabis) at a much younger age than non-Aboriginal youth (Currie 2001). We also find that First Nations people have double the rates of daily smoking (32 percent) than non-Aboriginal people. Moreover, one third of First Nations adults admitted to binge drinking compared to less than 20 percent for non-Aboriginal peoples. This is true also for youth (twelve to seventeen years of age).

Currie et al. (2013) argue that prescription drug use for non-medicinal purposes is between two and four times more prevalent among First Nations people than the general population. Webster (2012) shows that 9 percent of First Nations youth between the ages of twelve and seventeen self-report abuse of prescription drugs, while less than 6 percent of non-Aboriginal youth self-report abuse. However, for those living in urban centres as well as for those who have high cultural participation on the reserve, these rates are considerably lower. Until recently, First Nations culture was devalued. However, the degree to which Aboriginal peoples identify with and feel a sense of pride for their culture has a mediating effect on addictions and substance abuse. Young people who feel secure with their culture and are actively involved—for example by speaking a native language or participating in ceremonies—seem to have a resilience factor that reduces the probability of addiction and substance abuse (Currie et al. 2013).

The Canadian Centre on Substance Abuse claims that one in five people placed in hospital settings for alcohol-related illnesses are First Nations. They also report that alcohol psychosis among First Nations communities is more than four times the national average. Substance abuse is linked to many social and economic issues as well as health issues. Unemployment, family violence, criminal behaviour, suicides, and accidents are all closely linked to substance abuse.

Conclusion

Over the years the federal government has taken on considerable responsibility for providing health care to First Nations individuals and communities. A complex structure has been established that also involves the provincial/territorial and private sector in the provision of health care services for First Nations people. However, there appears to be a considerable resistance among federal and provincial officials to provide for the health of First Nations people. In the end, a complex and often poorly coordinated bureaucracy deals with First Nations health care issues. The bureaucracy involves hundreds of individuals within the federal government, hundreds of people in the First Nations communities, and millions of dollars to support these people and their programs. If the provinces can implement a health care system that is reasonably efficient and effective, why is the federal government unable to do so? And, more pointedly, why have First Nations people not closed the health gap between themselves and non-First Nations people?

A partial answer seems to lie in the fact that the per capita expenditure for First Nations health is much lower than for the general Canadian public. Second, the answer is partially contingent upon the policy and programs developed for a unique cultural group. There is little evidence in any of the health policies or programs that the unique cultural aspects of First Nations people are taken into account. In short, a foreign system has been imposed upon these people with little awareness of culture or respect for traditional healing.

Finally, we should note that individual health is embedded in the infrastructure of a community. We know, for example, that the introduction of running water and waste water management have dramatically increased the lifespan of Canadians, as well as enhancing overall wellness. Having more CAT scans and MRIs has only a marginal impact on quality of life and wellness. Yet we know that over 20 percent of the First Nations communities do not have safe water supplies, over 30 percent do not have a proper waste disposal system, and nearly half of First Nations communities have a lack of basic sanitary facilities.

Even more problematic is that in spite of this large and expensive bureaucracy over the past fifty years, there has been no creation of an adequate health care system that would alleviate the low level of wellness of First Nations communities. Moreover, no minister or responsible government official has been fired or lost his or her portfolio as a result of poor management of the health care crisis of First Nations people.

Chapter 7

Formal Education: Reading, Writing, and Assimilation

Introduction

First Nations peoples have long co-existed and organized their societies in harmony with their local environment. In First Nations culture, education is a lifelong process that affirms cultural practices at the same time as it provides knowledge and skills relevant to daily life (Cappon and Laughlin 2009). Children continue to be taught to think critically, to grow intellectually, and to contribute to their families and communities. Prior to the arrival of European settlers, First Nations people had their own established institutions, including education.

Over the past two centuries, policies established by government authorities have moved toward the elimination of traditional ways of Aboriginal life. These once strong and thriving nations have been relegated to reserves, isolated at many levels from the rest of Canadian society. We are now also coming to understand the traumatic impacts of the residential school system, an assimilationist system that failed Aboriginal children. These schools deliberately disconnected children from their languages, cultures, and families (Senate 2011). More recently, First Nations communities have begun to demand fundamental change: not only must their children have the opportunity to achieve their full creative and economic potential, but education must never again be used against them as a tool of control, disconnection, and alienation (Senate 2011).

Over the years, successive governments have done little to address the crisis in First Nations education. In many communities, only 30 percent of First Nations students will graduate from high school. First Nations students rarely attend a school with up-to-date libraries, state-of-the-art science and technology equipment, or athletic facilities. For the past four decades numerous reports have documented the problems in First Nations education: teacher training, retention and recruitment, the development of culturally appropriate curriculum, language instruction, parental engagement, and funding necessary to deliver a high quality education. In spite of these many reports, little of substance has been accomplished (Senate 2011).

A Brief History of First Nations Education in Canada

The history of First Nations education in Canada has been characterized by a clash of cultures, in particular with European conceptions of education. Moreover, Canadian educational systems have routinely excluded First Nations parents, elders, and entire communities from the education of their children. Historically, First Nations' formal education has primarily been a result of church or government educational philosophy, rooted in religious and secular ideology rather than pedagogy. The consequence is that many older First Nations people have a negative view of education, feeling little desire to encourage their children to pursue institutional learning.

First Nations teaching has longstanding roots in wholeness and balance. Kirkness (1999) describes how the development of the whole person was emphasized through teaching techniques involving storytelling and experiential strategies. Storytelling imparted key philosophical and ethical concepts, as well as reflecting experience, knowledge, and understanding (Sinclair 2010). These stories collectively map the creative and critical relationships of people, defining and maintaining interrelations within communities and with the environment (Innes 2013). Through this process, children learned traditional values such as humility, honesty, and respect. Boys and girls were taught to observe and analyze as well as to respect their environment. Education also endorsed independence and self-reliance as valued concepts, teaching young people through experiential learning (Kirkness 1999).

Early Mission Schools

As early as the seventeenth century Jesuit missionaries were involved in the religious education of First Nations children. Nevertheless, their mission to convert "heathens" to Christians was met with resistance from the First Nations communities. When the Jesuits (or Sulpicians or Basilians) converted a sufficient number of First Nations people to

Catholicism in a given location, they would then build a mission school. These mission schools isolated the children from the influence of parents, elders, and the community. By the late nineteenth century both the religious orders and the government held an attitude and ideology with regard to how First Nations education should be implemented. The religious orders promoted the view that First Nations people needed to convert to Christianity with minimal attention to be paid to other forms of education. The view among government officials was that First Nations children could not be "saved" and instead should be taught basic dress and manners and some farming techniques. Females should be taught basic cooking and household activities, like sewing and cooking. They were incapable, it was felt, of taking on much more. Moreover, if children were not secluded in a residential (mission) school, children's "tastes" would continue to be fashioned at home (Canada [Indian Affairs Branch] 1965) and thus defeat the entire process of educating them.

From first contact, missionaries played a crucial role in the education of First Nations children. Protestant and Catholic missionaries established schools, often with the support of the colonial government, to spread Christianity, move students along the evolutionary scale, and integrate them into secular mainstream society. As noted above, mission schools were seen to be the best strategy for "civilizing the natives" and assimilating them into settler Canadian culture. In the early twentieth century, the government changed its educational policy: rather than trying to transform First Nations children into successful members of the larger society, the government now sought to prepare them for success when they returned to the reserve. However, by the 1920s, the idea of an industrial school for First Nations students was completely abandoned (White and Peters 2010). Moreover, the educational curriculum for residential schools was simplified further for First Nations students; it was thought that minimal academic knowledge would be needed when they returned home. Education became very basic, and for those students that survived, few progressed beyond grade 6 before leaving the mission schools.

The residential school was a single focus of government First Nations education policy that lasted from 1830 until the late twentieth century. First Nations children were sent to boarding schools by consent or coercion; some of the children lived close to the school, while others were sent from many miles away. The central goal was to "civilize" and educate the students so they no longer abided by First Nations traditions. It was also to convert them to a form of Christianity. In short, the strategy was to assimilate First Nations children into the larger Canadian society, taking up mainstream values and norms. However, there was considerable discrimination, and this prevented First Nations people from successful integration into Canadian society.

The appalling conditions and overall negative impacts of the residential schools began to be understood by 1970, although the last residential school did not close until 1996. However, much of the information was withheld from the general public, from the initial revelations of physical and sexual abuse to later revelations of high mortality rate of First Nations children at the schools. It would not be until the publication of the report of the Royal Commission on Aboriginal Peoples (1996b) that the residential school system would be publicly characterized as a "failed policy." By closing the residential schools, government officials believe the problem to be solved. This ignores the historical trauma that continues to have adverse effects on First Nations peoples today. The public disclosure of Phil Fontaine in 1990 with regard to the physical and sexual abuse he sustained while in the residential school finally forced the public to face the impact of the government's policy and attempt to deal with it.

Residential Schools

From the opening of the first residential school in Brantford, Ontario, in 1831 to the last closure in 1996, approximately 130 schools were founded and hundreds of thousands of Aboriginal children were enrolled (Aboriginal Healing Foundation 2006). During this 167-year period, five generations of Aboriginal families spent their entire childhood in these schools. At its peak, the residential school system had eighty schools in operation across Canada. Although the stated purpose of the schools was to provide an education to Aboriginal children, they were subjected to continuous abuse in an attempt to assimilate them into mainstream culture (Mendelson 2006).

The policy of assimilation was buttressed by legislation (1894) that would allow police to arrest parents who did not send their children to school, as well as to forcibly remove children from their families. While the residential schools were established by the federal government, the operation and management was passed on to religious organizations. Over 60 percent of the schools were operated by the Roman Catholics. By 1940 the residential school system was in full operation across the country, housing an estimated 80,000 students. These schools processed more than 150,000 First Nations, Inuit, and Métis children over this period. As pointed out by Knockwood (2001), Milloy (1999), and Hamilton and Sinclair (1991), the schools were built of cheap material, employed staff that had little or no teacher training, were overcrowded, and provided little secular education for the students. When the Department of Indian Affairs reduced its grants, the quality of schooling fell substantially. In the end, an environment was created in which neglect and abuse ran rampant (Miller 2009).

Student experience in the residential schools has been and continues to be documented through the Healing Foundation as well as the Truth and Reconciliation Commission. Survivors have told of death from malnutrition and preventable diseases like smallpox. It is estimated that over one quarter of the students attending a residential school died while in attendance. Thus far, nearly 8,000 deaths have been accounted for by the Commission. The Truth and Reconciliation Commission noted that the odds of dying for children in an Indian Residential school was one in twenty-five; higher than the odds of dying for Canadians serving in WWII (one in twenty-six). Students were subject to extreme physical punishment for trivial acts, such as speaking their native language. Physical, mental, and sexual abuse was common in some schools, not only by the administrators and caretakers but also by older students. This last issue has become most problematic for people who were abused by their fellow students and now, as adults, find themselves living in the same community as their abusers.

At the same time, some residential school attendees have argued that the educational and assimilation experience was positive. Not all residential schools were abusive and coercive; there is some connection between student experience and a caring teaching staff. The new Indian Act, which was part of Bill C-428, abolished residential schools.

As more and more residential school survivors began to seek legal redress from the government, it became clear that a solution was needed. Government officials responded several different ways. First, they began to sue the churches that operated the schools. The courts, however, ruled that both the government and the churches were liable for damages. In 2001, the federal government created Indian Residential Schools Resolution Canada, a department designed to deal specifically with First Nations people bringing legal action against the government. Two years later it was clear (partially on the advice of the Canadian Law Association) that the courts would soon be clogged with thousands of cases; the courts would be mired in resolving these cases for years to come. The Dispute Resolution program was then established. However, it was complex and politically unacceptable to the courts, lawyers, and First Nations people and did not resolve the disputes any faster than before. As such, a new approach was enacted in 2006 by the Conservative government when the federal government, legal representatives of residential school claimants, and the lawyers for the various churches agreed to a Common Experience Payment. In this way, the process of dealing with residential school attendees began within the Indian Residential Schools Settlement Agreement.

The process begins with a lengthy search to determine if the applicant attended a residential school. Once this is confirmed, the individual is paid $10,000 for the first year and $3,000 for each additional year he or she attended a residential school. If the applicant is satisfied, the payment is made and the process ends. However, if the applicant is able to document additional abuse, an out-of-court process for the resolution of claims through the Negotiated Settlement Process can be pursued. As of 2013, $1.61 billion had been paid out to 99 percent of the 80,000 applicants in the Common Experience Payment process. The average payout was just under $20,000. In the Negotiated Settlement process, 730 claims were resolved and under the Independent Assessment Process hearings just over 4,000 claims were settled. The average payout for these claimants was just over $115,000 for a total of $500 million. In the end, nearly 32,000 claims have been resolved by the Independent Assessment Process with another 6,000 in process. The total compensation for this process has been nearly $3 billion.

These payments were not the choice of former students as a means of addressing this issue. Former students lobbied hard for full restitution and reconciliation instead of the arbitrary amount paid to them. Preliminary research suggests that about one third of the successful claimants have given the money to various charities and Aboriginal organizations; money was not the primary motivation for bringing a claim against the government. Rather, reconciliation was the underlying motive. Others have not applied for the funding: they feel that by accepting the money, they would be absolving the federal government of its actions.

In addition, the federal government implemented the Truth and Reconciliation Commission. This Commission was created after considerable turmoil in finding commissioners. Its goal was to prepare a historical record on the policies and operations of the schools. It would leave, as a legacy, a research centre that would be a permanent archive. In addition, the Commission has spent its moneys on Commemoration funding—creation of plaques, totem poles, theatrical pieces, museum exhibitions, and community gatherings. It also has created an archive for documents related to the experiences of residential schools. Thus far, 3.5 million documents have been made available although many of the churches that operated residential schools have not been forthcoming, particularly the Catholic Church. Finally, the Commission has held seven national events, bringing Aboriginal and non-Aboriginal people together, across the country. These were completed in 2014. The Commission is now writing up its final report.

The final report will not be completed and made public until 2016. However, the Commission has published its Interim Report, entitled *Truth and Reconciliation Commission of Canada: Interim Report* (2012). This report reveals the various activities that have been undertaken by the Commission since 2009. It also makes several recommendations focusing on educational support for residential school survivors, the process of reconciliation and how Aboriginal students in the residential schools can be honoured. Finally, it also provides a summary of what the interviewed survivors told the Commission. Over three quarters of the individuals interviewed revealed that the experience has had a significant impact in shaping their lives after leaving the residential school.

In 2015, the Commission released the Summary of the Final Report of the Truth and Reconciliation Commission: *Honouring the Truth, Reconciling for the Future*. The report identifies the residential school program as "cultural genocide" and calls for changes to government policies and programs related to Aboriginal peoples. It also makes ninety-four specific recommendations; specifically noting that reconciliation is not an Aboriginal problem but rather a Canadian problem that involves all Canadians including business leaders, as well as municipal and provincial governments. Some of the specific recommendations are to launch a national inquiry to investigate the violence exhibited by Aboriginal people and its relationship to the legacy of residential schools; launch a national inquiry into missing and murdered Aboriginal women; implement the United Nations Declaration on the Rights of Indigenous Peoples; establish a Royal Proclamation to be made by the federal government regarding its future actions with Aboriginal people; and for the federal government to renew treaty establishments and change the legal system to make Aboriginal people fully fledged partners in Confederation. Overall, the Commission sees education as a key element in achieving reconciliation and incorporating Aboriginal people into the social and economic fabric of Canada. At the same time, the Conservative government has not endorsed any of the recommendations and has argued that it will wait for the full report (six volumes) before responding.

The Indian residential schools experience continues to shape the lives of both reserve and urban First Nations peoples today. Among those urban First Nations peoples who say they (or a family member) were a student in one of these schools, three quarters report that this experience, or the experience of their family member, has had either a significant impact (50 percent) or some impact (23 percent) in shaping their lives (Aboriginal Healing Foundation 2003).

The Federal Role

Under the Constitution Act, 1867, the provision of education to Canadians is under the jurisdiction of provincial governments. The federal government is responsible for elementary and secondary education on reserves (federal responsibility for post-secondary education remains unclear). Responsibility for education to off-reserve First Nations youth as well as for those who wish to proceed beyond high school matriculation remains a much-debated issue.

As an agent of the federal government, AANDC has responsibility for First Nations primary and secondary education through its Elementary and Secondary Education Program. This program provides funding for educational services for on-reserve schools, reimbursement of tuition costs for students who attend off-reserve provincial schools, and other services such as transportation (Senate 2011). AANDC claims that it deals with educational programming just as it does for other service programming for First Nations people. On paper this means that AANDC takes the position of a funder, while First Nations communities themselves manage the education. However, in reality, AANDC still maintains considerable control, requiring First Nations communities to provide extensive reporting. AANDC claims to have a statutory obligation for education.

The AADNC *Report on Plans and Priorities* (2011–12) reports spending of about $1.65 billion for educational services in that year, with projections of $1.7 billion for 2013–14. Of that amount, about $1.55 billion was invested in First Nations education from kindergarten to grade 12, with more than $322 million to support post-secondary education for First Nations and Inuit students across Canada. AANDC provides about $14,000 per student, somewhat less in Manitoba and Saskatchewan.

Regardless of the real cost of capital and other support services, since 1996 there has been a 2 percent cap on annual increases in AANDC's education funding, including capital expenditures (Senate 2011). AANDC also provides approximately $200 million per year to support infrastructure costs for education facilities. In 2012, the federal government also agreed to invest $275 million over the next three years to build and renovate schools on the reserve. This money also was to be used for literacy programs and other services for First Nations students, as well as to strengthen the linkage between reserve and provincial schools. This funding supported approximately 116,400 elementary and secondary students, and about 22,000 post-secondary students.

The White Paper

In 1969, the Liberal government under Pierre Trudeau introduced an integration policy in its *Statement of the Government of Canada on Indian Policy*. At the core of this document was the complete integration of First Nations people into the existing provincial and territorial education systems. However, a wide coalition of agencies, churches, and organizations opposed this integration, and in 1970 the government withdrew the policy. The Conservatives reintroduced the discussion in 1984 when a leaked report (*Nielsen Task Force Report*, 1985) recommended that the concept of "Indian" be eliminated and reserves be abolished. Other initiatives by succeeding governments have tried to raise the issue but have found it a politically unviable policy. It would not be until 2011 that Harper's Conservative government introduced new legislation dealing with First Nations education. However, it was rejected by the Assembly of First Nations as well as regional chiefs. In 2014, a revised education policy (First Nations Education Act) was introduced but it also was rejected by First Nations people. As such, the federal government has withdrawn its policy paper.

Many scholars argue that First Nations and federal government representatives who negotiated the various treaties across Canada agreed that the treaties were to provide formal education to First Nations people as well as to future generations. This would allow, as Morris (1991 [1880]) pointed out, the supplementation of traditional educational practices with western teaching so First Nations people could live and prosper and provide for their people. However, over time these obligations of the federal government were forgotten or ignored. As noted above, the federal government attempted to initiate several policy documents that would relieve them of this obligation. While failing to phase out the federal governments' commitment to support education, it made arrangements with provincial officials so that provincial schools would take First Nations students (primary and secondary) on a "cost-recovery" basis. As such, if a local school was not available for First Nations students on the reserve, they would be bused to the nearest provincial school for their education. However, First Nations students would not receive any special curriculum, including language training, and they would be expected to succeed in the provincial educational curriculum.

Education Reform in the Twenty-First Century

In 1948 a Joint Parliamentary Committee on Indian Affairs submitted a report identifying the problems facing First Nations children in the educational system. Its recommendation was to begin a process by which First Nations students would be sent to provincial schools for their primary and secondary education, in order to hasten the assimilation process and to bring First Nations students into the new educational system. In 1967 the *Hawthorne Report* drew attention to the poor quality of First Nations education, and agreed that First Nations children should be placed in provincial public schools.

This policy shift increased the role of the provinces at the same time that it diminished the role of the federal government and churches in the education of First Nations children. Nevertheless, little was done to change the educational curriculum in reserve or provincial schools, including native languages, history, and culture. By 1970 nearly two thirds of First Nations students were attending provincial public schools. In the late 1970s the federal government began to place more management and administration of education into the hands of local First Nations communities. For example, Ottawa agreed to allow on-reserve schools to be operated by First Nations communities. However, control still remains with the Minister of Aboriginal Affairs and Northern Development and there has been no attempt to combine reserve schools into districts, as in the provincial case.

About 80 percent of all bands have an AANDC school in their community (particularly primary schools) and local control has yielded dividends in terms of attendance and graduation rates. Nevertheless, the quality of these schools and the educational attainment of students do not match their provincial cohorts. Some provinces and First Nations communities are taking steps to enhance the quality of the education curriculum for students. For example, recently the Saskatchewan government invested $3 million to improve education for First Nations students through supporting parents and elders in their children's education. In Alberta, the Kainai of the Blood First Nations have a new partnership with the Martin Aboriginal Educational Initiative and Scotiabank to launch an Aboriginal youth entrepreneurship program at the Kainai high school.

First Nations Control of Education

By 1972, First Nations leaders prepared a number of reports rejecting the plan to transfer all educational services for First Nations to provincial and territorial governments. *The Brown Paper*, *Wabung* and Harold Cardinal's *Red Paper* all countered the content of the federal government's White Paper, arguing for local control of education. The National Indian Brotherhood, precursor to the Assembly of First Nations, presented its vision of education in a report entitled *Indian Control of Indian Education* (1972). All these documents argued that the key to improving the education attainment of First Nations youth included parental responsibility, the provision of First Nations curricula, and First Nations local control of education. Many First Nations leaders argue that even though the government agreed to implement the policy of Indian Control of Indian Education, First Nations control has only meant limited administration of federal education programs and policies.

The policy of First Nations students attending provincial schools was seen as a failure. Facing discrimination, isolation, and a change in school and social environment, many students withdrew. Attendance dropped to 20 percent, grades were well below provincial averages, and graduation rates of these students seldom exceeded 15 percent.

In the end, the federal government fulfilled its treaty obligations to provide schools on the reserve, allowing the introduction of band-operated schools that reflected some local control and management by on-reserve residents. As a result of this change, school attendance increased, graduation rates improved, and the number of students going on to post-secondary educational institutions greatly increased. However, the quality of the education in these schools has not been at a level commensurate with the provincial public school system. The lack of teacher competencies, political interference in school operations, and lack of community and parental support have all affected the quality of education, particularly in the areas of math, science, and technology.

First Nations Education Today

Once the provincial school linkage was identified as a failed solution, First Nations once again argued for local control. As a result, nearly every First Nations community was provided with a school (mostly primary, but with some secondary). These federally funded schools are called "band" schools and are locally managed and controlled. Students can still chose between attending a band-operated school or a provincial/territorial public school. However, for many secondary students, there is no choice if the local community does not have educational services that extend beyond grade 9, and thus must attend a public school in a nearby community to continue their education.

According to AANDC, today there are over 500 band-operated schools in Canada. Current figures show that about 60 percent of all First Nations students attend band schools with the remainder attending provincial or private schools (see Table 7-1). Teachers at band-operated schools must be provincially certified to teach, and the school must follow the provincial curriculum. Some of these schools are supported by regional education service organizations that were initiated and funded by groups of First Nations, with additional support from AANDC. However, in most cases band-operated schools are independent institutions with few support systems to help with teaching or school administration. Teachers, for example, are not part of the provincial Teacher Association, and have no access to support from provincial agencies. Teachers are not able to access provincial training programs to upgrade qualifications or develop specializations, such as counseling or disability training (Senate 2011).

Barriers to Further Education or Training

Ever more First Nations students are completing primary and secondary schooling as well as going on to post-secondary education. In terms of

Table 7-1 First Nations Elementary and Secondary Education: Number of Full-Time Equivalent Students by Type of School, 2011–12

	BC	AB	SK	MB	ON	QC	Atlantic	National Total
Full-Time Equivalent Students:								
Band-operated schools	4,788	9,004	15,130	15,567	11,699	6,310	3,893	66,388
Provincial schools	8,192	6,648	3,434	5,392	6,007	9,001	2,190	40,863
Private schools	638	179	103	155	485	350	15	1,925
Federal schools		91			1,330			1,421
Total of Full-Time Equivalent (FTE) students	13,618	15,922	18,666	21,114	19,520	15,661	6,098	110,597*

*NOTE: Data rounded to whole numbers. Figures may not add up due to rounding.

Source: AANDC, www.aadnc-aandc.gc.ca/eng/1349140116208/1349140158945

those who continue on to college or trade school, the figures for First Nations youth are similar to non-Aboriginal youth. However, many First Nations youth never complete high school and their university completion rates are far lower than for non-Aboriginal people (Statistics Canada 2013b; CESC 2007; Statistics Canada 2008b).

A number of barriers are responsible for the low educational achievements. First, most young people who want to continue their education beyond high school feel they cannot afford university. This is true for both men and women. Second, young people feel that family and personal responsibilities are a barrier to further schooling; this was reported for two thirds of females, but only about 20 percent of males. Related to this is the barrier of personal health. Some people report that their personal health is an impediment to continuing their education. Time constraints are also a barrier; youth claimed to be too busy with little time to study if they continued their education. Another key matter is self-confidence and feeling unprepared for further schooling. Overall, about 40 percent reported that taking post-secondary courses was not a high personal priority; this was particularly true for men. Finally, many young First Nations people reported that while they might have wished to continue their education, the courses that were available did not match their interests.

Other barriers to obtaining a university education lie in the nature of the reserve educational system. First, as noted elsewhere, students graduating from high school do not have the requisite training to successfully transfer into university. Their math, science, and English competencies are not strong enough to gain entry or to complete university. Finally, many First Nations students lack the support from family and community in order to succeed in the post-secondary educational institutions.

The Education Gap

The gap in educational attainment between First Nations people and the rest of the Canadian population over the past century has been significant. The Auditor General of Canada (2004) estimated that it will take nearly thirty years, at the current rate of progress, for First Nations students to reach parity in academic achievement with other Canadians. Today, at least half of the on-reserve population aged twenty-five to thirty-four have not graduated from high school compared with 10 percent for other Canadians of the same age (see Figure 7-1). A comparison of the 2001 and 2011 data indicate that little progress has been made in improving the educational achievement rates for First Nations children. Figure 7-2 allows for a comparison between First Nations people and non-Aboriginal peoples of Canada.

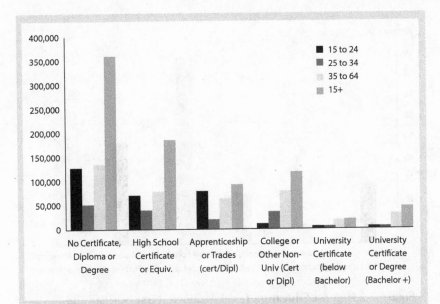

Figure 7-1 Level of Educational Achievement for First Nations People, 2011

Source: Statistics Canada 2008a, *Educational Portrait of Canada, Census 2006*; Statistics Canada 2013b, *Education in Canada: Attainment, Field of Study and Location of Study*; Statistics Canada 2013c, *The Educational Attainment of Aboriginal Peoples in Canada*

For decades, First Nations leaders have been asking the federal government to invest in the education of youth. They have pushed the government to drop its 2 percent increase limit. The increasing number of First Nations students, as well as the inflation rate, has meant that the low increases have been disproportionate to the growing population as well as the higher demand for education by First Nations peoples. The leaders of First Nations communities have argued for the establishment of reasonable, stable, and fair rate of growth. This means that the investments need to support renovations and new infrastructure as well as a system of education that supports students, teachers, and the community.

If First Nations people were able to increase their level of educational attainment in 2017 to the level of non-Aboriginal Canadians in 2001, it is estimated that an additional cumulative $71 billion would be generated in income for the federal and provincial governments. And, if the Aboriginal–non-Aboriginal employment rate gap and employment income gaps were eliminated, the contribution of Aboriginal Canadians to the Canadian GDP would increase to $160 billion (Sharpe et al. 2007).

In 2011, just over 40 percent of First Nations people had some postsecondary education. Women had more success in this regard. For the

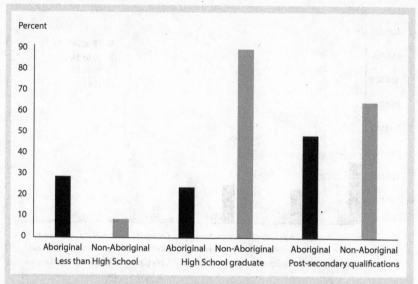

Figure 7-2 Highest Education Level Attained, First Nations and Non-Aboriginal Canadians (Age 25–64), 2011
Source: Statistics Canada National Household Survey 2011, *The Educational Attainment of Aboriginal Peoples in Canada*

trades, nearly 20 percent of men held a certificate; women were half as likely to hold a trade certificate. About 15 percent of women, and half as many men, attended or graduated from university.

Post-Secondary Education

In 1981, just under 3 percent of First Nations youth aged twenty-five to twenty-nine held a university degree. By 2006 this had increased to just over 5 percent. In the same time period, the proportion of those aged thirty-five to thirty-nine holding a university degree increased from just over 3 percent to well over 7 percent. And for those fifty to fifty-four in 1981, only 1 percent held a university degree compared to 9 percent in 2006. Today, about 10 percent of all First Nations people hold a university degree, compared with nearly one quarter in the general population. The results reveal that for most age groups, there has been a substantial increase in First Nations' university completion between 1981 and 2010. The increases in educational achievement for all cohorts for both male and female were about the same. However, even though the data show increases, the gap between First Nations people and other Canadians who achieved a university degree has increased from 1981 to

Table 7-2   Level of Post-secondary Education, by Gender and Age

| | Percentage of First Nations adults by gender and age group | | | | | | |
	Male	Female	18–29	30–39	40–49	50–59	60+
No post-secondary	52.2	47.2	65.6	40.8	37.5	39.8	60.8
Some post-secondary	25.6	19.3	20.2	25.4	26.0	23.6	15.8
Post-secondary degree/diploma	17.7	27.2	10.8	28.5	29.4	30.0	17.9
Graduate/ Professional degree	1.1	1.5	0.5*	1.1	2.1	2.1	1.2
Other	3.3	4.8	2.9*	4.1	5.1	4.46	4.34

* These figures are estimates.

Source: FNIGC 2012, 42

2006. Figure 7-2 and Table 7-2 reveal the level of post-secondary education for First Nations adults.

A New Approach in the Twenty-First Century

Recent efforts by the federal government to deal with First Nations education begins in the early twenty-first century (Government of Canada 2010). Specific agreements were signed between the federal government and various provinces in an attempt to standardize the delivery of education to primary and secondary students. In 2008 AANDC invested more than $70 million over a two-year period to support agreements with provinces and various First Nations communities. These funds were intended to improve the fiscal performance of First Nations schools as well as to help implement community-based plans for setting baselines and assessing the success of First Nations schools. Later that year, AANDC invested an additional $270 million over five years to develop and implement the First Nation Student Success program (since discontinued), the Education Information System to introduce students to internet technology, and the Education Partnerships program. Two years later, the government developed a "memorandum of understanding" framework with various provincial governments and First Nations leaders to engage in change for restructuring First Nations education. It was late in 2010 that AANDC created a national panel to discuss strategies for improving primary and secondary education outcomes. In addition, a new "comparable education" approach was implemented to ensure that First Nations students were able to compete successfully with non-Aboriginal students.

In 2011 the Auditor General produced a report on primary and secondary education for First Nations students that identified four major factors behind the inferior education that was available to First Nations students: lack of funding, lack of organizations to support the delivery of education to children, a lack of clarity about services available to First Nations children, and a lack of legislative base for First Nations education. As a result of this report, AANDC created a Canada–First Nations Joint Action Plan in which First Nations communities and AANDC would collaborate to improve the delivery of education on the reserves. In 2011 the Standing Senate Committee on Aboriginal Peoples completed its third annual report on First Nations education and made several recommendations.

During 2011–12, a federal government panel on Aboriginal education put forth several recommendations for improving Aboriginal education. The Panel's recommendations were as follows:

1. co-create a child-centered First Nations Education Act;
2. create a National Commission for First Nations Education to support education reform and improvement;
3. facilitate and support the creation of a First Nations education system through the development of regional organizations;
4. ensure adequate funding to support a First Nations education system that meets the needs of students, communities, and Canada as a whole; and
5. establish an accountability and reporting framework to assess improvement in First Nations education.

In October 2013, the federal government released a draft bill on First Nations education for consultation. As written, the bill would impose new obligations on First Nations communities, including forming school boards, appointing principals, setting education programs, and hiring an annual inspector. The draft bill, however, did not commit to more or even stable federal funding to meet the new requirements.

One year later a national panel of federal government officials and First Nations leaders presented a final report. This echoed, to some extent, the report by the Auditor General a year earlier. While AANDC was supportive of the recommendations, it took no steps to implement them. Instead, the federal government began to carry out consultations with First Nations communities in preparation of its draft bill, *Working*

Together for First Nation Students: A Proposal for a Bill on First Nations Education (2013d). There is little clarity about how much First Nations leaders were involved, and it was rejected by First Nations groups on the grounds that it did not incorporate their views. The federal government withdrew the bill, agreeing that it required revisions.

In 2013, this effort was put into federal legislation called the First Nations Education Act. In this proposed legislation, the federal government sees reserve schools as similar to provincial schools. The proposed act states that if a given First Nations school fails to meet provincial standards, the Minister of Education may appoint a temporary administrator to improve standards. This proposed act would allow the Federal government the right to create and enforce educational standards for reserve schools along with the power for AANDC to take control of the schools if they did not meet expectations.

First Nations' leaders as well as organizations such as the Chamber of Commerce, the United Church of Canada, and the Canadian School Board Association rejected the proposed Act, noting that the legislation has little resemblance to the actual recommendations put forth by the panel. Moreover, First Nations leaders note that they did not have any direct input into the initial draft of the Act. Others claim to have urged Ottawa to abandon the blueprint, saying it fails to meet the standards set out by the United Nations Declaration on the Rights of Indigenous Peoples. Still others argue that this unilateral development of the Act did not met the Crown's duty to consult and accommodate First Nations

The AFN passed a resolution in 2013 focusing on conditions they saw as necessary for the success of First Nations education. This resolution affirmed the need for government to respect and recognize First Nations rights, title, treaty and land rights, and jurisdiction. In addition it noted that the government must provide a statutory guarantee for funding and there is no unilateral right of government to interfere with the educational system on reserves. First Nations leaders claim they are determined to take on the responsibility for First Nations education, but it must happen on their terms. They argue that the atrocities during the residential school era are sufficient evidence that the federal government cannot be placed in a position of control over First Nations education. At the same time, First Nations leaders have proposed conditions that, if agreed to by the government, would be acceptable. Those conditions consist of First Nations control of education, a guarantee of adequate and stable funding over time, recognition of First Nations culture and specifically language in the curriculum, a process of joint (federal and First Nations) oversight of First Nations education, and the establishment of a permanent ongoing dialogue between First Nations leaders and government with regard to First Nations educational issues.

In early 2014, a new bill was brought forth to reform the primary and secondary education system with a revised First Nations Education Act. This new proposal addressed some of the concerns expressed by First Nations people, giving First Nations communities full control over education. Language and cultural programming would also be introduced into relevant communities. First Nations schools must acquire appropriate provincial certification for all teachers and must meet provincial standards with core curriculum and student competency. There would be monitoring of attendance records and graduation rates on reserves. If these rates are not within AANDC expectations, the government will intervene. A First Nations Education Authority would be established as a provincial school board to oversee the operations of the schools. Finally, a Joint Council of Education Professionals would be established to advise the Minister, monitor the activities of all First Nations schools, and prepare a five-year review of the proposed Act. The insistence that a "joint" oversight process be established is the result of the disastrous impact of the residential schools. First Nations students are given less funding on a per capita basis than non-Aboriginal students; First Nations people have been assured that funding would improve and that infrastructure issues would be addressed. Additional funds were requested to ensure that language and cultural issues are part of the school curriculum.

The federal government promised to designate nearly $2 billion over a seven-year period that would result in new schools. It also agreed that the AANDC budget for education would no longer be constrained by the 2 percent increase limits now in effect; rather, a 4.5 percent increase each year after 2016 would come into effect.

Some First Nations leaders have argued that the proposed act does not go far enough in giving First Nations people control over their education; rather, it simply allows them to administer and manage a provincial curriculum. It also gives the Minister of AANDC the right to intervene at any time, and replace First Nations leaders with bureaucrats to run the system. However, nothing in the new act will be implemented until after the 2015 election. First Nations people wonder if this would be another example of the reality falling short of official rhetoric. Moreover, the new policy being developed by government continues to align the First Nations educational system more closely with the provincial system, in effect offloading more responsibility to the provinces (Peters and White 2009).

While this document (First Nations Control of First Nations Education Act) was supported by the Assembly of First Nations on the condition that it would be the first step in dealing with First Nations education issues, regional chiefs and their organizations soundly rejected it. As a result, Sean Atleo, the Grand Chief of the AFN, resigned and the revised bill was removed from further consideration by the federal government.

Conclusion

The establishment of formal Canadian educational institutions and curriculum mostly bypassed First Nations children. The residential school system systematically denied an adequate education to First Nations children and youth over five generations.

Today we know that incorporating First Nations cultures and languages into formal education is essential. More recently, holistic models of education seek to examine education among First Nations people in a way that draws on their own cultures and languages. A key component of a holistic First Nations education is language, which is fundamental to learning given its impact on a culture's understanding and experience of the world. Languages express identities, are keepers of history, and contribute to human knowledge (Baker 2006).

We saw above that in 1972, the report *Indian Control of Indian Education* identified the need for greater control over First Nations education, more parental involvement in decision-making about their children's education, and better support for the promotion of First Nations languages and culture. First Nations people themselves have initiated the work on education reform. First Nations leaders have argued that education is not only a goal in itself but it also is a way to address poverty and increase participation in the workforce. At the same time, others have called for changed legislation and programs for First Nations students in a variety of audits and reports, including the *2011 Status Report of the Auditor General of Canada*, the Senate Committee report *Reforming First Nations Education: From Crisis to Hope*, and the report of the National Panel on First Nation Elementary and Secondary Education for Students on Reserve *Nurturing the Learning Spirit of First Nation Students*. These reports argue that education is the key to developing the potential for both individuals and communities. As the youngest and fastest growing demographic group in the country, First Nations youth are well positioned to capitalize on their potential. However, an educational system has to be in place to ensure that potential is achieved. Many stakeholders agree that it is imperative to create a strong education system that will both meet the needs of First Nations communities and empower students to participate in a thriving and successful Canada (Kroes 2009).

Even though the government's proposed First Nations Education Act was informed by the work of the National Panel on First Nation Elementary and Secondary Education, as well as consultations with some First Nations communities, it did not reflect their input and concerns. Today, the federal government claims it will work with every First Nations community as well as with provincial governments before it brings forth a new Aboriginal education policy (AANDC 2013b). At the same time, the federal government claims that the current structure of providing education is a non-system and the operation of the old education policy has produced a patchwork of rules and regulations. The new policy provides a tentative vision as to what the standards, services, accountability, and governance measures are and how they will be established for First Nations students. On the other hand, First Nations people argue that the government needs a new model of education; one that ensures that Aboriginal control and acknowledges that Aboriginal knowledge is an Aboriginal right (Battiste 2013). Moreover, Battiste claims that educational policies must be rethought to include Indigenous languages and science, as well as other fields of Aboriginal study in the curriculum. In short, she argues for a new knowledge system that incorporates both Aboriginal and non-Aboriginal thinking for the future.

Chapter 8

Land, Treaties, and Claims

Introduction

Aboriginal people and the federal government have negotiated approximately five hundred treaties over time, according to some estimates. The British Crown established solemn treaties to encourage peaceful relations between First Nations and non-Aboriginal people in 1701 in the land that is now Canada. Over the next two centuries, treaties were signed to define the respective rights of native peoples and settlers to use and enjoy lands that had traditionally been controlled and occupied by the Aboriginal peoples. Britain acquired the territory that is now Quebec with the Treaty of Paris in 1763, and a British military presence was established there. The French population greatly outnumbered the British, however, and relations had soured during the Seven Years War. Furthermore, the Treaty of Paris was difficult to enforce. To improve the balance of power in its favour, the British enlisted the support of First Nations people through a variety of treaties. But a new strategy was required to correspond to the new realities of the second half of the eighteenth century. Soldiers and veterans were guaranteed land rights in the region in exchange for loyalty to the Crown. First Nations Allies residing in the Quebec region were promised land and freedom from molestation. Out of these arrangements emerged the Royal Proclamation of 1763—the first real "treaty" of any substance. A year later, the Niagara Treaty (a Peace and Friendship treaty) established the principles of British and First Nations interactions (Ariss and Cutfeet 2012).

These treaties resulted from British concerns about both economics and demography. The war was over and the military was disbanding; there was less military power to maintain British control over the area.

Tensions with French settlers remained high, particularly as a result of raiding parties by British-allied First Nations groups against French settlers. Settler retaliation against First Nations groups likewise increased tensions. A permanent peace was required to bring stability to the region and cement British power.

The new regime brought changing patterns of European settlement. Settler views on land ownership and the establishment of capitalism were two radical changes that First Nations culture were forced to address. By the mid-nineteenth century, colonial Canada had implemented an institutionalized policy of assimilation. In addition, with the adoption of the early Indian Acts—the Act for the Better Protection of the Lands and Property of Indians in Lower Canada (1850) and the Act for the Gradual Civilization of the Indian Tribes in the Canadas (1857), for example—the control of First Nations by the federal government was put in place.

Pre-Confederation Treaties

Before settlers came to Canada, First Nations peoples had well-developed organizational and institutional systems for dealing with territorial disputes. The occupation of land was one key means of validating control. However, there were other forms of diplomacy used to maintain peace. For example, First Nations leaders held councils or protocol activities such as smoking the peace pipe, feasting, and exchanging ceremonial objects. These diplomatic strategies were designed to prevent direct confrontation. First Nations people knew well that it is easier to overcome disputes if each side shows respect for important symbols and acknowledges the substantive concerns of the other side; these traditions are reflected in First Nations diplomacy's process and product (Borrows 2005).

The era of Peace and Friendship Treaties was ushered in when the two parties (colonial government and First Nations) agreed to maintain peace while each side carried out their business. Given the nearly unlimited land and the few settlers at the time, this seemed like a reasonable strategy for the colonial government. And, for the most part, these "treaties" worked until the number of settlers began to increase and infringe upon the daily lives of First Nations people.

The establishment of these Peace and Friendship treaties involved a formal process that generally included song and ceremony to validate the treaty. As such, these treaties were a form of agreement that was very useful in securing peace. The famous "wampum belt" treaty of 1701 is illustrative of early First Nations treaties. Peace was also pursued through inter-societal activities among different First Nations groups. These informal strategies embodied lessons about overcoming differences with the careful valuation of interpersonal ties, among other things.

These early Peace and Friendship agreements between First Nations groups and government were carried out primarily in the Maritime region although there were some in Quebec and Ontario. Such treaties generally dealt with military and political relations and did not involve specific land transfers, annuities, trading rights, or compensation for rights limited or taken away. However, these early treaties are legal agreements and remain important today as First Nations people struggle to find and exercise their rights. Examples of Peace and Friendship treaties are those signed between the Mi'kmaq and the governor of Nova Scotia in 1760–61. These early treaties gave First Nations people the right to catch and sell fish for profit (including lobster). It was the content of these Peace and Friendship treaties that was argued in the Supreme Court of Canada in 1999 (*R. v. Marshall*) to eventually give Nova Scotia First Nations the Aboriginal right to engage in fishing (Coates 2000). Today the courts are beginning to re-visit these pre-Confederation treaties and have introduced new interpretations of First Nations access to different resources on the land and water.

While the land rights of First Nations peoples in Canada have not been treated uniformly, a consistent body of precedent and tradition developed that was utilized on new frontiers where fairly rapid settlement or resource exploitation was taking place. This involved negotiations by which First Nations peoples surrendered most of their territorial rights and in return gained various forms of compensation. Although numerous land surrender treaties had already been made in the Thirteen Colonies, it was not until after the American Revolution that the surrender and compensation model was first systematically used in Canada (Ray 1974).

By the 1770s there was a large increase in settler population in eastern territories; these settlers were interested in farming, lumbering, homesteading, and establishing businesses. In 1791 the British Parliament divided Quebec into the provinces of Upper and Lower Canada. The conciliar government in Quebec was abolished, and representative government in both provinces was established. Land was to be granted in freehold tenure in Upper Canada and could be so granted in Lower Canada if desired but only for non-First Nations people.

For the colonial government, treaties were little more than land cessions in return for once-for-all grants, usually in goods. However, some of the First Nations groups felt that the colonial government was taking on a trusteeship responsibility as part of the treaty because of the acceptance of First Nations protocol when the treaties were signed. Annuities, or annual payments for the ceded land rights, first appeared in a treaty in 1818 and thereafter became a staple component in all the treaties. At this time, providing reserve lands for First Nations people only occasionally comprised the surrender terms. Similarly, the right to continue hunting and fishing over ceded lands was rarely mentioned in the early written treaties. It was not until 1850, when treaties were negotiated by William Robinson, that First Nations peoples were granted all four items: once-for-all expenditures, annuities, reserves, and guarantees concerning hunting, fishing, and trapping. These early Robinson treaties then became the templates to be used by the federal government in almost all future treaties.

In terms of content, however, the southern Ontario treaties are less generous than subsequent agreements that provided far greater benefits to First Nations peoples. In addition, treaties negotiated in Ontario after 1830 were concluded in trust. Thus, the colonial government assumed responsibility for disposing of the ceded lands on the First Nation's behalf, with the proceeds of sales usually going to the particular First Nations people involved. Normally these funds would then be subtracted from other funds that might be allocated by government officials in support of First Nations people. The subsequent Robinson–Superior and Robinson–Huron treaties (1850–54) provided a template that would be used by future negotiators and would forever change the social and legal landscape of Canada. Subsequent treaties were intended to give recognition to First Nations interests in the land, to provide compensation, and to establish an orderly transition of land ownership from First Nations to the colonial government. These treaties also established the rules of the relationship between First Nations people and the federal government once the land was transferred.

Canadian Treaties

After Confederation, treaties would be made through the Canadian government. All the terms of the pre-Confederation treaties were considered the new government's responsibility. When the Hudson's Bay Company sold Rupert's Land in 1869, Canada took on the responsibility for negotiating with First Nations people residing in this area. However, the people who were subsequently appointed to negotiate treaties with First Nations people had little experience or familiarity with First Nations culture. As such, negotiators relied on the experience and tradition of the Hudson's Bay Company's treatment of First Nations people, as well as the written material that was available when the Manitoulin Island Treaty (1836) and Robinson Treaties of 1850s were negotiated.

From 1871 to 1877, Treaties 1 through 7 were signed with First Nations people (see Figure 8-1). The land taken by the Canadian government under Treaties 1 through 7 provided settlement land for immigrants to Canada. However, by the end of the nineteenth century, the pressures of settlement and resource development again brought about a new round of treaties. As such, Treaties 8 through 11, while differing in some respects from the earlier ones, were clearly modelled upon earlier treaties. The federal government engaged with First Nations peoples largely because its own agents felt that there would be violence against European settlers if treaties were not established. However, this perception was not based on specific threats from First Nations peoples, who simply wished to carry out direct discussions with the federal government for compensation for the lands they occupied prior to European settlement. After Treaty 1 was signed, the government did not seek alternative means for dealing with First Nations people and their land. As a

Figure 8-1 Pre-1975 Treaties of Canada

Source: Aboriginal Affairs and Northern Development Canada, www.aadnc-aandc.gc.ca/DAM/DAM-INTER-HQ/
STAGING/texte-text/htoc_1100100032308_eng.pdf

result, federal government officials simply based new treaties on prior ones. To a certain extent, First Nations negotiators were complicit in this process in that First Nations people insisted on treatment similar to that received by those who had signed earlier treaties. Nevertheless, over time, many First Nations negotiators demanded changes to the treaties as they were presented by federal negotiators in order to accommodate their special needs; however, the federal government negotiators refused to change the content of the treaties, with some minor exceptions.

The government of Canada received millions of acres of land from the surrender of First Nations land in these treaties. In return, 0.32 percent of Canada's land mass was set aside for reserves. Many irregularities emerged in the allocation of this land during this period; in some cases, treaty land entitlements would only be claimed many years later. While these entitlements are complex, they are legal obligations recognized in the Constitution that must be addressed by the federal government. The term *treaty land entitlement* is used to document land claims that flow from Treaties 1 through 11. There are two forms of land entitlement. The first is called initial or "late" entitlement, and this reflects the fact that the First Nations did not receive the land promised under the treaty. The second is a shortfall, which refers to the situation in which a calculation for the amount of land to be set aside did not include all the eligible population. Thus far, the federal and provincial governments have been reluctant to settle claims emerging out of the treaties. Nevertheless, these claims are slowly winding their way through the courts.

British Columbia is an anomaly in terms of establishing treaties with First Nations people. It is true that from 1849 to 1854 the colonial governor negotiated a series of treaties with the First Nations on Vancouver Island. However, after 1854 this was stopped as British politicians would not provide the governor with moneys to continue. Moreover, British Columbia settlers refused responsibility for negotiations with First Nations people and would not release public funds to settle land claims. As such, with the exception of part of Treaty 8 and the Vancouver Island treaties, none of the land in British Columbia has ever been "treatied out." Nevertheless, the early BC government agreed to establish reserves for First Nations people to clear the land for settlement. The British Columbia government, however, supplied considerably less land to First Nations people than did the federal government. When allotting land, non-Aboriginal settlers received 320 acres of land per homestead from the province while First Nations families were given much less, in most cases only 20 acres.

While the First Nations people in British Columbia continued to argue for title to their lands, after 1910 the provincial government refused to acknowledge their land rights or to establish any more reserves. Delegations were sent to Victoria and to Britain to argue for the rights of First Nations people. However, the provincial government insisted that First Nations had no rights; and even if they did, these rights had been extinguished through the implementation of provincial legislation over the years. British and Canadian authorities refused to accept the concept of First Nations land rights.

First Nations people continued to argue their case for land rights. In 1913 the federal government established a Royal Commission to look into the British Columbia allocation of lands to First Nations people. It also asked the Commission to examine whether the acreage provided to First Nations people should be adjusted. In 1916 the Commission published its report identifying lands to be added to and removed from existing reserves. The added land was to be twice the size of the subtracted land. The British Columbia government opposed the Commission's recommendations, but in 1923 finally accepted a negotiated version of the report. At this time the federal government passed an amendment to the Indian Act prohibiting the collection of funds by Aboriginal people for the advancement of a land claim. Anyone accepting money and acting on behalf of First Nations people anywhere in Canada was subject to fines and imprisonment. This amendment remained law until the middle of the twentieth century. As a result, Aboriginal groups became

What is a treaty?

Over many years, the Supreme Court of Canada has identified a number of conditions to determine if a document is a treaty. Thus far it has listed five considerations:

1. whether or not there has been continuous exercise of a right in the past and at present;
2. the reasons behind the Crown's commitment;
3. the situation prevailing at the time the document was signed;
4. evidence of relations of mutual respect and esteem between the negotiators; and
5. the subsequent conduct of the parties.

If the status of a given document remains unclear, evidence from external sources such as historians, anthropologists, and archaeologists, may be considered. Supreme Court rulings have demonstrated that their decision encourages and supports interpretations in favour of, and for the benefit of, First Nations people as part of fiduciary doctrine. The court's reasoning extends to the "Peace and Friendship" treaties of the eighteenth century.

powerless to press their claims. They were ignored by the federal government throughout the 1930s and 1940s.

Treaty Content and Format

Treaties 1 and 2 established the template that would be used for the next half century. They created reserve lands granting 160 acres per family. Annuities of $3 per person, a gratuity of $3 per person, and a school on each reserve were part of the treaty. Other promises were also made orally during the negotiations although most of these have been ignored by the federal government; only written documentation is considered legally binding. Over time the reserve allotment was increased to 640 acres per family of five. In the end, the federal government drafted treaties that were brief and uniform in content. Although constrained by these government-imposed limitations, negotiators were sometimes forced to make minor additions to a treaty. For example, the government negotiators for Treaty 6 were forced to add several benefits such as a medicine chest and provisions for relief in times of famine. In general, however, the government commissioners had by far the best of the bargaining. It turns out that the treaties were written by the government prior to meeting with First Nations groups and would be presented for signing. The terms of Treaty 9, for example, were determined by the Ontario and Canadian governments well in advance of discussions with First Nations people. Moreover, there is evidence that, in many cases, hard-won oral promises were "forgotten" by the government; in other words, these promises were never written into the formal treaty. Nevertheless, nearly all the treaties stipulate that First Nations people have the right to hunt, trap, and fish for food on unoccupied lands.

In their meetings with First Nations people, treaty commissioners always avoided discussing the nature or extent of First Nations land rights. Nevertheless, the written treaties always included statements that First Nations people surrendered their land rights. In many cases, the commissioners argued that the First Nations people had no land rights at all; if the First Nations leaders objected, the commissioners would ask missionaries or traders whom the First Nations people trusted to coerce them to sign. In the end, however, First Nations treaties were never brought before Parliament for discussion or vote. Instead, the treaties were presented to cabinet and ratified by an order-in-council. This suggests that they were accepted by the federal government, both as a recognition of First Nations land claims and as a means of their negotiation and resolution.

In the end, between 1871 and 1923, the federal government signed eleven treaties with First Nations people across Canada. Once these treaties were signed, government officials began to actively encourage settlers to take up fee simple ownership of land, engage in agricultural activities, settlement, and resource development. These treaties are often referred to as the "Numbered Treaties." The Numbered Treaties cover Northern Ontario, Manitoba, Saskatchewan, Alberta, and parts of the Yukon, the Northwest Territories, and British Columbia. According to the government, under the terms of these treaties, the First Nations who used and occupied these lands, gave up their rights to the land and it was then transferred to the Crown. In exchange, the federal government agreed to provide for such things as reserves and other benefits like farm equipment and animals, annual payments, ammunition, clothing, and the right to hunt, fish, and trap. The Crown also made other promises, such as maintaining schools on reserves and providing teachers or educational help to the First Nations communities named in the treaties.

Two Views of Treaties

Each party had a very different conception of the meaning of these treaties. We saw earlier that treaties were not unknown to First Nations peoples who had a clear understanding of the "nation-to-nation" concept of resolving conflict. For the federal government, negotiating a treaty was a legalized formality in which First Nations people would cede their lands, thereby extinguishing all future claims and rights. They also saw these treaties as a first step toward assimilation and integration of First Nations people into western-style capitalism.

A further distinction is the attitude toward the ceremony surrounding the treaty. From the perspective of First Nations leaders, signing was part of a process enveloped in First Nations protocol. There were a number of events, ceremonies, and discussions that took place prior to and during the negotiations. For example, the smoking of the pipe, feasts, horsemanship displays, drumming, singing, and discussions of kinship all were part of the process and demonstrated, from a First Nations perspective, that the treaties were more than signed documents. Most of the Crown representatives at these events had little understanding of the significance of such ceremonies and events. As one commissioner noted, after a long day of discussing the content of the treaty, the Indians return to their camp to drum, dance, and sing all night.

For First Nations, treaties are solemn pacts that establish future, ongoing relations. Treaties were seen to be flexible in time and space. First Nations' interpretation of the treaties suggests they understood that they would receive some government support in the future, including protection, to ensure the survival (both cultural and physical) of their people. In signing a treaty, First Nations people believed that they would be giving the new settlers the right to use some of their lands, but not relinquishing full title. It is unlikely they comprehended the concept of "extinguishment" of all title and rights forever given that such words were never used in either the oral commentary (so far as we know) or within the treaty itself. Signing the treaties confirmed for First Nations people that the Crown was dealing with them as a sovereign nation. It is clear that during the treaty negotiations, First Nations people believed that individuals did not own the land but rather land was a collective interest. Since they had a sacred trust with the creator to take care of the land, First Nations people believe that it is their duty to take over the stewardship of land, plants, and animals.

The Fight for Land

As Borrows (2005) points out, First Nations peoples' pre-eminent thoughts are about land. They occupied land in Canada prior to the arrival of the settlers; land was their life and their life was their land. However, over the past 250 years First Nations peoples have been largely dispossessed of their lands. They feel that this has endangered their survival as a people and culture. Moreover, First Nations peoples regard their traditional lands as sacred and therefore integral to their culture and identity. Their goal is to continue living on and occupying territories that have provided for their ancestors for thousands of years. First Nations people argue that much of the conflict between Aboriginal and non-Aboriginal people is about land. Non-Aboriginal people are obsessed with owning and controlling land that First Nations people now have. At the same time, First Nations peoples want to hold onto their traditional territories and resources to preserve their ancient relationships with the land. They feel that the previous occupation by their ancestors as well as their relationship with the creator entitles them to occupy and use the land and as such, they have struggled to resist further removal from their territories. Therefore, First Nations peoples have engaged in civil disobedience to protect and sustain their relationship to the land (Borrows 2005).

First Nations people feel an ancestral connection to their traditional territory and want Canadians to understand that their traditional territories are not just part of their cultural heritage, but also a fundamental part of the people themselves (Elsey 2013). The federal government's position is that First Nations land claims must be established using western rules of continued and unbroken occupancy and use. As such, the courts reason that First Nations people must present proof of exclusive ownership or control over a particular geographical region if they want to successfully claim rights over that land. First Nations peoples argue they do not have written materials to support their claims of continuous control over a geographical region since theirs is an oral culture. They use oral history to depict their use and occupancy of the landscape through the use of certain sites, sacred areas, and territorial boundaries of each First Nations group. The validity of these claims is often illustrated by comparing the stories of each Aboriginal group. As Elsey (2013) points out, many of these stories serve to illustrate the connection between the land and the culture of the First Nations group. The stories allow the First Nations community to build history with their land and reflect a sense of identity of the people with regard to the land.

First Nations people believe that the earth was created by a power external to human beings, and since they were the first to be placed on the land, they have a responsibility to act as stewards. Given that humans had no hand in making the earth, they also have no right to possess it or dispose of it as they see fit; the possession of land by humans is unnatural and unjust. The value most Indigenous peoples place on the land around them is not economic but an emotional and psychic attachment. Elsey (2013) observes that First Nations people's world view is beyond dualistic thinking—mind versus body. Instead they view their environment as part of their selves which is "enfolded" into the fabric of their body as their own experience. The geographical region in which First Nations people live, through their stories and use of the land, provides the history of the people and it is inseparably connected to their First Nations identity (Elsey 2013).

Interpreting the Historical Treaties

The interpretation of the word "treaty" has evolved over the past two centuries in its application to First Nations people. While in the international context there is a consensus on the nature of a "treaty," the meaning of this word has been limited over time in its application to First Nations' agreements. This slippery redefinition has been used to deny First Nations their international status. First Nations treaties in Canada are not considered to be international treaties nor are they seen as contracts; rather they are understood to be a special class that resists categorization within existing legal standards. The courts have not yet established what exactly these agreements are, although First Nations people have always believed they were "nation-to-nation" treaties.

Treaties have several possible legal interpretations. In one sense they can be seen as agreements between two sovereign nations (as they are understood by First Nations). But the federal government of Canada, as evidenced through legislation and court decisions, does not interpret the treaties in the same manner. Ariss and Cutfeet (2012) claim that at the time the treaties were signed, the Crown understood First Nations as peoples with the rights of sovereignty. The Supreme Court decisions since 1982 also have given some credence to these treaties as being "nation-to-nation" agreements.

An alternative interpretation is that treaties are contracts. Prime Minister Pierre Trudeau publicly stated that treaties are analogous to contracts and thus must be dealt with as such. Contracts can be revised, terminated, and resolved through the courts if there are differences of interpretation. Treaties can also be seen as pieces of legislation. This interpretation is plausible; many treaties were written before such legislation as the Indian Act. As such, it is a legal means of establishing an orderly relationship between people and may be understood to be analogous to legislation. The recent court decision that declared that the Manitoba Act was nothing more than a treaty gives some legal credence to this kind of interpretation.

Ross (2003) points out that the written text of a treaty is only one aspect that needs to be taken into consideration. The Supreme Court has pointed out several times—for example in *R. v. Sparrow* (1990), *R. v. Marshall* (1999), *R. v. Sioui* (1990), and *R. v. Badger* (1996)—that the oral terms of the negotiations must be considered in order to fully appreciate the obligations and responsibilities of the signatories. Furthermore, the Supreme Court has ruled that treaties must be interpreted in a manner that maintains the integrity of the Crown. As such, any limitations set out in the treaty that restrict the rights of First Nations people must be narrowly construed.

Nevertheless, many Canadians feel that treaties are no more than outdated contracts between a group of First Nations people and the federal government. The oral component of the treaty is irrelevant. There also is a belief that, since the treaties are old, the agreements within them can be breached. However, in a Supreme Court decision concerning hunting rights (*Simon v. The Queen*, 1985), the court held that treaties were neither contracts nor international instruments. They are to be regarded as agreements *sui generis*, that is, unique but existing in force and binding.

The inclusion of treaty rights in section 35 of the Constitution confirms the treaties' original constitutional status (Borrows 2010). Moreover, the introduction of section 35 in the Constitution has meant that the Crown can no longer ignore Aboriginal rights, interests, or perspectives. Adding to this discussion is Henderson's (1997) argument that treaties between First Nations and the Crown are basic constitutional documents; this fact has been ignored through most of Canada's history. Upon close analysis of the various pre- and post-Confederation treaties, the content of these treaties suggests that First Nations people were familiar with the process of negotiating treaties; the negotiations prior to the signing of each treaty reflect the specific needs of different First Nations.

There are some examples where the courts have negated a treaty's legitimacy. For example, in *R. v. Sylliboy* (1929) the Mi'kmaq Treaty of 1752 was judged by the court to be nothing more than an agreement between First Nations people and the British Governor; neither party had any right to enter into a treaty. The Mi'kmaq in particular were defined as "uncivilized savages" with no legal rights. However, new principles of treaty interpretation have emerged, some recognizing Aboriginal law. For example, in *R. v. Marshall No. 1*, the justices found that the Mi'kmaq Treaty of 1752 was about reconciliation and mutual advantage for both groups.

Ariss and Cutfeet (2012) point out that a key component in the understanding of a treaty is recognizing the common interpretations of the parties when they signed the treaties. It is clear that the First Nations' objective was to establish a lasting relationship with the Crown; they also wanted to help the Crown while also protecting their livelihood. Courts also have found that the promises made in treaties must be placed in their historical, political, and cultural contexts to clarify the common intentions of the parties and the interests they intended to reconcile at the time. In short, the courts have begun to interpret treaties beyond the technical ("on the face of it") texts by considering historical and social contexts. Today, sole reliance on written documents is considered insufficient for rendering a decision; oral components of the treaty negotiations must be included. Another limitation of the current legal system is that the relationship between First Nations people and the land is always characterized in terms of a "commodity," ignoring the psychological attachment.

The Supreme Court of Canada also has ruled that treaties should not be interpreted as if "frozen in time"; rather, interpretation should take place in the context of modern times. Moreover, treaties should be "liberally" interpreted in terms of First Nations understanding at the time of the signing. The justification for the "liberal interpretation" of the treaties is based on the courts acknowledging that the Crown composed the treaties, and as such the treaties likely reflect the Crown's intentions more than those First Nations signatories. In addition, there is some recognition that there were considerable inequalities in cultural and practical communication at the time of signing. First Nations people were not fully appreciative of the treaties' full meaning. Thus, the new principles require that courts acknowledge and recognize the viewpoints of First Nations people in the treaties, and allow external evidence demonstrating this. The courts have stated that this principle is core to the honour of the Crown; treaties were "sacred" agreements between First Nations people and the government cemented mutually binding obligations.

The federal Crown agrees that treaties with First Nations people are legal agreements that set out promises, obligations, and benefits for both parties. This interpretation has been confirmed by the courts. Nevertheless, all treaty rights already in existence in 1982 (the year the *Constitution Act* was passed), and those that came afterwards, are recognized and affirmed by Canada's Constitution. However, while on the interpretation of treaties, the federal government on many occasions has failed to honour their content.

Civil Disobedience

When First Nations peoples signed treaties with the Crown it was agreed that the Crown would ensure they received benefits. These benefits covered a wide range of allowances such as twine, ammunition, education, health care, food in the event of famine, housing, and exemptions from taxation. However, all too often over the years the Crown has failed to fulfill the conditions of the treaties. On such occasions, First Nations peoples have used their physical presence to influence legislative and policy choices, at times exercising civil disobedience as a response to the loss of lands, resources, and other agreed-upon conditions in the treaty. They have done this by physically disrupting non-Aboriginal people's access to government offices or public transportation routes or by other tangible techniques that have inconvenienced non-Aboriginal peoples. Even though the RCMP have defined Aboriginal people as one of the top five "threats" to national security, such instances of civil disobedience are always in exceptional circumstances and when other avenues of justice are not possible (McCarthy 2013; RCMP 2014a; Toledano 2015). In 2007, the RCMP reported to CSIS that there is considerable concern by federal government officials as well as the policing community about the potential for unrest in Aboriginal communities and argued that there is a rise in the level of militancy among Aboriginal people (Dafnos 2015). In these reports the RCMP and CSIS have identified Aboriginal people as potential sources of domestic terrorism and thus have embarked upon a strategy of monitoring and infiltrating various groups (Groves and Lukacs 2011; Diabo and Pasternak 2011). Nevertheless, the history of physical occupations and re-occupations is an important one in First Nation–Crown relations. In the end, First Nations people have engaged in overt conflict such as blockades because of a failure by other parties to recognize and affirm First Nations land and resource rights and because third parties, particularly government, fail to address the effects of this denial (Borrows 2005). Over the past thirty years conflicts have taken place across the country: Anishinabe Park, Moresby Island, Barrie Lake, Temagami, Old Man River, James Bay, Labrador, Oka, Lubicon Lake, Gustafsen Lake, Cape Croker, Mount Currie, Clayoquot Sound, Sun Peaks, Burnt Church, and Grassy Narrows, to name a few. In each instance, First Nations people feel there is ample justification for these actions (Hedican 2013).

Why have First Nations resorted to overt conflict in an attempt to settle their claims? In some cases the federal government has failed to honour its treaty agreements. Also, many of these claims were not settled when they should have been, as a result of the Indian Act preventing First Nations people from obtaining legal recourse. In other cases the federal government has objected to the claims, forcing matters into the courts where biases in the law work against many First Nations' claims. Some First Nations claims have been lost as a result of the courts adhering to western legal principles. In still other cases, First Nations people feel that they have a moral right to land that goes unrecognized by Canadian legal or political institutions. For these reasons, they feel civil disobedience becomes necessary. Finally, in some cases, First Nations people argue that conflict is an important process. It brings their issues to the forefront of politics and the media, and it affords them "a seat at the table." It also provides a catalyst for social cohesion among First Nations people as well as with other like-minded organizations, such as environmental or religious groups.

Types of Claims

There are four major types of First Nations claims facing the federal government: comprehensive land claims, specific claims, general litigation claims, and claims arising from the legacy of Indian residential schools.

Comprehensive land claims are unresolved First Nations rights and land title issues. In 2012 there were eighty-one comprehensive land claims that were under negotiation, accepted for negotiation, or under review. A second type of claim is a specific claim that deals with past grievances with regard to obligations under treaties or the management of First Nations' assets by the federal government. There are currently 443 specific claims under negotiation, accepted for negotiation, or under review. There is a third type of claim: legal proceedings for 533 general litigation claims are being pursued through the courts. Finally, there are thousands of claims being addressed through AANDC with respect to the legacy of Indian residential schools. A further discussion of comprehensive and specific claims is presented later.

AANDC has developed a provisional liability test for the above claims; it estimates that the bill is just above $11 billion. An additional $4 billion has been identified as possible liability for claims still to be confirmed. In addition to money set aside, AANDC has also accumulated title to land that will be used to settle some of the claims. These lands are held by AANDC for the sole purpose of future settlements of land claims.

Modern Day Treaties and Claims

First Nations land claims, until recently, were either suppressed or simply not defined as bona fide claims. There was an understanding by the federal government that the 1888 *St. Catherines Milling and Lumber Co.* case clearly ruled, once and for all, on the issue of Aboriginal title. This case (ruled on by the Privy Council) held that First Nations people had no Aboriginal rights to land. What they did have was the right to use and occupy (usufructuary rights), but even that was dependent upon the good will of the Crown. Moreover, until the passage of the revised Indian Act in 1951, First Nations people had to obtain the federal government's approval before they could launch legal proceedings.

While AANDC is the major federal agency to deal with First Nations people and their land claims, it is beholden to the Treasury Board, the Department of Justice, and the Prime Minister's Office; all of these bodies may overrule any negotiations that AANDC might have approved. The excessive reliance on the courts is reflected in the 2010–11 AANDC budget, which reveals the highest expenditure for legal fees of any federal department, including Revenue Canada.

In 1930, under the National Resources Transfer Agreements, an arrangement allowed three western provinces to take control over land and resources, thereby matching the powers of Quebec and Ontario. These agreements extinguished the treaty rights for First Nations to engage in hunting, trapping, and fishing commercially but expanded their right to engage in subsistence activities throughout the provinces. In short, the National Resources Transfer Agreement trumped the content of the Treaties in all of the western provinces. The courts accepted this agreement.

Modern Treaties (Comprehensive Settlement Claims)

From 1923 until 1973, the federal government carried out business on the basis that all outstanding land claims had been settled. After the 1973 *Calder* case, Indian Affairs created the Office of Native Claims to deal with all First Nations claims. By 1981, however, only twelve of the approximately 250 claims submitted to the government had been settled and no comprehensive land claims had been resolved. As a result, a broad consultation process with First Nations leaders was undertaken to improve both policy and process. At that time the federal government ceased applying the statutes of limitations and the doctrine of laches (western common law allows courts to turn down claims where the claimant had waited too long—the doctrine of laches) in relation to First Nations claims. Both policies had prevented many claims from moving forward, particularly specific claims.

Thus many land claims have lain dormant for over half a century until the recognition of Aboriginal rights in the *Calder* decision. The introduction of the Charter of Rights and Freedoms in 1982 confirmed the existence of First Nations land rights. Under the Constitution Act 1982, existing Aboriginal and treaty rights were recognized and affirmed. Prior to 1982, the Crown could unilaterally extinguish Aboriginal rights if it did so with plain and clear intent. Since 1982, however, the Crown no longer has that power, although the Crown can still infringe upon existing Aboriginal rights if it meets the criteria established by the courts.

The federal government created the Comprehensive Claims policy in 1973 and affirmed it later in 1981. The claims process is laden with bureaucratic hurdles. For example, before a claim is accepted, it must be reviewed by the Department of Justice and the Treasury Board. Once the negotiation process is in place, many other federal departments also review the case and the recommendation made by AANDC. It should be noted that in some cases, AANDC has recommended settlement of a claim only to have it rejected by other departments. The Prime Minister's Office is the final decision maker. To date, the federal government has settled twenty-four comprehensive claims with Aboriginal people in Canada. The first fifteen comprehensive claims settled by government covered 4 million square kilometres and were supplemented by capital transfers to Aboriginal groups of $2.2 billion.

Comprehensive land claim settlements deal with areas such as northern Quebec, Yukon, NWT, and British Columbia, which are the major regions where numbered treaties had not been established. As such, these areas were ripe for negotiating modern-day treaties. The first North American modern treaty was established in Alaska in 1973 and this became an initial template for Canada as it began to discuss land claims in the 1970s. The first of these modern-day treaties in Canada was the James Bay and Northern Quebec Agreement, signed in 1975. A decade later the Inuvialuit Final Agreement was signed, encompassing 90,000 square kilometres. The Nunavut settlement was established in 2000. With those settlements, attention then focused on Yukon and British Columbia. British Columbia had taken the position that provincial laws and the settlement of the area by colonists superseded First Nations land rights and claims. However the courts reminded the provincial government that First Nations land rights could not be extinguished indirectly. Rather, this process would have to take place via specific and direct legislation. Since the province had not done this, First Nations land rights still existed and required resolution. As such, British Columbia has become very active in attempting to settle land claims over the past decade (see Figure 8-2).

The cost of carrying out an investigation for a land claim is borne by the First Nations community making the claim. The federal government is prepared to provide the First Nations group with an "up front" loan with the proviso that if the group is successful in pursuing its claim, the money must be returned. In a case where the group is unsuccessful, the money does not have to be returned. However, the federal government has taken the stance that if negotiations with First Nations groups over land claims are not moving "forward," they will stop the negotiations and refuse to pay any additional money to allow the case to proceed. The process has become so complex that the government has produced several documents outlining the process of dealing with First Nations groups and managing dispute resolutions (*Guide for Federal Implementers of Comprehensive Land Claims and Self-Government Agreements*; *Guide for the Management of Dispute Resolution Mechanisms in modern Treaties*; *A Federal Implementer's Guide to Reviews in Self-Government and Comprehensive Land Claims Agreements*). There is also a Cabinet document that informs various federal departments as to their role and responsibilities with regard to dealing with modern treaties.

One of the major recommendations presented by the Royal Commission on Aboriginal Peoples (Canada 1996) was that the federal Crown create a trilateral relationship (federal–provincial–First Nations) with regard to establishing new treaties. This recommendation was accepted by the federal government and is now in implementation in British Columbia. By 2013, fifty-four First Nations, representing over 70 percent of British Columbia's First Nations, were active in treaty negotiation through the tripartite lands commission. The province then

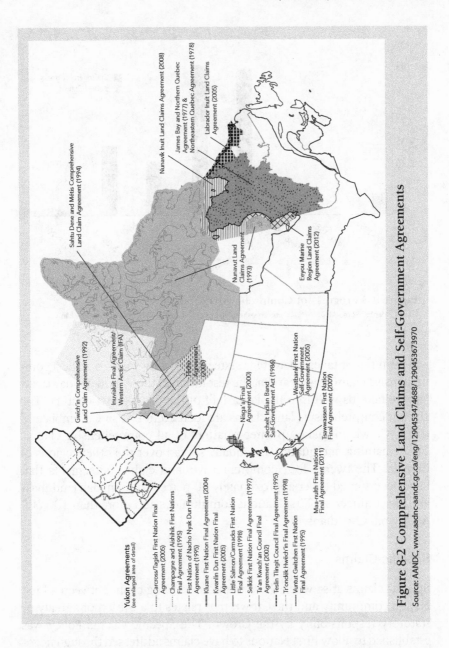

Figure 8-2 Comprehensive Land Claims and Self-Government Agreements

Source: AANDC, www.aadnc-aandc.gc.ca/eng/1290453474688/1290453673970

established a Treaty Negotiation Advisory Committee in 1996 to provide input and advice to the government with regard to establishing treaties in the province and settling outstanding claims by First Nations peoples.

Figure 8-3 shows the number of comprehensive claims initiated and settled over the past four decades; the number of claims in progress far exceeds the number that have been settled.

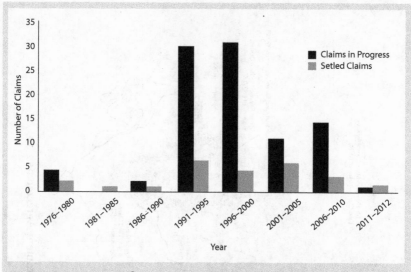

Figure 8-3 Progress of Comprehensive Claims, 1976–2012
Source: Adapted from AANDC 2015a, *Comprehensive Land Claims and Self-Government Negotiation Tables*

Given that it takes on average sixteen to twenty years to settle a comprehensive claim, it is clear that the resolution of these modern-day treaties will take us well into the latter half of the twenty-first century. The current comprehensive land claims are focused in British Columbia and the NWT which make up three quarters of all comprehensive claims. The remaining one quarter are equally spread over the other regions of Canada. The twenty-four comprehensive land claims agreements that have been signed cover approximately 40 percent of Canada's land mass and affect ninety-six First Nations communities and more than 100,000 Aboriginal Canadians.

Specific Claims

Specific claims arise when there is an outstanding claim between a First Nation community and the Crown that relates to a breach of a treaty or statutory responsibility by the Crown. The Specific Claims Policy was established to allow First Nations to have claims addressed through negotiations with the government rather than fighting their claim in court. In 1982, the federal government outlined its specific claims policy with the publication of *Outstanding Business: A Native Claims Policy*. Further amendments were made to the policy in the early 1990s. Then, in 2007, a new policy, titled *Justice at Last: Specific Claims Action Plan*, was created in an attempt to facilitate the resolution of specific claims as well as produce certainty for government, the private sector, and all Canadians. One year later the Specific Claims Tribunal Act came into force, allowing Aboriginal groups to file with an independent tribunal those claims that are not accepted for negotiation or not resolved through mediation within a three-year time period. Alternatively, First Nations may choose to follow a legal process through the courts to resolve their claim without going through the above processes.

Specific claims deal with events that need to have taken place at least fifteen years prior to the First Nation submitting their claim. However, the federal government decides whether or not to accept a claim based on criteria they have established, regardless of what First Nations people think. As such, historically many First Nations claims were rejected because they fell under the statutes of limitation or under the doctrine of laches—although the government has more recently stated they will not invoke these conditions in hearing a specific claim. However, the acceptance of a specific claim for negotiation is not an admission of liability by the federal government. Moreover, in the event that no settlement agreement is reached and litigation ensues, the federal government reserves the right to plead all defenses available to it, including limitation periods, laches, and lack of admissible evidence.

The average time it takes for a specific claim to be resolved is now over thirteen years. For many years the number of claims submitted per year was greater than the number resolved. Inventory and backlog continues to grow. However, while new claims are submitted each year, the recent policy has helped decrease the backlog (see Figure 8-4). For

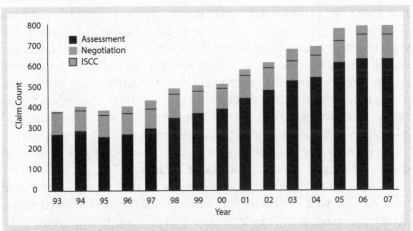

Figure 8-4 Growth of Specific Claims in Federal System: 1995–2007

Note: ISCC is the Indian Specific Claims Commission.

Source: Reproduced from AANDC 2007, *Specific Claims: Justice at Last*, 4

example, in March 1996, 746 specific claims had been received by government. Of those, 151 had been settled by negotiation, 40 settled by litigation, and 95 were being negotiated; 286 were under review, files were closed on 98, and 76 were rejected. By March 31, 2013, there were 337 claims in the inventory and 1,124 concluded claims (which could mean rejected, resolved, or closed).

Conclusion

More recent interpretations of treaties and land claims have suggested that the actions of the federal government were not so much a careful and deliberate scheme to displace First Nations people. Rather, the main goal was to open the country for settlement. Currently, there is debate among historians regarding the government's plan for First Nations policy in the West. Some argue that the government had no plan at all while others claim that a governmental plan did exist, but was vague. Other historians argue that the government intended merely to extend pre-Confederation First Nations policy to the post-Confederation period, following the precedents set by the Robinson Treaties and the Manitoulin Island Treaty. Whether the federal government had previously considered a plan or not, it did have clear objectives in its treaty dealings. Treaties were necessary to facilitate the opening of the West to settlement and to promote First Nations' assimilation into European settler society. Settlement of the Prairies was far and away the most significant consideration for the government in its determination to sign treaties.

The federal government negotiated treaties in areas needed for transportation lines or which were good farmland. Areas with little potential for settlement, such as the North, were left uncovered by treaty. The government felt that treaties and land settlements in desirable areas should be settled before the natives realized the value of their lands, thereby ensuring that the government could procure cheap and favourable terms. Immediate catalysts for each of the specific numbered treaties varied, however. First Nations interference with surveying and telegraphing crews was significant in several areas. A determination to remove any danger to incoming settler and railway crews also prompted the government to negotiate the Prairie Treaties.

Treaties 1 and 2 were negotiated because settlers were being stopped from moving west of Portage La Prairie, while Treaty 3 allowed immigrants safe passage to the West and secured the railway route. The catalyst for Treaty 4 consisted of First Nations interference with the geological survey which was establishing the border between Canada and the United States, and Treaty 5 secured a source of timber for the settlers.

Finally, Treaty 6 was motivated by the First Nations refusal to allow telegraphing crews on their lands, and concerns regarding the safety of settlers prompted negotiations for Treaty 7. Although the immediate catalysts were different in each case, all of the numbered treaties were negotiated by the federal government primarily on the basis of pressure for settlement and transportation.

Although the federal government is responsible for providing First Nations communities with access to legal services for claims disputes, these communities are responsible for making payments (including interest) on loans. The federal government, given its comparatively unlimited access to financial resources, can "drag on" the claims process through appeals, thereby undermining potential for First Nations successes. Even in a win, the cost of the process may exceed the value of the claim. As such, in many cases First Nations communities have had little choice but to halt the legal process. The federal government is now pursuing an "own-source revenue" program that forces self-governing Aboriginal groups to contribute to the costs of their own government activities. As such, the federal government will reduce its transfer of funds to these groups over time as they generate their own money through levying taxes or by generating other sources of income.

Chapter 9

The Urbanization of First Nations People

Introduction

Since the mid 1950s, the federal government has been persuading First Nations people to relocate from reserves into urban centres. In 1958, Citizenship and Indian Affairs Branch initiated a program that would support First Nations people to move into cities for employment and "a better way of life." By the 1970s, Indian Affairs was providing financial support by way of rent and other needs, with funding also going toward Friendship Centres across Canada to provide integration services for First Nations people. Central Mortgage and Housing Corporation also provided First Nations people with funds for the purchase and repair of off-reserve houses. These agencies were non-statutory, providing funds only to non-profit organizations. At the time there was a belief that First Nations people could better integrate into mainstream society if they were in cities.

By the 1970s, urban migration was well underway, with over half of the First Nations population moving to cities. However, with high fertility rates and decreasing rates of mortality, the on-reserve population did not substantially decrease. It is important to note that the rights of urban First Nations people remain unclear, unlike the rights of those Aboriginals living on reserves. For example, the question of collective rights in an urban context has yet to be tested in the courts (Luffman and Sussman 2007).

In the late twentieth century, the federal government introduced the Urban Aboriginal Strategy, focusing on developing partnerships among the federal and provincial governments, municipalities, and urban-dwelling First Nations peoples. Part of this strategy was to improve coordination and collaboration among service providers. However, in the end, the federal government was unable to bring about a close collaboration of service agencies for urban First Nations people, although in some regions such as Ottawa, municipal governments have established Aboriginal Working Committees, which created a working relationship between the municipal government and other stakeholders.

In the past, the federal government has focused solely on issues confronting reserve First Nations communities. This singular focus is a reflection of how government thinks about First Nation communities, which tends not to include urban First Nations communities (Wilson and Peters 2005). At the same time, these old "top down" social-economic development models implemented on the reserves have been applied to further development in urban communities (Mendelson 2004). However, these social-economic models have not been successful in promoting economic development of First Nations in urban centres. A new approach is needed that responds directly to the changing issues, while also helping to foster the creative potential that exists in urban First Nations communities (Foley 2008).

However, one of the major barriers to economic development or entering the labour force for First Nations people living in urban centres is that they are still considered to be immigrants in a foreign land— misplaced, unable to meet the norms of urban dwellers, and woefully unskilled to take part in the modern economy and urban way of life. Many Canadians see urban First Nations people as displaced "cultural curiosities." When First Nations people do move to the city, there is often a conclusion on the part of mainstream Canadians that they are choosing to abandon their cultural heritage. Those who remain on the reserve, by contrast, are seen as "resisting" integration and participation in Canadian society (Belanger 2011).

A number of researchers have identified key urban issues for First Nations people, but there has been little research or policy development on these issues. Most of the focus has been on issues related to land or treaties, the Indian Act, or taxation. Until recently, even the Assembly of First Nations had expressed little interest in dealing with urban issues for First Nations people. Bill C-31 (1985) set the stage by allowing individual Bands to determine their membership lists. Many bands established stringent membership rules such that First Nations individuals connected to that band but living in an urban centre are excluded and cannot easily participate in reserve politics or economic activities. Nevertheless, serious efforts are now being made to address some of the issues facing urban First Nations people.

Role of Government

For over a century, the federal government has claimed that its fiduciary responsibility was limited to First Nations people with status, or registered Indians, and even that responsibility ended at the reserve boundaries. However, over the past two decades this policy has been revised such that now, many federal programs for First Nations people are delivered in cities in what Abele and Graham (2011) call "status-blind" fashion— Métis, Inuit, and non-status Indians are all equally eligible. In 1996, the fledgling Centre for Municipal–Aboriginal Relations was created and partially supported by federal moneys. Its mandate was to produce an effective Aboriginal and municipal coalition focused on building relations based on the principles of respect, sharing, and mutual responsibility. A year later the Urban Aboriginal Strategy was created by the federal government as a four-year program, which has been extended to the present. The federal Task Force on Urban Issues (2002) concluded that the issues facing First Nations people living in urban centres across Canada needed to be addressed. It recommended better coordination of intergovernmental policy delivery as well as action on poverty, employment, and housing (Abele and Graham 2011). All these activities, plus the tremendous growth in the number of First Nations people permanently residing in urban centres, has propelled the issue onto the radar of policy makers, practitioners, and service-providing organizations.

The Urban Aboriginal Strategy was created to meet the specific needs of First Nations people living in urban centres. In addition to providing funding, the federal government partners with other levels of government, Aboriginal and community organizations, and the private sector. These partnerships include a variety of programs, funding arrangements, and the administration of projects. These collaborative efforts are meant to support various initiatives that will enhance the economic and social participation of all First Nations people living in Canadian cities (Siggner and Costa 2005). At present there are seven different federal agencies that support the Urban Aboriginal Strategy, including Aboriginal Affairs and Northern Development Canada, Human Resources and Skills Development Canada, Western Economic Diversification Canada, Public Health Agency of Canada, Public Safety Canada, Department of Justice, and Canadian Heritage.

The central goal of the Urban Aboriginal Strategy is to better deal with issues facing First Nations people living in cities, aiming to increase their social participation in various institutions. Through these efforts, the government aims to target appropriate socio-economic needs of urban First Nations people, coordinate the implementation of appropriate policies, and develop linkages and policy integration with different stakeholders. The Strategy funds projects that focus on investments in three areas: improving life skills; promoting job training, skills, and entrepreneurship; and supporting Aboriginal women, children, and families.

The Urban Aboriginal Strategy also was established to create partnerships with other federal departments, provincial and municipal stakeholders, Aboriginal communities, and the private sector. It is hoped that together these parties can make strategic investments to enhance the economic and social participation of First Nations people in Canada's cities. The Urban Aboriginal Strategy is unique in that it also invests in building capacity within the urban Aboriginal community.

How successful has this strategy been? There is a lack of clarity in the Strategy's stated goals and objectives, such that it is difficult to ascertain its impact. Thus, we have little empirical data to assess the impact of the Strategy even though it has been in operation for some time.

Demographics of Urban First Nations

In the mid 1950s, the number of First Nations people living in urban centres numbered in the hundreds. Most of these early urban residents were women who had married a non-status person, and thus were required to leave the reserve; or, they were young single men in search of excitement and possibly employment. For many, their residence in the city was considered temporary, and they relocated often between the reserve and the city. Over the past half century, this has changed. Since 1970, the urban segment of the First Nations population has increased from 13 percent to 41 percent while the proportion residing in large urban centres has increased from 7 to 31 percent. The average annual growth rate for First Nations people in the ten major urban centres in Canada varies, but over time but it has continued to increase. Between 1951 and 1981, the First Nations population residing in Canadian cities experienced considerable growth. For the period of 1951 to 1971, a 12 percent growth rate was recorded. This fell to just under 10 percent in the period from 1971 to 1981. The percentage of First Nations people living off-reserve increased from 17 percent to 28 percent during this time. This period of growth began to level off between the 1980s and the beginning of the twenty-first century. During that time the annual average growth rate hovered just below 5 percent each year.

Since 2000, there have been substantial levels of growth in urban areas, particularly for prairie cities. Table 9-1 shows the urban population in 2011. There is wide variation in the increases from 2001, with Montreal showing a 60 percent increase, Halifax a 52 percent increase,

Table 9-1 Aboriginal Population, Proportion of Census Metropolitan Area (CMA), and Population Increase from 2001–2011

City	Aboriginal population in 2011	Proportion of CMA (%)	% Change (2001–11)
Halifax	5,820	1.4	+52
Ottawa-Gatineau	30,570	1.8	+56
Montreal	26,280	0.5	+63
Toronto	36,995	0.5	+37
Thunder Bay	10,055	8.3	+23
Winnipeg	78,420	10.0	+24
Regina	19,785	8.9	+10
Saskatoon	23,895	9.3	+7
Calgary	33,370	2.5	+29
Edmonton	61,765	5.1	+29
Vancouver	52,375	1.9	+11

Source: AANDC, aadnc-aandc.gc.ca/eng/1100100014298/1100100014302

and Calgary and Edmonton about a 29 percent increase. Cities with long-standing Aboriginal populations reveal much smaller increases given there was already a large population at the beginning of the twenty-first century. Nevertheless, they still show substantial increases over the decade. However, since 2006 the increases in the cities identified have started to stabilize. First Nations population growth has slowed, and for the past decade most cities have experienced a roughly 4 percent increase each year during that time. Today, about 90 percent of the urban First Nations population lives in one of twelve cities. Almost 10 percent of the Winnipeg population is First Nations; Saskatoon and Regina have similar proportions. In other cities, First Nations people make up between 2 and 5 percent of the city's population. However, if we look at smaller urban centres like Prince Rupert and Prince Albert, the First Nations population makes up well over a third of the total population (Statistics Canada 2008b). These increases in the urban First Nations population are a result of complex factors. It may be connected to people leaving the reserve to work and live in the city as well as a high birth rate. Another factor may be related to how people declare their ethnicity on census forms (Guimond 2003b). We also note that the reserve population is commensurately increasing as the urban population increases. While the First Nations birth rate is higher, urban birth rates do not provide a full explanation of the large increases in First Nations population living in the city. For many, the loss of Indian status forced them to relocate to one of Canada's urban centres. Moreover, children who lost or were denied Indian status could not return to the reserves. In other cases, students leaving residential schools often chose the urban centres, given that knowledge of their traditional culture and language had been lost. Even their kinship remained partially unknown (Innes 2013). In the end, it is probable that all three of these explanations combine to reflect the huge increases in the number of urban First Nations people.

Urban First Nations people are much more mobile than the urban non-Aboriginal population. Roughly half of the First Nations population residing in the city claim to have moved between censuses, compared to only about one fifth of the non-Aboriginal population. The Urban Aboriginal Task Force (2007) argues that this high mobility rate is tied to poverty and the limitations placed on finding suitable housing. This high rate of mobility creates major challenges for service provision, particularly services like education, employment training, and housing. Only about half of the urban First Nations population can speak an Aboriginal language; this is much lower than the on-reserve population.

There is a significant income gap between First Nations and non-Aboriginal people. While this gap is slowly decreasing, it is predicted that it will take more than 60 years to close (Wilson and Macdonald 2010). However, Parriag and Chaulk (2013) point out that for urban First Nations people, the trend is somewhat different. Overall, they find that urban First Nations reveal a different income profile than rural. They show that one third of urban First Nations make between $40,000 and $80,000, and that one quarter make above $80,000. These patterns reveal that there is an emerging middle income group (Anderson 2013) and that over one half of the urban First Nations people were earning above $40,000 and 26 percent were earning over $80,000. When these figures are compared with non-Aboriginal urban people, we find that one third make between $40,000 and $80,000 and 40 percent make above $80,000. This reveals a gap between the incomes of the two groups. Table 9-2 shows urban First Nations socio-economic attributes compared to non-Aboriginals, in both large and smaller urban areas.

The urban Aboriginal population in Canada is very young, with nearly one third under the age of fifteen compared to 17 percent of the non-Aboriginal population. Table 9-2 shows that there are more First Nations women than men in urban areas, while the reverse is true on First Nations reserves. Many single women move with their children to cities. Nearly one in four families is lone-parent. While the percentage of urban First Nations children in low-income families declined in the

Table 9-2   Socio-Demographic Attributes of Urban and Non-Urban Aboriginal People by Size of Urban Area

Selected Indicators	Urban Areas < 100,000 Population				Urban Areas >100,000 Population			
	Aboriginal Identity Population (%)		Non-Aboriginal (%)		Aboriginal Identity Population (%)		Non-Aboriginal (%)	
	2001	2006	2001	2006	2001	2006	2001	2006
% of population aged 15–19 < high school	26	19	18	14	24	18	14	16
% of population aged 25–44 with university degree	5	7	14	16	10	13	28	33
Unemployment rate	18.4	12.7	8.2	6.6	18.5	10.6	8.1	6.1
Average total income (all sources)	$20,552	$26,134	$27,046	$32,331	$21,499	$27,029	$31,956	$37,594
Average employment (full time) income	$35,469	$41,406	$39,716	$46,204	$34,714	$41,861	$45,973	$54,267
% receiving government transfer payments	18.8	16.5	14.8	14.3	16.4	15.0	10.0	9.6

Incidence of low income before tax among "economic families"	33.8	25.5	11.2	9.2	37.0	31.2	14.3	13.8
Incidence of low income before tax among unattached individuals	56.9	50.1	37.7	34.6	57.7	58.4	39.5	38.7
% of children under age 15 in low income families	43.1	36.2	17.4	15.3	50.0	44.8	20.6	20.5
Lone parent families as a % of all Census families	25	23	16	16	27	24	17	17

Source: AANDC, aadnc-aandc.gc.ca/eng/1100110001429B/1100110001430Z

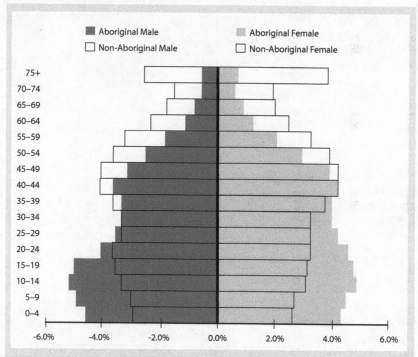

Figure 9-1 Age and Gender Distribution of the Urban Aboriginal and Non-Aboriginal Populations, Canada, 2006
Source: AANDC, aadnc-aandc.gc.ca/eng/1100110014298/1100110014302

early twenty-first century, the percentage of such children is still more than twice that of non-Aboriginal children in low-income families.

Living in the City

The initial First Nations residents of the city were transients or sojourners, coming and going in relatively quick succession. The First Nations population in cities was "churning" with this traffic that did not remain long enough to establish networks or develop a sense of community cohesion. The city was not a home, reflected in the fact that few First Nations people participated in its social and economic structure.

Since the turn of the twenty-first century, however, a number of independent and government surveys have carried out studies of First Nations people living in urban centres across Canada. The survey results reveal that, overall, residents in the city are largely first generation; in other words they were born and raised somewhere other than where they currently live. At the same time, most of them are long-term residents (more than twenty years) in the city. Only a small group are second- and third-generation residents of an urban environment. Nevertheless, First Nations people living in the city feel they have a future here and can make a positive difference to their community. This difference, they believe, will make their community a better place to live and provide non-Aboriginal people with a better understanding of First Nations people. Research also has found that despite their different linguistic and cultural backgrounds, most remain oriented strongly toward their First Nations cultural identity (Restoule 2005). We also find that the composition of urban First Nations people is much different than it was fifty years ago. Previously, the First Nations composition in any city reflected the nearby First Nations communities. As such, early enclaves of First Nations people in urban centres was homogenous in culture, language, and region of origin. However, today we find a mosaic of First Nations identities residing in the city and the First Nations (and Aboriginal) population is diverse and multi-ethnic.

Nevertheless, government officials still do not see that urban First Nations people have developed new social and political strategies to deal with the urban context; instead, too often First Nations people are treated as though they were living on the reserve. They see urban First Nations people as a heterogeneous cultural mosaic who have abandoned their cultural heritage such that the federal government has little responsibility for them. The courts have disagreed with this stance; the Federal Court of Canada's decision regarding *Misquadis* (2002) explicitly recognized that urban First Nations communities are similar to rural First Nations communities and are thus the responsibility of the federal government. Moreover, the *Esquega* (2007) case also contributed to the understanding that urban First Nations communities should be recognized as a political community. As such, they require outside funding. For example, courts have ruled that Human Resources and Skills Development discriminated against urban First Nations in their failure to fund necessary infrastructure to facilitate integration into the social and economic institutions of urban centres (Belanger 2011).

First Nations Identity

The legacy and effects of the Indian residential schools experience persists among urban First Nations peoples. The Urban Aboriginal Peoples Survey results show that a majority of urban First Nations peoples across cities have been affected, both physically and mentally, by attending Indian residential schools. There is considerable evidence that this experience has had an impact in shaping their lives (Aboriginal Healing Foundation 2007). However, as we saw in Chapter 7, it should be noted that not all individuals who attended residential schools feel the experience was totally negative; some former students recall a positive experience, while for others it was mixed.

When asked about their family and kin, many First Nations peoples do not know their family tree well, but First Nations peoples are much more likely to know their family history than non-First Nations peoples. Nevertheless, the establishment of the residential schools had a great impact on dispersing and disbanding kinship networks (Innes 2013). Nonetheless, urban First Nations people are proud of their identity, and may even be more so than non-First Nations people (Peters 2010). First Nations peoples in cities learn about their family tree from a variety of sources but parents and grandparents are key sources of information, especially for youth. Others point out that education is a critical channel for learning about First Nations identity. Moreover, few people report hiding or even downplaying their Aboriginal identity while in the city. First Nations peoples in urban centres have considerable respect for their heritage and express strong pride in their identity.

Coming to the City

The decision to move to a city is a result of both push and pull factors. For First Nations men, the predominant reasons for moving to the city are related to family, education, and work opportunities. At the same time, there were no major "push" factors aside from a lack of job opportunities on the reserve. Most men find life on the reserve quite satisfying except for the employment situation. First Nations women, by contrast, report that their decision to move was based on family and education. Some felt they needed to escape a "bad family situation" on the reserve, and hoped that the city might provide a better environment for child-rearing. In addition, given the difficulties of obtaining a post-secondary education on the reserve, education is also a strong pull factor for females.

Staying in the City

When urban First Nations people are asked to name the location of their "home," nearly three quarters of them report the "city." A limited number claimed that their "ancestral home land" was their home. Urban First Nations peoples' "sense of place" is predominantly defined by the city in which they currently live. Put another way, the current First Nations urban population is a permanent population. As such, many First Nations people feel their current city residence is their "home," particularly those who are first-generation urban dwellers. Overall, most First Nations urban residents do not intend to move back to their homeland at any point in their life. However, for even those non-movers, social and economic factors may change and they may return either temporarily or permanently to the reserve.

Most urban First Nations people claim to enjoy working and living in the city. Five reasons for enjoying the city were recorded: the improved standard of living, the availability of recreational activities and entertainment, the proximity of family and friends, better employment opportunities, and social acceptance. Nevertheless, urban Aboriginal people are as likely to feel that they belong to an Aboriginal as to a non-Aboriginal community. Many say they belong to a mostly First Nations or equally First Nations and non-Aboriginal community. Maintaining a connection to members of their own First Nation community and other First Nations people in their city is important to a majority, although given the multi-ethnic makeup of urban First Nations people, this can present difficulties.

First Nations people living in the city are clear as to which components of their traditional culture are the most important and need to be shared with the younger generation. First and foremost is language, followed by ceremonies, spirituality, music, customs and traditions, elders, and art. A considerable number of urban First Nations people also feel family values are an important aspect of Aboriginal culture to be passed on to the next generation.

Connecting with the Home Community

Regardless of origin, gender, or duration in the city, most urban First Nations people stay connected with their communities of origin. At the same time, while some of them believed that they would return to the reserve someday, the data reveal that only a minority return to take up permanent residence back on the reserve. The lack of housing and employment, as well as poor educational facilities, keeps people from returning to the reserve. Others, whose band refused them membership, have no desire to return home. Nevertheless, urban First Nations people retain a cultural connection to their home communities or to those of their parents or grandparents. Their links to their home communities are based upon strong family and community ties and reflect links to both contemporary as well as to traditional First Nations culture. Those individuals who have high incomes are more likely to stay connected with their home communities than those with lower incomes.

Urban Aboriginal Organizations

Until the 1970s there were few urban Aboriginal organizations that were able to help newcomers navigate the maze of bureaucratic structures to find housing, health services, and employment. We saw above that some of the first organizations to arise in urban centres were Friendship Centres. Early Friendship Centres were mainly conduits to help individuals adjust; in other words, helping people integrate into an urban labour market as well as to locate affordable housing. Early Aboriginal organizations acted as buffers between formal systems and community members. However, today this has changed. Aboriginal organizations play a unique role as sites of mobilization and community-building (Proulx 2003; Silver and Hay 2006). Through their intimate knowledge of the community, they have become more effective at program interventions than governments at any level. Anderson (2013) shows that First Nations residents are strong collaborators with municipal and community organizations, enhancing the quality of life of city residents.

Urban First Nations people report considerable contact with various mainstream service-providing organizations, particularly banks, schools, and the health care system. In addition, half of the current urban First Nations peoples at least occasionally use and rely on First Nations services and organizations. In some cases, member organizations provide general information as well as confirmation of First Nations identity. Regardless of the degree of contact with non-Aboriginal services, all First Nations people agree that specific services are important, particularly in the case of addiction programs, child and family services, and housing services (Environics 2010).

The use of First Nations service-provider organizations is more common among First Nations peoples in larger cities like Toronto and Vancouver, cities noted for the greater availability of First Nations cultural activities. These large cities have over time built considerable support services for First Nations people. On the other hand, residents of Regina (40 percent) are the least likely to use First Nations services and organizations. Frequent use of First Nations services and organizations is also more common among First Nations peoples aged forty-five years and older and those who are less affluent. The data reveal that the use of these services and organizations steadily declines as household income increases. Finally, Aboriginal services and organizations are equally important to long-time residents and those who are new to their city (for example people who arrived in the city within the last two years).

In 2012 the Government of Canada transferred three Aboriginal programs from Canadian Heritage to Aboriginal Affairs and Northern Development Canada: the Aboriginal Friendship Centres Program, Cultural Connections for Aboriginal Youth, and Young Canada Works for Aboriginal Urban Youth. It was hoped that the transfer would more fully integrate the services of these organizations into other federally supported programs. Since then, other urban Aboriginal organizations such as Calgary Urban Aboriginal Initiative have become the brokers of many different federal and provincial programs. The government claims that the financial support of these Aboriginal organizations will be more cost effective, as well as better able to coordinate federal and provincial efforts to support urban and off-reserve Aboriginal people.

It is clear that for urban First Nations social and economic development, Aboriginal organizations make a difference (National Association of Friendship Centres 2009). We know that they operate less as independent organizations, but rather as "member" organizations through a holistic integration to other spheres of life, such as the cultural, the social, and the political. We also know that First Nations community members play an important advocacy and brokerage role, as well as providing a mechanism for support (cultural and otherwise) for some early stage migrants to the city (Silver and Hay 2006). With respect to economic development, Peters (2011) and others have pointed out that steady growth in the size and complexity of urban First Nations organizations has created employment opportunities for an emerging professional class of First Nations people. It also generates skill sets and experiences that can be used in the pursuit of entrepreneurial goals. However, even though the major urban centres have a substantial multicultural First Nations population, there is a notable absence of First Nations-owned businesses, organizations, and First Nations-specific services.

Returning to the Homeland

For those individuals who have moved to the city, we find that roughly a third return to their home community, either temporarily or permanently. It is also true that a large number of First Nations city dwellers tend to move back and forth between the reserve and the city. The question arises as to why and when First Nations people decide to stay in the city or return to their homeland—temporarily or permanently. Given the dynamic nature of residential mobility for First Nations people, it is evident there are a number of "push" and "pull" factors that determine the extent of that mobility. First of all, the linkages with their homeland, and whether these are strengthened or weakened by social and legal events, help determine the decision (Environics 2010). Second, the size of the First Nations population and its cultural composition have an impact on the decision to stay or leave. Third, the ability to find a job that will sustain the individual or family will influence whether or not the individual remains in the city. Overall, we find that the size of the city and the size and composition of the First Nations population, as well as the services offered, have a major impact on the decision of First Nations people to stay in the city. However, even for those who remain in the city, their linkages with rural homelands remains strong.

First Nations Communities in the City

First Nations peoples define their community primarily as family and friends. As such, they are more likely to feel they belong to a First Nations community than to a non-Aboriginal one even though they may be spatially distant from each other. This is not true for all First Nations peoples, some of whom feel they belong to both a First Nations as well as a non-Aboriginal community. Nevertheless, community is defined as the people in their neighbourhood, members of their own cultural group, and other Aboriginal people in the city. At the same time, urban First Nations peoples have as many close non-Aboriginal as Aboriginal friends. The results show that First Nations friends are more common among older urban First Nations peoples, whereas young people are more likely to have as many non-Aboriginal friends as First Nations friends.

First Nations peoples living in the city are more likely than not to say there are some, if not a lot of, Aboriginal cultural activities in their community. There are however notable variations in this perception by city, socio-economic status, age, and strength of Aboriginal identification. Those urban First Nations with more education and higher income show greater awareness of Aboriginal cultural activities in their cities than those with low education and income. Overall, a majority of First Nations peoples participate in the various cultural activities that are available in their city. However, it seems that young people participate less in these cultural activities than the older generation.

Perceptions of Non-Aboriginals in an Urban Setting

Living in the city affords First Nations people interactions with non-Aboriginal people in many different dimensions of their life. This phenomenon is not the case for non-Aboriginal people interacting with First Nations people. Evidence shows there is a general belief by First Nations people that non-Aboriginal people carry a wide range of negative stereotypes of them, most commonly of alcoholism and drug abuse. These stereotypes influence the opportunities available to First Nations people while also affecting their well-being. Overall, First Nations people are able to identify at least one difference between themselves and non-Aboriginal people. The general belief is that there are many differences, especially in terms of value systems and cultural heritage, between First Nations and non-Aboriginal people. At the same time, there is a belief among First Nations peoples that the negative impressions held by non-Aboriginal people are improving, especially among those who are familiar with Aboriginal tradition and culture. We also know that these perceptions vary considerably between different cities (Environics 2010). The regional variations reveal that urban First Nations perceptions about non-Aboriginal people are shaped by the city in which they live.

We also know that many urban First Nations residents have experienced discrimination. This is particularly true for older residents, women, and urban First Nations people living in Saskatoon and Regina. However, the discrimination varies by time and place, and is seen in the labour market, educational institutions, health services, and even various retail outlets. Nevertheless, there is a general view among urban First Nations people that they are accepted by non-Aboriginal people; they recount many positive exchanges with non-Aboriginal people, which have shaped their lives for the better.

Settlement Patterns

While the federal government has been a supporter of First Nations people's relocation from reserves into cities, officials did not fully understand the implications of such a widespread movement of people. Their general concern was assimilation and the eradication of any "Indianness" of the people. It should be noted that there has been an absence of community opposition to First Nations people residing in certain areas of the city, as we have sometimes seen for example when foreign immigrants move into certain areas of a city (Parriag and Chaulk 2013). Nevertheless, social class has become an important issue for urban communities and neighbourhoods. Having low income housing or shelters for the homeless has become a major issue in many neighbourhoods in urban centres.

Thus, the urbanization of First Nations people has produced a backlash from certain segments of the urban population. However, it seems more focused on social class than on ethnicity. Urban non-Aboriginal peoples are concerned with low-income people moving into their neighbourhoods and affecting the value of their housing. Community spokespersons argue that allowing low-income residents into the community will bring crime, drug use, and other activities that are perceived as not prevalent in their community. They also are worried that schools, religious institutions, and community associations will be negatively influenced by these low-income populations. As such, many cities have rules restricting the number and placement of low-income dwellings in certain urban zones. Second, municipalities also have expressed concerns about ethnic or class ghettoization. In the end, while there is little evidence to support the ghettoization hypothesis for almost any ethnic group in Canada, many communities have opposed the placement of subsidized housing units near their single home dwellings.

The data reveal that First Nations people are not, contrary to popular perception, segregated in any parts of a large urban centre with the exception of Winnipeg and Regina. While there may be higher concentrations of urban First Nations people in inner city areas, the concentration does not represent a ghettoization of First Nations people. In most urban centres across Canada, First Nations people are highly dispersed throughout the city. For example, in Edmonton, which has a high urban First Nations population, there is not one census tract or enumeration area where more than 20 percent of the population are First Nations people. In summary, contrary to the fears of some non-Aboriginal people, the data reveal that First Nations people are residing in diverse regions across the city. This diversity and dispersion is supported by the work of Anderson (2013), who points out that today there is strong evidence of an emerging middle-class First Nations population in the city.

Social Issues in Urban Centres

A number of social issues have emerged as First Nations people have settled in cities across Canada. Issues such as domestic violence, social support, homelessness, and unemployment are all on the table for municipal governments. Domestic violence, addiction, and petty crimes are all symptomatic of a marginal, poor population residing in an urban centre. However, it is also true that there are organizations that prey upon the isolation and social exclusion of First Nations people; a significant issue worth mentioning here is gang membership.

First Nations Gangs

Over time, the increase of First Nations people in urban areas, their marginal existence, and their exposure to prejudice and discrimination have produced a unique form of social exclusion. These excluded individuals are primarily young, male, and unable to enter the labour market. It is estimated that nearly one quarter of all gang members in Canada are First Nations people. These young men and women make up the nearly 1,000 gang members in the prairie provinces, with Saskatchewan as the epicentre. These gang members are usually between the ages of fifteen and twenty-four and are mostly male, although females are certainly allowed into gangs if they demonstrate their commitment and follow orders from the leaders. Females may also provide sex (as a form of slavery). Like other gangs, First Nations gangs are likely to have names, a "branded" colour and style of clothing, and recognizable tattoos to reveal membership (Totten 2010). First Nations gangs also are similar in many other respects to non-Aboriginal gangs: they engage in criminal activities to make money for luxury goods such as drugs and alcohol. However First Nations gangs differ considerably from non-Aboriginal gangs in that they have a unique organizational structure and hierarchy. As Totten (2010) points out, at the core of the gang is the leader or boss. Next are the "veterans," who have been in the gang for a considerable time and have extensive social and criminal networks in the city. Further from the core are the members or affiliates of the gang, individuals who engage in most of the criminal activities. Finally, there are the "strikers" and the new recruits. These individuals are not yet considered "full" members and as such are expected to engage in extreme criminal activities to demonstrate their allegiance. These strikers are potentially the most violent even though they might not generate significant money for the gang.

Most members of a gang are recruited by existing members and are shown that they can "bond" with the gang. This provides some structure to their lives. Real and perceived threats from rival gangs maintain high social cohesion. In addition, each member is assigned a specific role which carries with it a certain status. Movement up the hierarchy is also possible if member actions are supportive of the gang and demonstrate superior organizational skills or simply daring behaviour. However, membership also has a functional aspect. It provides the member with self-respect and self-esteem; it furthermore secures employment and income that many members would otherwise be without (Totten 2010). Some of the more lucrative activities of First Nations gangs are drug distribution and domestic sex trafficking. Sex trafficking generally occurs in "triangles" such that females are moved from one city to the next. For example, one triangle is Calgary–Edmonton–Vancouver. However, with the heavy oil sands developments in both northern Alberta and Saskatchewan, sex trafficking also involves a flourishing trade among the oil and mine workers.

Strikers and new recruits have high levels of internalized violence such as drug use, self-injury, and suicide. Most of their activities beyond routine crime are directed toward other gang members who threaten (or are perceived to threaten) the gang (Totten 2008). In the end, most violence is between gangs; data reveals that First Nations gangs do not often exhibit physical violence against non-Aboriginals. However, we find that in many gang conflicts, family and kin members are found in different gangs. Totten (2010) argues that these individuals have much higher rates of internalized violence. For example, these young people have high levels of self-hatred that drives them to engage in self-injurious behaviours, sometimes leading to death.

Conclusion

As Norris and Clatworthy (2011) point out, the high rates of in-and-out migration creates a "churn" that can affect service delivery in areas of education, health, and social services. Regardless of whether the churn has a high or low impact on urban immigration or emigration, the demographic composition of the urban First Nations population can be problematic for service providers as well as for policy analysts. Moreover, we have seen that the extent of migration to and from the cities varies across regions. These differences reflect the history of migration for First Nations people, natural increase in city size, legislation changes, and ethnic mobility. As Guimond et al. (2009) point out, poorly designed policy can emerge without a full understanding of the forces that affect First Nations migration.

While in the mid-twentieth century migration from the reserves contributed directly to the growth of First Nations population in cities across Canada, this is no longer the case. Today we find that many First Nations people have decided to permanently settle in urban centres along with their offspring. The higher rate of fertility of First Nations people also accounts for some of the increase. Moreover, the sheer size of the First Nations population on the reserves has meant that even if a smaller percentage of people from the reserve move into the city, the numbers are substantial. We also find that cities that have a long history of First Nations populations have developed their own institutional structures to deal with new incoming First Nations people. As such, they mediate the number that "return" to the reserve and thus also contribute to the growing First Nations population in the city.

There is a sense of cultural vitality among urban First Nations peoples in Canadian cities. The belief that First Nations people cannot be economically successful in urban centres without the loss of some cultural authenticity is poorly supported by research. There is a confidence in their ability to retain cultural identity in the city. Maintaining Aboriginal languages, as well as customs and traditions, is a priority for many urban First Nations people. However, we find that urban First Nations youth are the least attuned to First Nations culture in their communities. Nevertheless, urban First Nations people embrace pluralism, even more so than non-Aboriginal people (Environics 2010). Finally, Aboriginal organizations clearly help First Nations peoples make significant choices about their cultural, economic, and social affairs; as well, for some, they sustain a sense of collective identity in the city.

Most Canadians have forgotten that many of today's urban centres are situated in areas that had been settled by First Nations people many centuries ago. In this sense, it could be argued that First Nations people are now just beginning to reclaim their urban history. Moreover, the relocation of reserves as cities evolved around them (in addition to the illegal surrenders of reserve lands near city boundaries) are all factors contributing to the physical removal of the First Nations population from modern urban space. This is partially what led to the belief that First Nations people are "new" to the urban centres. Finally, the creation of roads and fences marking property boundaries reinforced the notion that urban centres are foreign institutions for First Nations people. Within urban centres, many municipalities built on federal and provincial colonialism in their dealings with First Nations people. However, the extent to which they replicated the form varies from region to region. As such, we find that municipal government orientation toward First Nations peoples varies from place to place; this may explain why some urban centres are considered more "friendly" by First Nations people.

The trend toward an increasing number of First Nations people residing in major urban centres is clear. New social networks and a developing middle class will result in an increased presence through political and social activities (Anderson 2013).

Chapter 10

Aboriginal Rights, Self-Government, and Sovereignty

Introduction

When the Privy Council made its historic decision in 1888 (*St. Catherines Milling and Lumber Co.*), the federal government considered the issue of Aboriginal rights to be settled. This decision found that First Nations people had no Aboriginal rights or title. What they did have, according to the Council, was usufructuary rights. Such rights established the right to occupy and use lands when the Crown approved. However, for the past four centuries this decision has been a contested terrain for First Nations peoples. They continue to fight for their rights. In 1973 the Supreme Court (*Calder*) acknowledged, for the first time, that Aboriginal rights were held by First Nations people, independent of the Crown. Even the Liberal government in power at the time had to accept that this decision would fundamentally change how the Crown would deal with First Nations people.

For decades the federal government refused to accept any aspect of the inherent right of self-government for First Nations people. However, the Inherent Rights Policy (Canada 1995) acknowledges the right of Aboriginal self-government. This policy allows that First Nations self-government is appropriate for matters internal to the First Nations communities and only those issues that are unique to their culture, traditions, and institutions (Belanger and Newhouse 2004).

The federal government has refused to accept the argument that First Nations people have sovereign rights. While First Nations people continue to argue for sovereignty, the federal government continues to resist. In *R. v. Sparrow* (1990), the Supreme Court addressed the issue of constitutional versus Aboriginal rights. The Court's ruling specified that there is no doubt that sovereignty and the ability to carry out legislation with regard to land or title is vested in the Crown; only Canada's federal and provincial governments can exercise governmental power, as established under the Constitution. Nearly a decade later, the federal government would develop a policy stating that First Nations people had the inherent right of self-government but not sovereignty. With the subsequent patriation of the Constitution in 1982 and the introduction of the Charter of Rights and Freedoms, Aboriginal rights were given constitutional recognition. These new laws changed the Crown's relation with First Nations people. Prior to 1982, for example, treaty rights were subject to unilateral federal modification or extinguishment; today, this is no longer possible. Section 35 of the Charter has become a major vehicle by which First Nations people can assert their Aboriginal rights. However, in the Charter, Aboriginal and treaty rights are not defined. It was the intention of the Supreme Court that further litigation would sort out the boundaries of those rights. And, over time, the Supreme Court of Canada has established criteria to determine whether or not a given activity or claim is an Aboriginal right. Nevertheless much more clarification is required (Belanger and Newhouse 2008) as First Nations people continue to expand and exert their claims to many different Aboriginal rights.

The federal government claims that an Aboriginal right is a common law right, not a statutory right, and only the courts can determine the existence of such a right. As such, the federal government cannot unilaterally declare these rights or create them through the passage of legislation. The above principles have been stated by the federal government in their attempts to deal with First Nations people over the years. However, it has been the duty of the courts to interpret the legislation. As such, the courts have intervened, influencing legal principles by providing interpretations of the principles and subsequent legislation. During the nineteenth and twentieth century, the federal government simply denied the existence of First Nations rights and title with little input from First Nations people. First Nations were unable to participate in the legal system to contest that belief. However, recently the courts have come to recognize the Crown's responsibilities and the distinctiveness of First Nations culture. Surprisingly, the courts also have dealt with gaps in First Nations policy given that First Nations people have been unable to create or implement policy. Consequently, some court decisions have set out new principles but left the implementation of those principles to the federal government.

Constitutional Context

The Canadian Constitution is a kind of "fundamental law" that sets out the nature of the federal government, the basic principles of government operations, and establishes the laws of the land. There is also an "unwritten" side to the Constitution, customary ways the federal government has operated over time, known as "conventions." Conventions are as important as the written Constitution but notoriously more difficult to interpret and equally hard to enforce. For example, when Prime Minister Pierre Trudeau wanted to unilaterally repatriate the Constitution, the Supreme Court allowed that from a constitutional perspective, he might do so. However, there was a "convention" that required him to consult with the provinces. The new Constitution contains the majority of the acts that made up the Canadian Constitution of 1867, such that many of the same legal and political questions with respect to First Nations people remain.

It has been argued that the federal government acted in accordance with the Constitution until 1995; in that year, Prime Minister Brian Mulroney declared that First Nations people had inherent Aboriginal rights to self-government. However, critics have argued that this was a violation of the Constitution. The argument goes as follows: given that Canada is a constitutional monarchy, sovereignty is held only by the federal Crown. Sovereign powers are distributed and controlled by the Constitution and operate in accordance with constitutional law. Thus, if the federal government is sovereign, how can a lesser government have any right to self-government? One way this can happen is by the federal Crown delegating certain powers to lesser governments (such as provincial governments). However, since the Constitution distributes all legislative jurisdiction to Parliament and the Provincial Legislatures, and this is both exclusive and exhaustive, there are no "left-over" self-government issues to be taken up by another level of government—such as a government comprised of Aboriginal people (Rustand 2010). Thus, if the federal government wishes to delegate legislation to Aboriginal people, it may do so; however, it is then a matter of delegation, and not a matter of an "inherent" right to self-government. Nevertheless, the acceptance of Aboriginal self-government has now been in effect for nearly twenty years and thus it might qualify as a "convention."

Changing Views of Aboriginal Rights

Aboriginal rights have undergone an evolution since the Royal Proclamation of 1763. For years, the federal government argued that

Aboriginal land rights originated with the Proclamation. In more recent times, however, the courts have acknowledged that Aboriginal people have some Aboriginal rights. Nevertheless, what they encompass, how they are expressed, and the nature of those rights still remain unclear. In 1996, the Supreme Court of Canada (*Van der Peet*) identified the criteria that Aboriginal people would have to meet in order to establish an Aboriginal right. At the same time, Parliament has shown little appetite to clearly spell out the specifics with regards to Aboriginal rights. At the same time it is also unwilling to accept First Nations' perspectives on this matter. As such, the courts are in the position of defining Aboriginal rights. They have reluctantly accepted this task but admit they are not trained to provide a definitive answer. In the meantime, First Nations people argue that their voices are rarely heard in the debate. First Nations people appreciate the courts' efforts, but they also make the point that any definitions will reflect the settler bias of law; in other words, they feel First Nations' conceptions of rights are being ignored.

Aboriginal Views

First Nations people argue that Aboriginal rights are given to them by the Creator. For First Nations people, the Royal Proclamation of 1763 simply affirmed their Aboriginal right and title. First Nations people believe that Aboriginal rights are inherent and collective. In this context, "inherent" means self-originating in a First Nations people, independent of Crown sovereignty or the Constitution. It means that Aboriginal rights exist because Aboriginal peoples lived in Canada prior to European colonization and enjoyed their own societies, political systems, laws, and forms of government (McNeil 2006a). These Aboriginal rights also include a number of other areas of human endeavor, such as education, self-government, hunting, fishing, trapping, and land ownership.

The courts claim that the establishment of an Aboriginal right is contingent upon the "right" being central to the culture of the First Nations community. Henderson and Barsh (1997) find this criterion objectionable and problematic. First of all, it allows the courts to determine what is "integral" to a First Nations culture. In addition, this process cannot make a distinction among all the cultural elements that comprise First Nations culture. In other words, it assumes that each aspect of First Nations culture is independent of every other aspect and that there is a hierarchy of importance among cultural components. Henderson and Barsh (1997) argue that this kind of thinking is judicial fiction; they liken it to the claim that an ecosystem is the same after the removal of a few incidental species.

Boyer (2014) provides an excellent example of how change occurs in First Nations law and culture in her discussion of the Haudenosaunee concept of "adding to the rafters" (referring to adding new logs to a longhouse), which allows for new norms and laws to be added to the Great Law of Peace, so that future generations can adapt to the changes in their lives over time. The First Nations understood that change takes place over time and each community had to find a way to incorporate that change into their norms, values, and laws. In short, First Nations people understand their culture is not "frozen" and evolves over time. First Nations people also argue that the Supreme Court's insistence that any Aboriginal right has to meet the "distinctive culture" test is misplaced. This kind of argument fails to acknowledge the continually changing nature of culture. The claim that a right has to reflect a "pre-contact" way of life for a specific First Nation is simply wrong (Henderson and Barsh 1997). This component has been modified to an extent in the *R. v. Sappier* (2006) and *R. v. Gray* (2006) cases, establishing that a practice can be an Aboriginal right if it is related to survival or if it is a practice that is engaged in by other First Nations people.

The View of the Federal Government

The federal government of Canada argues that Aboriginal land title, as a sub-category of Aboriginal rights, lies within the jurisdiction of Parliament. This includes jurisdiction to govern the land. Aboriginal title is nothing more than a "property right" and a "burden on the Crown." The Crown claims that First Nations people have no ownership of the land and that Aboriginal rights are nothing more than common law rights that can be restricted by government legislation at any time as long as that legislation meets the criteria outlined in the Supreme Court's definition of extinguishing Aboriginal rights.

Historically, the federal government of Canada has taken the position that all Aboriginal rights have been extinguished by Canadian law (implicitly or explicitly). However, after the ill-fated 1969 White Paper—in which the Liberal government attempted to abolish the legal status of "Indians"—was defeated, a new awareness of "Indigenous" emerged among First Nations people across Canada. With the subsequent *Calder* decision in 1973, a growing political consciousness emerged among First Nations communities. In addition, many other Canadians showed their support for Aboriginal rights and demonstrated to the federal government that First Nations issues such as Aboriginal rights required more attention (McNeil 2006a).

In the late 1970s, this political awareness focused on the desire to make constitutional changes with respect to Aboriginal issues. As the Liberal government first introduced its suggested changes in the 1970s, there was some hope among First Nations people that they would finally see the beginning of real change. However, by the early 1980s, the provincial governments rejected the proposed constitutional changes by the federal government. As such, the federal government decided to "go it alone."

The revised 1980 proposal for constitutional change omitted any reference to Aboriginal people or the issues they had raised in the earlier round of negotiations. This "critical incident" brought Aboriginal people from across Canada to unite in a single cause. In addition, groups such as churches, women's organizations, and other non-governmental organizations gave their support to Aboriginal people. In a last-minute change of heart, Peter Lougheed, then premier of Alberta, offered a compromise: Aboriginal and treaty rights would be reinstated in the proposed Constitution Act, along with the word "existing" to be placed before the terms "rights" and "treaties." As a result, the revised Constitution Act was approved and existing Aboriginal and treaty rights are now embedded in the Constitution.

Constitution Act, 1982, and the Charter of Rights and Freedoms

In 1982, Canada repatriated its Constitution and added, as Part II to the Constitution, the Charter of Rights and Freedoms. The Charter acknowledges the existence of Aboriginal peoples, affirms their existing Aboriginal and treaty rights prior to 1982, and establishes that Aboriginal rights are legally enforceable rights recognized by Canadian common law.

Aboriginal Issues in the Charter of Rights and Freedoms

The relevance of the new Charter to Aboriginal issues is limited to an extent to four sections: 15, 25, 28, and 35 although other sections may come to be important in the future. However, it would seem that section 35 has become the most widely used and has, thus far, yielded the most change in Aboriginal–non-Aboriginal relations. We address each section.

continued

Section 15 states:

> 15(1) Every individual is equal before and under the law and has the right to the equal protection and equal benefit of the law without discrimination...
> 15(2) Subsection (1) does not preclude any law, program or activity that has as its object the amelioration of conditions of disadvantaged individuals or groups including those that are disadvantages because of race, national or ethnic origin....

Thus section 15 provides that all individuals are equal before and under the law and have the right to equal protection. These equality rights do not preclude laws, programs, or activities designed to assist disadvantaged individuals or groups.

Section 25 permits the courts to balance such rights with the rights of Aboriginal people. It says:

> 25 The guarantee in this Charter of certain rights and freedoms shall not be construed as to abrogate or derogate from any aboriginal, treaty or other rights and freedoms that pertain to the aboriginal people of Canada including:
>   (a) Any rights or freedoms that have been recognized by the Royal Proclamation of October 7, 1763 and
>   (b) Any rights or freedoms that now exist by way of land claims agreements or may be so acquired.

Section 28 states:
Notwithstanding anything in this Charter, the rights and freedoms referred to in it are guaranteed equally to male and female persons.

Finally, section 35 states:

> (1) The existing Aboriginal and treaty rights of the Aboriginal peoples of Canada are hereby recognized and affirmed.
> (2) In this Act, Aboriginal peoples of Canada include Indian, Inuit and Metis people of Canada
> (3) For greater certainty, in subsection (1), treaty rights includes rights that now exist by way of land claims agreements or may be so acquired.

The significance of the Charter is that Canada acknowledges that these rights emerged from the traditions practised by Aboriginal people prior to the arrival of Europeans. In addition, the Charter recognizes that Aboriginal rights are collective in nature; rights are held by an Aboriginal community even if they are enjoyed by individuals (such as hunting rights). This recognition of collective rights is a unique component in the Constitution. Finally, the Charter also recognizes Aboriginal treaty rights. Here, regardless of the nature of the treaty—Peace and Friendship treaties, numbered treaties, or modern treaties—the treaty is legally binding. For example, in a recent court case it was decided that the Manitoba Act was, for all purposes, a treaty and the provisions within it have to be upheld.

The Charter guarantees political rights to all Canadian citizens and acknowledges the civil rights of each individual. It should be noted that prior to the Charter, a Bill of Rights had been in operation since 1960. However, the Canadian Bill of Rights was only a federal statute and not a constitutional document. And, as a federal statute, it was limited in scope, easily amended by Parliament, and had no application to provincial laws. The new Constitution changed all of that. In the end, the Charter and specifically section 35, represent a major change in Canadian law. In terms of Aboriginal relations, it means that the federal and provincial governments must justify infringements or extinguishment of Aboriginal rights. Moreover, if there is infringement, then some sort of compensation must be available.

The repatriation of the Constitution and the introduction of the Charter of Rights and Freedoms have fundamentally changed the federal government's relations with Aboriginal people. Moreover, as Aboriginal communities came to understand these important changes to Canada's constitution, they began to bring forward challenges to previous actions by the federal government. This has led to considerable involvement by the courts in assessing the propriety of government action as well as how to "right the wrongs" of the past.

Aboriginal Rights

Over the past three decades, aspects of Aboriginal rights have worked their way through the courts. The courts have focused on the protection of Aboriginal practices or activities such as fishing, but not on the protection of Aboriginal culture itself (Christie 1998). The courts also have made it abundantly clear that they are not the only institution that needs to address Aboriginal rights; the federal government has singularly failed to do so. Rather, the government has left it to the courts to make decisions (which the government may then denounce if they are not to its liking). As such, the courts, and in particular the Supreme Court, have begun to set a vision for Canada regarding Aboriginal people in the face of inaction by the federal government.

In making decisions, the Supreme Court has observed that all cases coming before them are on a "case-by-case" basis, and no single case sets a precedent for future cases. However, as ever more decisions are made by the Supreme Court, a body of law is developing that will constrain the decisions of future courts.

First Nations people have criticized the Supreme Court, arguing that the singular focus on the "legal" aspects of a case has diminished other concerns. For example, the limitations of tort law and the rejection of alternative forms of dispute resolution has angered many First Nations people. In the litigation regarding the residential school experience, Aboriginal people argued that it is based on the narrow grounds of tort law and conceptions of issues such as harm, wrongdoing, and compensation (Llewellyn 2002). In the tort system involving residential school claims, a claimant must file a complaint, complete a lengthy application form, and provide intimate details of all incidents of abuse. The process of filing a charge is so daunting that the existing tort law is ineffective for most First Nations people who were abused. Even if they do decide to proceed, the cost of a lawyer is beyond the financial resources of many. Moreover, the current legal system has a narrow conception of "harm"; the harm is restricted to the harm suffered by an individual. A family or community cannot be brought into the litigation system to claim harm. Finally tort law focuses on "winners" and "losers" and the process of engaging in compromise is not part of the process.

First Nations people want the Crown to concern itself with relationships and to build one of mutual concern, respect, and dignity. Residential school victims sought an alternative dispute resolution strategy: a form of "restorative" justice where the issue of compensation was only of secondary interest. The government rejected these principles and chose tort law, which allowed them to sidestep these issues and focus on the settlement. Llewellyn and Howse (1998) and Hughes and Mossman (2005) claim that First Nations people wanted a process that focused on repairing the relationships. Restorative justice is founded on the concept of restoring social relationships of equity. Achieving social equity requires that the system attend to the relationships among the individuals, groups, and communities involved. Moreover, as Llewellyn (2002) points out, in restoring relationships, all parties must be concerned with both the harm and with its relevant contexts and causes. If the relationships among the parties are to be restored, the assessment must be expanded beyond the single dispute at issue. The underlying conflict must be addressed and resolved. The aim of restorative justice is thus an ideal of social equity. As such, restorative justice deals with restoring the relationships between the wrongdoer and the victim, wherein the rights and dignity of both are respected. The objective of this form of justice is not to restore the relationship to the state it was before the wrongdoing but its goal is the restoration of the relationship to the ideal of social equality (Ross 1996).

Overall, the Supreme Court of Canada has defined Aboriginal rights as an element of custom, a practice, or a traditional activity that is integral to the culture of a First Nations community claiming a "right" that has not been extinguished prior to 1982. The court also has defined

Aboriginal rights as communal rights and not individual rights; this is the case even though any individual wishing to enter the legal system is required to bring the case before the courts. As such, First Nations individuals may carry out those rights only by virtue of belonging to a First Nations community that historically existed and continues to exist today.

The courts, over time, have established several steps that must be undertaken to determine whether an activity is an "Aboriginal right." Step 1 is to determine whether or not there is an "existing" Aboriginal right. This requires that the court consider five issues. In this process, the First Nations complainant must first of all precisely identify the "right" in question; if it is too general or vague, the courts will not proceed to evaluate it. The court then poses three questions:

1. What is the nature of the action that the applicant is claiming to be an Aboriginal right?
2. What is the nature of the government regulation or statute that is being impugned?
3. What is the pre-contact practice of this right?

Let's take the common real-life example of a First Nations community claiming an Aboriginal right to operate a gambling casino. The first step is for the First Nations to clearly state the right: the right to operate a high-stakes gambling casino independent of provincial and federal law. The next relevant question relates to the nature of the federal statute being impugned. In this case, it would be the Criminal Code of Canada that controls all gambling in Canada. The Criminal Code defines the types of gaming activities that are illegal. The provinces, in turn, are assigned responsibility to regulate legal types of gaming, such as casinos, lotteries, and so on. Finally, the court would ask if this was an activity carried out in the First Nations community prior to settler contact. If the three criteria were met, the court would then move to the next stage in defining a "right" (see for example *R. v. Pamajewon*, 1996)

Step 2 assesses whether an activity is an Aboriginal right or not and involves determining the right's geographical character; in other words, is it site specific? The applicant must then provide evidence as to where the traditional activity took place and how it was practised. Step 3 asks the question of history. Here the claimant must provide evidence that gambling existed in the site identified in step 2 prior to contact with the settlers. In most cases oral evidence is not accepted. As such, historical archival evidence needs to be presented to the courts to support the case. Step 4 addresses the issue of "continuity." This element focuses on whether or not the activity claimed as a right was practised historically *and* whether or not the practice is still being carried on today. The courts have noted that the activity today does not have to be identical to the historical activity, but it must be reasonably close. The fifth and final step is key: determining if the activity being claimed as a right is "integral to a distinctive culture." The court has been very clear that this criterion is key to their decision. They have stated that to convince the court that an activity is integral to a distinctive culture, the Aboriginal claimant must do more than just demonstrate that an activity, tradition, or custom was an aspect of, or took place in, the Aboriginal community to which he or she belongs. The claimant must demonstrate that the activity was a central and significant part of the First Nations community's distinctive culture. In other words, this activity must be a key component of the First Nations' cultural makeup.

If the claimant fails to provide enough information to support any of the above criteria, the court will rule that the claimed activity is not an Aboriginal right. These are stringent criteria set out by the courts; the activity being claimed as a right cannot be the result of coming into contact with settlers. First Nations communities argue that these criteria are problematic for two reasons. First of all, culture is not stagnant but rather changes over time. However, the current criteria do not take this into consideration. In addition, in many cases the federal government itself coerced First Nations people to assimilate and thus lose some cultural and traditional activities, leaving little evidence of them today. The continued insistence by the courts that only "written" evidence is acceptable runs counter to an oral society. First Nations people argue that these criteria were created by the courts with no consultation. Finally, First Nations people claim that the context of information being dealt with in the courts is not taken into consideration. They go on to argue that if context were taken into consideration, it would allow for a more complete interpretation of the activity being claimed as a right. For example, when the Gitxan-Wet'suet'en land claim came before the courts, the issue of civilization, continuity of culture, and conflict became issues before the courts. In this court case the Crown argued that only historical documents could be introduced as evidence. These are documents that "say what they mean, mean what they say," that any adult with reasoning ability could understand. In short, the courts argued that contextual and historical information regarding the document was irrelevant to understanding the document's meaning.

The courts also have ruled on Aboriginal title, which they consider a subset under the general rubric of Aboriginal right. In its decision on the *Delgamuukw* case of 1997, the court identified a test that is now the guide to determine whether an Aboriginal claim to title over a land area is protected as an Aboriginal right. The criteria used by the Supreme Court emerged out of the *Baker Lake* (1980) and *Guerin* (1985) cases. The test reviews four criteria. First, the members of a First Nations group must show that they and their ancestors were members of an organized society. Second, they must show that the organized society occupied the territory over which they claim Aboriginal title. Third, the occupation of the territory was to the exclusion of other organized societies. The BC Court of Appeal later noted that it is possible to occupy land without the exclusion of other peoples, and this condition is mediated on that principle. Finally, the occupation had to be an "established fact" when England asserted sovereignty (Office of the Treaty Commissioner, nd)

The second question that arises with regard to Aboriginal rights is whether or not they can be extinguished. This issue emerged from the *Sparrow* case and built upon the idea of the *sui generis* nature of Aboriginal rights. The courts have said that the extinguishment of Aboriginal rights is a burden of the Crown (Christie 1998). Only Parliament has the power to unilaterally extinguish Aboriginal rights. If Parliament wishes to do so, it must have a clear and transparent plan. If an Aboriginal right exists, the Crown must then make a case for extinguishing that right. It begins by asking if the Aboriginal right has been extinguished and then follows that question with "How was it extinguished?" The courts have stipulated that the Crown has to ask two fundamental questions. First, does the legislation being proposed by the Crown have the effect of interfering with an existing Aboriginal right? And if the answer is "yes," then further questions are posed. Is the limitation a reasonable one? Do the limitations of the proposed legislation impose undue hardship on First Nations people? Does the legislation deny the rights holders of their preferred means of exercising that right?

In addition, the Crown has to justify the infringement on a right. Here, new questions are posed: is the legislation in question sufficiently important to warrant an infringement of a right? The limitations in the legislation must be reasonable and justified using a "proportionality" test that meets the following criteria: Is the legislation designed to achieve the desired goal? Does the legislation impair rights as little as possible? Is the goal of sufficient importance to introduce the legislation? And what is the proportionality between the effects of the legislation and the goal desired by the legislation? Underlying the doctrine of Aboriginal rights, the courts wish to develop a process and a commitment to protecting practices and traditions that were a historically important component of a specific First Nations community.

The courts have ruled that the doctrine of Aboriginal rights exists and under the Constitution, that doctrine must be recognized and affirmed. Moreover, the courts have ruled that section 35 of the Charter should be liberally construed. When documents introduced as evidence are vague or unclear, the courts should resolve the litigation in favour of First Nations people. Nevertheless, in a twist, the courts have ruled that the onus of proving a *prima facie* infringement on an Aboriginal right lies on the individual or group challenging the legislation. Thus, if an individual believes that there has been a Charter breach, he or she must prove it.

Self-Government

The history of First Nations self-government is long, although for over a century, government officials ignored First Nations claims or denied the existence of self-government. However, as far back as 1983, the *Penner Report* recommended that the federal government recognize First Nations as a distinct order of government and take steps leading to self-government. Ten years after the *Calder* case, the Constitution Act established that Aboriginal rights and treaty rights both existed and may be acquired, recognized, and affirmed. Moreover, in 1990, the Supreme Court (*Sparrow*) ruled that extinguishing Aboriginal rights must be done with clear and plain intention. If not, then those rights continue. In *Delgamuukw* (1997), the Supreme Court confirmed that Aboriginal title existed and it is a right to the land as well as to hunting, fishing, and trapping. Then, in 2005, the BC Supreme Court ruled that self-government is an Aboriginal right, thereby solidifying the 1995 announcement by the federal government that First Nations self-government was inherent.

Although the federal government recognizes the inherent right of self-government, this only means that First Nations peoples have the right to govern themselves in a limited fashion. The key question becomes this: self-governance with regard to what activities? From the perspective of the federal government, First Nations people can only govern themselves in relation to issues that are internal to their communities and integral to their unique cultures. There also is agreement that, given the different circumstances of First Nations peoples across the country, this inherent right will not be uniform. As such, the self-government arrangements for each First Nations community will need to be tailored to meet its unique needs.

Self-Government of What?

If Aboriginal people have the right of self-government, what does it entail? First of all, the Government has said it must operate within the framework of the Canadian Constitution. Second, it must take place in collaboration with the provinces/territories. Third, the inherent right of self-government does not, from the federal government's definition, include a right of sovereignty as understood by international law and will not result in sovereign independent Aboriginal nation states (Belanger 2008).

It is clear that the federal government is not prepared to hand over full self-government to First Nations communities. On the other hand, it does seem willing to extend self-government to issues such as membership, marriage, education, health, policing, property rights, housing, hunting, and taxation. In addition, the federal government has stated that there are other potential areas for self-government even though these domains do not fully meet the criteria of being integral to Aboriginal culture or being strictly internal to an Aboriginal group. These include the administration of justice, parole, environmental protection, fisheries, and gaming. Finally, there are some issues over which the federal government is not willing to surrender control, including sovereignty, defense, central banking, currency, national law, federal telecommunications, navigation and shipping, postal services, and the census.

Both First Nations and the federal government have laid out their case as to what they would negotiate as part of self-government. Consider as a metaphor a box containing all the domains over which First Nations have power of self-government. First Nations are arguing that they begin with a full box: all issues are to be considered for First Nations self-government. By contrast, the federal government counters that First Nations groups have no self-government—in other words, the box is empty but the government is willing to put some issues into it. In terms of what could fall under First Nations self-government, the federal government has suggested categorizing the following issues thusly:

Aboriginal: Issues such as governing structures, elections, internal constitutions, marriage, membership, education, hunting on aboriginal lands, housing, local transportation, property rights, natural resource management. Some of these may require harmonization with federal and provincial laws.

Federal: Issues such as sovereignty, defense, external relations, treaty making, national economy, trade, intellectual property, currency, criminal law, broadcasting and telecommunications, postal service, census.

Ambiguous: Issues such as gaming, migratory bird management, correctional facilities, labour, administration of justice issues.

The federal government feels that some agreements on self-government can be undertaken through the implementation of treaties, legislation, contracts, and Memoranda of Understanding. Nevertheless, one of the main impediments to self-government is the insistence by the federal government that the fiduciary obligations they have for First Nations people may be affected by these new agreements. The federal government argues that as First Nations governments exercise jurisdiction and take over control over decision making that affects their communities, they also will have to assume greater responsibilities for the exercise of those powers. As such, over time the federal government's responsibilities will decrease and eventually will disappear.

Approaches to Self-Government

McNeil (2006a) points out that there have been three different approaches taken by the courts to determine whether or not First Nations have inherent self-government:

1. freestanding Aboriginal rights,
2. linking rights of self-government to other Aboriginal and treaty rights, and
3. residual sovereignty.

The first two approaches are well-known by the courts. However, neither has produced decisions that would allow a differentiation between them. The third approach has not yet been introduced.

In addressing the issue of self-government, the courts must first establish what jurisdiction (scope) is being claimed. Are they considering territorial or personal jurisdiction? Are they considering exclusive or concurrent jurisdiction? And, are they considering legislative, executive, or judicial jurisdiction (McNeil 2007)? Then, they must address another question: is the jurisdiction inherent or delegated?

We now turn to the issue of scope. How much authority do First Nations people have over their own affairs? Has the authority been limited to specific matters such as land and water? As noted above, the federal government is clear about what it is prepared to include in the self-governance "box"; but, as we saw above, the list of items that the government includes in this box differs from the First Nations' list.

The issue of exclusive versus concurrent jurisdiction needs to be determined if self-government is to work. Again, there is considerable disagreement between the federal government and First Nations people as to who has exclusive rights over certain issues. Government officials tend to prefer concurrent jurisdiction given that this is the model they know best. It provides the ability to intervene in jurisdictional issues of First Nations communities at any time or place. On the other hand, First Nations people claim that some issues are exclusively under their own jurisdiction, while others may be concurrent. For example, the Nisga'a hold exclusive rights over certain issues and these cannot be changed unless Aboriginal, federal, and provincial authorities all agree to make the change.

Canadian courts have addressed the issue of scope and have decided that in order to claim jurisdiction over an activity, the First Nations community must meet the "integral to the distinctive culture" criterion. The point of this test is to determine the right of self-governance. Here, the First Nations community must show that the issue is historically an integral component of their society and that it remains so today. In short, this test limits self-government claims to matters that were integral to First Nations cultures prior to European contact and that can be claimed to be integral still. After a century of court decisions regarding the scope of Aboriginal jurisdiction, the result is as follows: First Nations people do not have general rights, but they do have some specific rights. Furthermore, First Nations people must provide evidence that a specific right existed prior to European settlement.

Aboriginal View of Self-Government

First Nations peoples feel that self-government is a way to regain control over their affairs and to preserve their culture. In addition, First Nations people see self-government as an "inherent" right, based upon the long occupation and stewardship of the land before settlers arrived. They feel that self-government is a responsibility given to them by the Creator and reflects a spiritual connection to the land. First Nations people want Canadians to recognize and accept that they had established governments prior to European settlement. Finally, First Nations peoples draw upon international law to support their claims, such as the Declaration of the Rights of Indigenous Peoples (2007), signed by Canada in 2010 but partially rejected in 2014.

What do First Nations people expect when they claim self-government? They see their political authority as emerging from a spiritual basis, not a secular basis. They see self-government as being conferred on their people by the Creator. As a gift from the Creator, self-government can neither be given nor taken away. As such, First Nations people are clear that self-government is inherent with spiritual origins embedded within a holistic perspective of the world.

Moreover, First Nations people argue that if the Creator had not given Aboriginal people authority over a particular matter, it was then retained by the Creator; as such, settlers have no right to claim an interest. As McNeil (2007) argues, even if there were limitations on the authority given to First Nations people, it would not create a jurisdictional vacuum that could be filled by the colonizer. For First Nations people, the relationship between the Creator and themselves means there is an understanding that the place of humans in the natural world is equal to other elements of the natural world, such as animals, rocks, and plants, although First Nations people have a responsibility to ensure that all components of the natural world are respected and in balance.

Alternative Approaches to Self-Government

An alternative approach to self-government can be found in British Columbia, where both the provincial and federal governments negotiated self-government with First Nations. The first twenty-first-century treaty with the Nisga'a Nation reveals that the province of British Columbia agrees that the Nisga'a Nation have the inherent right of self-government. In the treaty, the BC government, after negotiating with the Nisga'a Nation, outlines the jurisdictional boundaries of the Nisga'a government. This treaty was challenged in the courts. The argument that was brought forward held that the Canadian Constitution did not allow for Aboriginal government, given that all the legislative powers had been divided between the provincial and federal governments under the Constitution Act, 1867. In 2001 the BC Supreme Court ruled that self-government is an Aboriginal right. Specifically the Court ruled that the Aboriginal right to self-government was one of the underlying values of the Constitution, and that this right remained outside the powers that were distributed to Parliament or the provincial legislatures. Thus, there is a strong legal argument in favour of First Nations' self-government. The court upheld the constitutional validity of the self-government provisions of the Nisga'a treaty. It ruled that First Nations people have decision-making authority over land and all other Aboriginal and treaty rights. Under this approach, the scope of jurisdiction is set out in the treaty. In short, under this interpretation of self-government, First Nations people start out with an empty box of jurisdictional issues and the onus is on them to fill this box by proving Aboriginal rights (McNeil 2007).

A different approach would hold that since First Nations people were independent sovereign nations at the time of contact, they held all-encompassing rights. In this perspective, the onus is on the government to show how certain rights were diminished or extinguished through legislation, executive decree, or negotiations. Thus, in this scenario, the box is full and only those issues that have been specifically diminished are removed from the box.

Self-Government Today

The road to self-government began with the Supreme Court decision (*Calder*) that found that if there is an Aboriginal historic presence on the land, Aboriginal title can be recognized as common law without the support of federal or provincial government. This decision was followed in 1982 by the creation of section 35 of the Canadian Constitution Act that states Aboriginal and treaty rights are affirmed. Eight years later the Supreme Court, in the *Sparrow* (1990) and *Sioui* (1990) decisions, ruled that these Aboriginal rights would remain in place unless there was clear and explicit evidence they were extinguished. By 1997 (*Delgumuuku*), the Supreme Court confirmed that Aboriginal title exists and that when dealing with Crown land, the government must consult with Aboriginal people.

Self-government agreements are now defined as bilateral agreements between the federal government and a First Nations community. Sometimes the agreement is part of a comprehensive settlement but there are cases where it is a stand-alone agreement, as in the Westbank First Nation Self-Government Agreement. Provincial governments may be involved in these agreements but all of them are signed under the 1995 Aboriginal Inherent Self-Government Policy that recognizes that First Nations need the authority to act (Krehbiel 2008). Under the new policy, First Nations can also retain land use and planning authority for land that is outside the treaty settlement area.

As more First Nations communities take on (de-facto) inherent self-government, it is important to note that they do not act in isolation but operate within a network of federal, provincial, territorial, and municipal governments and share jurisdictional issues. However, the question becomes this: who has the ultimate decision-making powers? This is known as paramount decision making. And also, when are the decision-making processes concurrent? In other words, at what point do both governments have some decision-making rights? McNeil (2010) argues that in the case of First Nations jurisdictional conflicts between First Nations and federal or provincial governments, First Nations jurisdiction will be paramount. In cases where First Nations people chose not to invoke jurisdiction, federal or provincial jurisdiction will be paramount.

When the First Nations Land Management Act (1999) was passed, it recognized the ability of First Nations to enact laws respecting the development, conservation, management, use, and possession of land on the reserve. This means that the band council can establish laws with regard to the control of land use and development. As of today, there are over fifty First Nations that have signed off on the Framework Agreement and another twenty that are engaged in the process of signing (Krehbiel 2008). Poelzer (nd) shows that self-government is the current means by which First Nations people can formalize their relationship to their lands and resources as well as preserve their culture. And, in doing so, they will have the necessary autonomy to make decisions about their future.

Sovereignty

The issue of sovereignty has plagued both philosophers and legal experts. The plethora of definitions that currently exist give evidence to the problematic nature of the concept. However, for most purposes, it means simply the legal power to rule people and territory. While the theoretical definition is easy to present, establishing the boundaries of such a definition has proven elusive and the practical considerations have likewise proven difficult.

First Nations claim sovereignty and the right to self-determination because they had their own government and economies prior to the arrival of the settlers. As such, First Nations leaders argue that sovereignty and governance exist independent of British constitutional law (Henderson 2008). However, over the history of Canada, Canadians have tried to follow a European tradition of linking a government with sovereignty and then looking for a model of First Nations government that would facilitate Aboriginal self-rule (Bish 1990). First Nations people have argued, contrary to this approach, that there is an inherent right of First Nations people to create and control their own affairs. As such, First Nations people will create different governments for different purposes and there may well be more than one form of government that different First Nations people devise. In summary, from a First Nations perspective there is no one single model of governance; rather there are different models for different peoples and for different functions (Bish 1990). However, all demonstrate that each First Nations community has the sovereign rights to rule and control their members. All this talk about self-determination and sovereignty by First Nations people does not mean that they have aspirations of secession from Canada. Quite the contrary, First Nations people are comfortable being part of Canada and accept Canadian rule. On the other hand, what they do want is to determine their lives without continuous and pervasive intervention by the federal and provincial governments.

Cornell and Kalt (2010) point out that at the heart of nation building is the question of sovereignty—who is in charge of making decisions? While for nearly a century First Nations peoples have advocated for decision-making power over their own affairs, the federal and provincial governments have resisted such a change. Moreover, the federal and provincial governments continue to argue that their definition of treaty rights, Aboriginal rights, funding obligations, and fiduciary duties are correct and that the definitions of these concepts that have been put forward by Aboriginal people are wrong. Rather than seek a resolution to these differences, the federal government is reluctant to negotiate issues such as self-determination unless its own definition is used. The Auditor General (2006) noted in her assessment of the British Columbia negotiations with First Nations people that after more than ten years of negotiations and $726 million spent on the negotiation process, there were no treaties, no resolution on self-government, and no settlement of a single comprehensive land claim. The entrenched view by provincial and federal governments that their way is the only way has failed to produce solutions, good governance structures in First Nations communities, or a better quality of life for First Nations people.

The source of inherent jurisdiction is, for Aboriginal people, the Creator with whom Aboriginal people have a special relationship. In short, it is part of a divine birthright given to Aboriginal peoples. Monture-Angus (1999) argues that sovereignty is the original freedom conferred to First Nations people by the Creator rather than a temporal power. However, from a non-Aboriginal perspective, the source of jurisdiction of Aboriginal governments is seen in more secular terms. For example, the Supreme Court has ruled that jurisdictional rights of First Nations people emerge from the fact that they occupied lands long before the arrival of European settlers in what is now Canada. For most Canadians, the jurisdictional rights emerge from pre-existing sovereignty of First Nations or have been delegated by the federal government. In short, the origins of jurisdiction take on a factual or historical basis and not a spiritual one (McNeil 2010).

Conclusion

There is considerable evidence that self-government is a necessary condition for communities and nations to make progress in improving the well-being of their citizens (Graham 2007). First Nations people themselves agree that self-government is necessary if they are to prosper (Ekos 2001). Thus it would seem that the federal government and First Nations people agree that self-government is a major component in the creation of good governance while also improving economic development in First Nations communities. If it had passed, the Charlottetown Accord would have "constitutionalized" the right of First Nations people to self-government. That said, there have been major difficulties in reaching self-government agreements over the past three decades. Moreover, the government wants to establish a single template that will provide a "universal formula" or nation-wide approach to the creation and implementation of First Nations self-government. However, there is considerable resistance by both federal and provincial governments to allowing First Nations communities to create and shape their own paths and structure of self-government. In addition, the federal government still wishes to impose its definition of self-government and fails to appreciate that no outside agency can impose good governance. For good governance to occur, strong political commitment must come from within the First Nations community. Finally, good self-government has a balanced system in which the various components have appropriate impact. For example, the government sector should be balanced with an independent media and the active participation of voluntary organizations. Finally, it should be noted that there are a number of regulatory voids facing First Nations communities. While some of these are being addressed, it has taken the government half a century to finally implement legislation to deal with these. For example, because provincial law relating to land does not apply to reserves and there is little federal legislation dealing with land development, Aboriginal communities do not enjoy the legislative protection of neighbouring non-Aboriginal communities in areas such as water, waste, and natural resource management (Krehbiel 2008). However, in 2010 the federal government passed the First Nations Certainty of Land Title Act; this resolved some of the gaps between federal and provincial legislation such that industrial and commercial development projects on reserve lands can now take place. This is a step in the right direction, but it is interesting that the government knew about the problem for fifty years before addressing it.

The Supreme Court of Canada has, from a different perspective, concurred that First Nations people have an inherent right of self-government based on the understanding that First Nations people occupied lands and practised their own distinctive cultures prior to European contact. However, this perspective is at odds with the Aboriginal understanding of the source of jurisdiction. Many Canadians view their legal system as more secular and derived. Some Canadians argue if First Nations people are to be given self-government rights, these have to emerge from the fact that federal/provincial/territorial governments delegate those rights. However, in the end, while there is considerable resistance to First Nations claims of inherent rights, Canadian law has made it very clear that First Nations people have the inherent right to self-government.

From a policy perspective, there also has been considerable pressure to accept Aboriginal self-government. The 1966 *Hawthorn-Tremblay Report*, the 1972 *Red Paper*, the 1973 *Council of Yukon Indians Land Claim* proposal, and the 1977 *Federation of Saskatchewan Indian Government Paper* all pointed to the need for Aboriginal self-government. Then, in 1985, the *Penner Report* more forcefully and clearly articulated the advantages of Aboriginal self-government. The government of the day did not accept the idea of Aboriginal self-government nor its constitutional entrenchment. A decade later, however, the federal government announced its policy to implement the inherent right to Aboriginal self-government. This was soon followed by the recommendations of the Royal Commission on Aboriginal Peoples. Even with such a legal basis and policy support, the question still remains: how this will be put into operation?

Conclusion

The ongoing legacy of colonization, the devastation of the residential school system, the removal of children to foster care beginning with the "Sixties scoop," the silencing of Aboriginal voices, the loss of traditional roles, and ongoing discrimination all affect the social inclusion, as well as the health and well-being of Aboriginal peoples (Masching 2009). Although these are all issues many Canadians would like to forget, they cannot be written out of history. The federal government's new approach to "solve" the Aboriginal "problem" has been an attempt to buy its way out of the past. When the payment is made, regardless of the terms, government officials pronounce that the matter is settled; all parties should now "move on." First Nations people are not prepared to accept this "once and for all" settlement approach, which fails to address the underlying issues behind First Nations people's marginalized position in Canada.

A review of past federal governments' actions with regard to First Nations people reveals an astonishing number of policies, bills, programs, and financial investments. At the same time, there is no single piece of legislation, policy, or program that has met with the whole-hearted support of First Nations people. For example, when Bill C-31 was passed in 1985 First Nations people were assured that the discriminatory component of the Indian Act had been removed. Then, after the courts agreed with First Nations people that the new legislation was itself discriminatory, Bill C-3 was passed, again over the objections of First Nations people. We now wait for further court action on this controversial bill.

By no stretch of the imagination could it be found that any of these extensive pieces of legislation, programs, or polices have led to a better life for First Nations people. In the end, there is no government vision for the enhancement of the social and economic position of First Nations people in Canada. Instead, we see more "patchwork" legislation, inappropriate policies, and an ongoing adversarial relationship between the federal government and First Nations people. Moreover, most of the programs implemented to "support" First Nations people still remain "pilot" projects that last between one and five years, at which point funding is removed, regardless of the program's success. Even the most recent First Nations Education Act falls short, with no guarantee that the funding will ever be provided.

A myriad of policies have been introduced over the past decade; even so, there remains little evidence that they are consistent or well integrated with other federal or provincial policies. For example, in 2010 the First Nations Certainty of Land Title Act allows for the registration of on-reserve commercial real estate development that mirrors the provincial land titles system. This barrier had been identified by First Nations people more than fifty years ago. The passage of the First Nations Land Management Act allows First Nations communities to use their self-government authority over their lands and monies derived from the use of that land (Canada 2013). To illustrate the demand for such legislation, today more than thirty First Nations are operating under their own land codes and seventy more have expressed an interest in taking on self-government and control over their lands.

Some positive actions have been taken by the federal government, but they have been neither voluntary nor visionary. For example, more than seventy specific claims have been settled in the past six years with a bill of more than $1 billion. Comprehensive claims are moving forward but only on the conditions set by the federal government. These conditions are not based on fairness or justice, but rather upon settling with the least cost. Moreover, First Nations people point out that they are paying for the costs of settling claims when in fact the federal government incurred the cost by refusing to settle the claims as provided by the Treaties. Overall, we see that the government expends huge sums of money when dealing with First Nations communities each year. Aboriginal Affairs and Northern Development Canada's annual budget now exceeds $10 billion. This is only one of many departments offering services to First Nations people.

Nevertheless, the past three decades have seen major changes in government–First Nations relations. These changes have resulted from court decisions dealing with issues that Parliament refuses to settle. These court decisions have generated considerable angst among many Canadians, a result of the decisions themselves, but also the costs. Over the past two decades, the courts have given legitimacy to the issue of Aboriginal rights, although from a First Nations perspective the definition of these rights is extremely narrow. Nevertheless, there is a sense of clarity in the Supreme Court of Canada's decisions regarding the Crown's dealings with First Nations people. Prior to these court decisions, the Crown (both federal and provincial) was largely blind to the matter of First Nations people's rights. In the end, the Crown exploited the land and resources of First Nations people with no regard for Aboriginal rights. The Supreme Court has now declared that the Crown (both federal and provincial) has a constitutional obligation to consult and accommodate First Nations when a policy or project is being proposed—for example a pipeline, mine, or dam—that has or may have an impact on their Aboriginal rights or title. While the level of this obligation or accommodation varies by the nature of the policy or project, it is in effect even prior to any legal confirmation of any Aboriginal rights or title (First Nations Leadership Council 2013).

The recognition of Aboriginal rights began with the 1973 *Calder* decision. For the first time in modern history the Supreme Court of Canada formally acknowledged the existence of Aboriginal rights. The Supreme Court's decision was the first time that the Canadian legal system acknowledged Aboriginal title to land; such title existed outside of, and was not simply derived from, colonial law. This decision was followed by a number of cases that confirmed Aboriginal rights. Then, in the beginning of the twenty-first century, the *Taku* (2004), *Haida* (2004), and *Mikisew* (2005) decisions definitively entrenched the notion of Aboriginal rights and the duty to consult and accommodate. It dismissed the Crown's position that it had *de facto* control over lands and resources without regard to the claims of First Nations peoples. It also laid to rest the Crown's claim that when a treaty with a First Nations community was in place, the terms of the treaty ended the Crown's obligations toward that First Nations group. Thus, the Crown could do anything it wanted with the lands and resources within the treaty area without having to consult with the First Nations community. The Supreme Court decisions reminded the Crown that its behaviour toward First Nations people had to meet the conditions of the Constitution (section 35) and ensure the "honour of the Crown" by exercising its duty to consult and accommodate.

The Supreme Court clearly outlined this "duty" in the *Haida* and *Taku* decisions. In both cases the Court reminded the Crown that this duty is based on three principles: relationships, recognition, and reconciliation. Since these two ground-breaking decisions by the court, a review of lower-court decisions will reveal that in many cases the courts failed to take this into consideration, and did not adequately respect the special relationship that exists between the Crown and First Nations people. In many of these cases, the lower courts have lost their way in enforcing the principles outlined by the Supreme Court. As such, sometimes the courts have chosen to take a pragmatic approach to resolve conflicts between the Crown and First Nations. In these cases, the justices' decisions follow the principle of "least harm to the status quo"; as such, in many cases, decisions do not address the principles of relationships, recognition, and reconciliation embodied in the principles of consultation and accommodation.

As the Supreme Court has pointed out, given the federal government's position of power when working with First Nations people, it had a duty to ensure clear recognition of their rights, to devise strategies in aid of reconciliation, and to establish long-term trust relationships. These principles are basic to the Constitution and to the honour of the Crown.

Relationship

This principle acknowledges that there is a special (*sui generis*) relationship between the Crown and First Nations people. When the Crown claimed sovereignty over the land that now comprises Canada, it precipitated an obligation to treat First Nations people fairly and to protect them from exploitation. As such, it is important that consultation with First Nations people take place in a responsible fashion. This special relationship remains today and is acknowledged by the recent *Eyford Report* (2013).

Recognition

The second principle refers to the Crown's recognition of Aboriginal rights as embodied in the Charter of Rights and Freedoms. Aboriginal rights have been recognized by common law with regard to First Nations who occupied the land prior to the European settlers entering the country. English law has been very clear in its acceptance that First Nations people possessed pre-existing rights in the land. It recognizes those rights in the absence of a treaty; with the signing of a treaty, however, those rights are extinguished. In many cases, however, the conditions of a signed treaty were never fulfilled. In such cases, is the treaty rendered null and void? Moreover, in many parts of Canada, there is an absence of historical treaties; this is the case in British Columbia, Northern Quebec, the Yukon, and the Northwest Territories. However, beginning with the signing of the James Bay Cree comprehensive claim, modern treaties are now dealing with the recognition of First Nations rights. Equally important is the Crown's readiness to fulfill the conditions of these new treaties. What land still remains to be resolved is primarily in British Columbia, where the provincial government has not settled First Nations' land issues and even contemporary treaties have not been signed. Nevertheless, court decisions have clearly ruled that First Nations' traditional activities such as leadership selection, marriage laws, and land stewardship prior to European settlement are recognized by the federal government and are at the core of the common law concept of Aboriginal rights (First Nations Leadership Council 2013).

Reconciliation

The final principle and perhaps the most important component of the "duty to consult" is the reconciliation dimension. In the Supreme Court's definition, the Charter of Rights and Freedoms clearly identifies that its purpose is to protect First Nations' interests that emerge from their occupation and use of the land in an organized and structured manner prior to the arrival of European settlers. Thus, the Crown has a duty to address the concerns of the First Nations people whose lands are being used by others and resolve issues of reconciliation and consultation. The Supreme Court has observed that any process of consultation must be linked to reconciliation. Reconciliation cannot take place if the Crown feels no obligation to take Aboriginal rights into consideration when addressing issues related to land and resources. In other words, consultation is not simply the manner in which Government achieves reconciliation. In the end, the courts have said that reconciliation has to restore the First Nation–Crown relationship such that mutual trust and confidence are in place. The relationship between First Nations and government must exhibit a pattern where each of the two parties exercising their authority over the lands and resources represent their respective constituencies, trust each other, and embrace reconciliation. Once there is a commitment to a pattern of trust and mutual respect with regard to making decisions about lands and resources, reconciliation will have been achieved.

At the same time, the Crown vigorously argues that the law does not stipulate "there is a duty to agree." This is correct. However, in making such an argument, there is the implication that discussion is all that is required with regards to First Nations people; beyond discussion, any actions are possible regardless of First Nations objections. This stance also omits the obligation to "accommodate." In taking such a stance the Crown disregards the three Rs discussed above that make up the basis of section 35 as interpreted by the Supreme Court of Canada.

As a result, civil disobedience is beginning to take on a life of its own. History tells us that the frequency of blockades, protest movements, and "sit-ins" is increasing. The entire "Idle No More" movement is a public statement that First Nations people are no longer willing to be passive recipients of policies and programs that the federal government unilaterally imposes. First Nations people want to join with other Canadians in building a vision for their children. They want to have a say in the creation of the future of Canada and to have Canadians recognize their contributions to the development of the new Canada.

In addition, the "duty to consult" means that the Crown is to share information, solicit information, listen carefully to the concerns of First Nations peoples, and change their proposed action based upon information received during the consultation process (First Nations Leadership Council 2013). Thus, if consultation is to work, the rights of First Nations peoples must be recognized by the Crown. Furthermore, the Crown must acknowledge that it has a "relationship" with First Nations people that cannot be ignored. Moreover, legal experts suggest that not only should Canadian jurisprudence achieve reconciliation with Aboriginal peoples but also that this accommodation or adaptation should protect Aboriginal governance rights and provide opportunities for their expression (Morellato 2003). Moreover, if the three Rs are not pursued by both the Crown and First Nations, the conflict between the two parties will never be fully resolved.

Bibliography

AANDC (Aboriginal Affairs and Northern Development Canada). 2004. *Specific Claims Snapshot*. Ottawa: AANDC.

———. 2007. *Specific Claims: Justice at Last*. Ottawa: AANDC.

———. 2010. *Annual Report*. Ottawa: AANDC.

———. 2011. *National Assessment of Water and Wastewater Systems in First Nation Communities: Release of Final Reports*. Gatineau: AANDC.

———. 2011–2012. Report on Plans and Priorities, Ottawa.

———. 2012. *Report Creating the Conditions for Economic Success on Reserves*. Ottawa: AANDC.

———. 2013a. *Creating the Conditions for Economic Success on Reserve Lands: A Report on the Experiences of 25 First Nation Communities*. Ottawa: AANDC.

———. 2013b. *Developing a First Nation Education Act*. Ottawa: AANDC.

———. 2013c. *Progress Report: Specific Claims, 2012–2013*. Ottawa: AANDC.

———. 2013d. *Working Together for First Nation Students*. Ottawa: AANDC.

———. 2013e. Registered Indian Population by Sex and Residence. Ottawa: AANDC.

———. 2015a. *Comprehensive Land Claims and Self-Government Negotiation Tables*. Ottawa: AANDC.

———. 2015b. *National Summary on Specific Claims*. Ottawa: AANDC.

Abdelal, R., Y. Herrera, A. Johnston, and R. McDermott. 2009. "Definition, Conceptualization and Measurement Alternatives." In *Measuring Identity*, edited by R. Abdelal, Y. Herrera, A. Johnston, and R. McDermott, 17–33. New York: Cambridge University Press.

Abele, F., and K. Graham. 2011. "What Now? Future Federal Responsibilities Towards Aboriginal People Living in Cities." *Aboriginal Policy Studies* 1: 162–82.

Aboriginal Healing Foundation. 2003. *Aboriginal People, Resilience and the Residential School Legacy*. Ottawa: Aboriginal Healing Foundation.

———. 2006. *A Healing Journey: Final Report Summary Points*. Ottawa: Aboriginal Healing Foundation.

———. 2007. *Suicide among Aboriginal People in Canada*. Ottawa: Aboriginal Healing Foundation.

Aboriginal Justice. 1991. *Report of the Aboriginal Justice Inquiry of Manitoba*. Ottawa: Department of Justice.

Aboriginal Nurses Association. 2001. *Aboriginal Victimization in Canada*. Ottawa.

Aboriginal Survey. 2013. *The Education and Employment Experiences of First Nations People Living Off Reserve, Inuit, and Metis: Selected Findings from the 2012 Aboriginal Peoples Survey*. Ottawa: Statistics Canada.

Aboriginal Task Force. 2008. *Aboriginal People and the Labour Market: Estimates from the Labour Force Survey, 2008–2010* Ottawa: Statistics Canada.

Alcantara, C. 2013. *Negotiating the Deal*. Toronto: University of Toronto Press.

Ali, A., and M. Crain. 2002. "Institutional Distortions, Economic Freedom, and Growth." *Cato Journal* 21: 86–93.

Ali, S. 2009. *Mining, the Environment, and Indigenous Development Conflicts*. Tucson: University of Arizona Press.

Allan, B., and J. Smylie. 2015. *First Nations, Second Class Treatment*. Toronto: Wellesley Institute.

Amnesty International. 2004. *A Human Rights Response to Discrimination and Violence Against Indigenous Women in Canada*. New York: Amnesty International.

Anaya , J. 2013. "Statement upon Conclusion of the Visit to Canada." http://unsr.jamesanaya.org/statements/statement-upon-conclusion-of-the-visit-to-canada

Anderson, A. 2013. *Homes in the City*. Toronto: University of Toronto Press.

Anderson, T., ed. 1992. *Property Rights and Indian Economies: The Political Economy Forum*. Lanhan: Rowan and Littlefield.

Anderson, T., and D. Parker. 2006. "The Wealth of Indian Nations: Economic Performance and Institutions on Reservations." In *Self Determination*, edited by T. Anderson, B. Benson, and T. Flanagan, 54–69. Palo Alto: Stanford University Press.

Ariss, R., and J. Cutfeet. 2012. *Keeping the Land*. Halifax and Winnipeg: Fernwood Publishing.

Asch, M. 2014. *On Being Here To Stay*. Toronto: University of Toronto Press.

Assembly of First Nations. n.d. *Fact Sheet: First Nations Education Funding*. Ottawa: Assembly of First Nations.

———. 2010. *First Nations Control of First Nations Education*, Ottawa: Assembly of First Nations.

———. 2012. *A Portrait of First Nations and Education*. Ottawa: Assembly of First Nations.

Auditor General of Canada. 2004. *Report of the Auditor General*. Ottawa: House of Commons.

———. 2006. "Chapter 5: Management of Programs for First Nations." In *Status Report of the Auditor General of Canada to the House of Commons*. Ottawa: House of Commons.

———. 2009. "Chapter 4: Treaty Land Entitlement Obligations." In *Status Report of the Auditor General of Canada to the House of Commons*. Ottawa: House of Commons.

———. 2011. *Report of the Auditor General*. Ottawa: House of Commons.

———. 2014. "Chapter 5. First Nations Policing Program." In *2014 Spring Report of the Auditor General*. Ottawa: Public Safety Canada.

Bains, R. 2014. *Myths and Realities of First Nations Education*. Vancouver: Centre for Aboriginal Policy Studies, Fraser Institute.

Bakan, A., and A. Kobayashi. 2000. *Employment Equity Policy in Canada: An Interprovincial Comparison*. Ottawa: Status of Women.

Baker, C. 2006. *Foundations of Bilingual Education and Bilingualism*. Clevedon, UK: Multilingual Matters.

Battiste, M. 2013. *Decolonizing Education: Nourishing the Learning Spirit*. Saskatoon: Purich Publishing.

Belanger, Y., ed. 2008. *Aboriginal Self Government in Canada*, third edition. Saskatoon: Purich Publishing.

———. 2011. "The United Nations Declaration on the Rights of Indigenous Peoples and Urban Aboriginal Self-determination in Canada: A Preliminary Assessment." *Aboriginal Policy Studies* 1: 132–61.

Belanger, Y., and D. Newhouse. 2004. "Emerging from the Shadows: The Pursuit of Aboriginal Self-Government to Promote Aboriginal Well-Being." *Canadian Journal of Native Studies* 24: 129–222.

———. 2008. "Reconciling Solitudes: A Critical Analysis of the Self-Government Ideal." In *Aboriginal Self-Government in Canada: Current Trends and Issues*, third edition, edited by Y. Belanger, 1–19. Saskatoon: Purich.

Belanger, Y., G. Weasel Head, and O. Awosoga. 2012. "Housing and Aboriginal People in Urban Centres: A Quantitative Evaluation." *Aboriginal Policy Studies* 2: 4–25.

Bell, C. 2014. *R. v. Daniels: Jurisdiction and Government Obligations to Non-Status Indians and Metis.* Queens University: Institute of Intergovernmental Relations School of Policy Studies.

Benjamin, C. 2014. *Indian School Road: Legacies of the Shubenacadie Residential School.* Vancouver: Nimbus Publishing.

Bish, R. 1990. "Community Models of Indian Government." Paper presented at the National Indian Government Conference, Osgoode Hall Law School, Toronto, October 3–5.

Bland, D. 2012. *Time Bomb: Canada and the First Nations,* Toronto: Dundurn Books.

Borrows, J. n.d. "Wampum at Niagara: The Royal Proclamation, Canadian Legal History, and Self Government." www.sfu.ca/~palys/Borrows-WampumAt Niagara.pdf

———. 2005. "Crown and Aboriginal Occupations of Land: A History and Comparison." http://www.attorneygeneral.jus.gov.on.ca/inquiries/ipperwash/policy_part/research/index.html

———. 2010. *Canada's Indigenous Constitution.* Toronto: University of Toronto Press.

———. 2012. *Recovering Canada: The Resurgence of Indigenous Law.* Toronto: University of Toronto Press.

Bougie, E., P. Fines, L. Oliver, and D. Kohen. 2014. "Unintentional Injury Hospitalizations and Socio-Economic Status in Areas with a High Percentage of First Nations Identity Residents." *Health Reports* 25: 145–56.

Bougie, E., K. Kelly-Scott, and P. Arriagada. 2013. *The Education and Employment Experiences of First Nations People Living Off Reserve, Inuit, and Métis: Selected Findings from the 2012 Aboriginal Peoples Survey.* Ottawa: Statistics Canada.

Boyce, J. 2013. *Adult Criminal Court Statistics in Canada: 2011–2012.* Ottawa: Statistics Canada.

Boyer, Y. 2014. *Moving Aboriginal Health Forward.* Saskatoon: Purich Publishing.

Bradford, T. 2012. *Prophetic Identities: Indigenous Missionaries on British Colonial Frontiers, 1850–1875.* Vancouver: University of British Columbia Press.

Brave Heart-Jordan, M.Y.H. 1995. "The Return to the Sacred Path: Healing from Historical Trauma and Historical Unresolved Grief among the Lakota." *Dissertation Abstracts International* 56: 3742.

Brennan, S. 2011. "Violent Victimization of Aboriginal Women in the Canadian Provinces, 2009." *Juristat,* Catalogue No. 85-002-X. Ottawa: Statistics Canada.

Brewer, M. 2010. "Social Identity Complexity and Acceptance of Diversity." In *The Psychology of Social and Cultural Diversity,* edited by R. Crisp, 123–45. Chichester, UK: Blackwell.

Brodsky, G. 2014. "McIvor v. Canada: Legislated Patriarchy meets Aboriginal Women's Equality Rights." in *Indivisible: Indigenous Human Rights,* edited by J. Green, 123–45. Halifax: Fernwood Publishing.

Brown, L. 1994. "Community and the Administration of Aboriginal Governments." In Royal Commission on Aboriginal Peoples, *Seven Generations.* Ottawa: Libraxus. (CD-ROM)

Brown, M.R. 2012. *Aboriginal Participation Major Resources Development.* Ottawa: Public Policy Forum.

Bruce, S. 2000. "The Impact of Diabetes Mellitus among the Métis of Western Canada." *Ethnicity and Health* 5 (1): 47–57.

Bruce, S., R. Kliewer, T. Young, T. Mayer, and A Wajada. 2003. "Diabetes among the Metis of Canada: Defining the Population, Estimating the Disease." *Canadian Journal of Diabetes* 27: 442–48.

Bryce, P. 1922. *The Story of a National Crime: Being a Record of the Health Conditions of the Indians of Canada from 1904–1921*. Ottawa: James Hope and Sons.

Brzozowski, J., A. Taylor-Butts, and S. Johnson. 2006. "Victimization and Offending among the Aboriginal Population in Canada." *Juristat* 26: 67–82.

Bumsted, J., L. Kuffert, and M. Ducharme, eds. 2011. *Interpreting Canada's Past*, fourth edition. Toronto: Oxford University Press.

Burleton, D., and S. Gulati. 2012. *Debunking Myths Surrounding Canada's Aboriginal Population*. Toronto: TD Economics.

Cajete, G. 2004. "Philosophy of Native Science." In *American Indian Thought: Philosophical Essays,* edited by A. Waters, 87–102. Malden, MA: Blackwell.

Calverley, D. 2010. *Adult Correctional Services in Canada: 2008–2009*. Ottawa: Statistics Canada.

Canada, Government of. 1965. *The Education of Indian Children in Canada*. Toronto: Ryerson Press (Originally published by Indian Affairs Branch, Education Department, Ottawa).

———. 1969. Statement of the Government of Canada on Indian Policy. White Paper. Ottawa.

———. 1985. Nielsen Task Force Report. Ottawa.

———. 1987. *Report to Parliament Implementation of the 1985 Changes to the Indian Act*. Indian and Northern Affairs Canada. Ottawa: Queen's Printer.

———. 1995. *The Government of Canada's Approach to Implementation of the Inherent Right and the Negotiation of Aboriginal Self-Government*. Ottawa.

———. 1996. The Report of the Royal Commission on Aboriginal Peoples. Ottawa.

———. 1997. Gathering Strength: Canada's Aboriginal Action Plan, Ottawa: Indian Affairs and Northern Development.

———. 2010. *A Progress Report on Aboriginal Initiatives from the Government of Canada, 2009–2010*. Ottawa: Indian Affairs and Northern Development.

———. 2013. *First Nations Land Management Act*. Ottawa: Aboriginal Affairs and Northern Development Canada.

Canadian Academy of Health Sciences. 2014. *Improving Access to Oral Health Care for Vulnerable People Living in Canada*. Ottawa: Canadian Academy of Health Sciences.

Canadian Bar Association. 2010. *The Logical Next Step: Reconciliation Payments for All Indian Residential School Survivors*. Toronto: Canadian Bar Association.

Canadian Chamber of Commerce. 2013. *Opportunity Found: Improving the Participation of Aboriginal Peoples in Canada's Workforce*. Ottawa: Canadian Chamber of Commerce.

Canadian Community Economic Development (CCED Network). 2013. *Recommendation for the Federal Sustainable Development Strategies, 2013-2016*. Montreal: CCED.

Canadian Council for Aboriginal Business. 2011. *Promise and Prosperity*. Toronto: Canadian Council for Aboriginal Business.

———. 2012. *Community and Commerce*. Toronto: Canadian Council for Aboriginal Business.

Canadian Council on Learning. 2009. *The State of Aboriginal Learning in Canada: A Holistic Approach to Measuring Success*. Ottawa: Canadian Council on Learning.

Canadian Criminal Justice Association. 2000. *Aboriginal Peoples and the Criminal Justice System*. Ottawa. http://www.ccja-acjp.ca/en/aborit.html.

Canadian Education Statistics Council (CESC). 2007. *Education Indicators in Canada: Report of the Pan-Canadian Education Indicators Program 2007*. Ottawa: Statistics Canada.

————. 2009. *Federal Data Scan: Aboriginal Data in Statistics Canada's Education Data Source*. Ottawa: Statistics Canada.

Canada Mortgage and Housing Corporation. 2006. *Urban Aboriginal Households: A Profile of Demographic, Housing and Economic Conditions in Canada's Prairie and Territories Region*, Socio-economic Series 06-024. Ottawa: CMHC.

Canadian Human Rights Commission. 2004. *Protecting Their Rights: A Systemic Review of Human Rights in Correctional Services for Federally Sentenced Women*. Ottawa: Canadian Human Rights Commission.

Cannon, M. 2004. "Bill C-31—An Act to Amend the Indian Act: Notes toward a Qualitative Analysis of Legislated Injustice." Paper presented at Congress, Winnipeg, June 6.

Cappon, P., and J. Laughlin. 2009. "Redefining How Success is Measured in Aboriginal Learning in Canada." Paper presented at the OECD World Forum on Statistics, Knowledge and Policy, Charting Progress, Building Visions, Improving Life. Busan, Korea, October.

Carter, S. 1990. *Lost Harvests: Prairie Indian Reserve Farmers and Government Policy*. Montreal: McGill-Queens University Press.

Chandler M. 2005. "Suicide & The Persistence Of Identity In The Face Of Radical Cultural Change." Presented at the Assembly of First Nations National Policy Forum, April 19.

Chandler, M., and C. Lalonde. 1998. "Cultural Continuity as a Hedge Against Suicide in Canada's First Nations." *Transcultural Psychiatry* 35 (2): 193–211.

Chansonneuve, D. 2007. *Addictive Behaviours among Aboriginal People in Canada*. Ottawa: Aboriginal Healing Foundation.

Charbonneau, Hubert. 1984. «Trois siècles de dépopulation amérindienne.» In *Les populations amérindiennes et inuit du Canada : Aperçu démographique*, edited by L. Normandeau and V. Piché. Montreal: Presses de l'Université de Montréal.

Charron, M., C. Penney, and S. Senecal. 2010. *Police Reported Crime in Inuit Nunangat*. Statistics Canada Catalogue no. 85-561-X. Ottawa: Statistics Canada.

Chartrand, L. 2013. "Failure of the Daniels Case: Blindly Entrenching a Colonial Legacy." *Alberta Law Review* 51: 181–90.

Chartrand, L., and C. McKay. 2006. *A Review of Research on Criminal Victimization and First Nations, Metis and Inuit Peoples 1990 to 2001*. Ottawa: Policy Centre for Victim Issues, Research and Statistics Division, Department of Justice.

Christie, G. 1998. "Aboriginal Rights, Aboriginal Culture and Protection." *Osgoode Hall Law Journal* 36: 447–84.

Clairmont, D., and R. Linden. 1998. *Developing and Evaluating Justice Projects in Aboriginal Communities: A Review of the Literature*. Ottawa: Solicitor General of Canada.

Clatworthy, S. 2005. *Indian Registration, Membership and Population Change in First Nations Communities*. Winnipeg: Four Directions Project Consultants.

————. 2013. Personal correspondence.

Clatworthy, S., and M.J. Norris. 2007. "Aboriginal Mobility and Migration in Canada: Trends, Recent Patterns and Implications, 1971–2001." In *Aboriginal Policy Research: Moving Forward, Making a Difference*, edited by J. White, S. Wingert, D. Beavon, and P. Maxim, 145-167. Toronto: Thompson Educational Publishing.

Clatworthy, S., M.J. Norris, and E. Guimond. 2009. "A New Open Model Approach to Projecting Aboriginal Populations." In *Moving Forward, Making a Difference*, edited by J. White, S. Wingert, D. Beavon, and P. Maxim, 141–63. Toronto: Thompson Books.

Clement., J. 2009. "University Attainment of the Registered Indian Population, 1981-2006: A Cohort Approach." In *Aboriginal Education*, edited by J. White, J. Peters, D. Beavon, and N. Spence, 69–106. Toronto: Thompson Books.

Coates, K. 2000. *The Marshall Decision and Native Rights*. Montreal and Kingston: McGill-Queen's University Press.

Comack, E. 2012. "Colonialism Past and Present: Indigenous Human rights and Canadian Policing." In *Indivisible: Indigenous Human Rights*, edited by J. Green, 115–34. Halifax: Fernwood Publishing.

Comack, E., L. Deane, L. Morrisette, and J. Silver. 2013. *Indians Wear Red: Colonialism, Resistance, and Aboriginal Street Gangs*. Halifax: Fernwood Publishing.

Commission on First Nations. 2004. *Planning for Prosperity: First Nations, Intergovernmental Cooperation and Treaties*. Victoria: BC Treaty Commission.

Congress of Aboriginal Peoples. 2007. *Where Does the Money Go? Proactive Disclosure of Grants and Contributions for Aboriginal People*. Ottawa: Congress of Aboriginal Peoples.

Cook, E-D., and D. Flynn. 2008. "Nine Aboriginal Languages of Canada." In *Contemporary Linguistic Analysis: An Introduction*, sixth edition, edited by W. O'Grady and J. Archibald, 318–34. Toronto: Pearson Longman.

Cooke, M., and D. Bélanger. 2006. "Migration Theories and First Nations Mobility: Towards a System Perspective." *Canadian Review of Sociology and Anthropology* 43: 13–32.

Cornell, S. 2002. *The Harvard Project Findings on Good Governance*. Vancouver: BC Treaty Commission.

Cornell, S., and J. Kalt. 1992. *Reloading the Dice: Improving the Chances for Economic Development on American Indian Reservations*. Los Angles: American Indian Studies Center.

———. 2000. "Where's the Glue? Institutional and Cultural Foundations of American Indian Economic Development." *Journal of Socio-Economics* 29: 443–70.

———. 2006. *Two Approaches to Economic Development on American Indian Reservations: One Works, the Other Doesn't*. Boston: Harvard Project on American Indian Economic Development.

———. 2010. *Sovereignty and Nation Building: The Development Challenges in Indian Country Today*. Boston: Harvard Project on American Indian Economic Development.

Correctional Services Canada. 1999. *Demographic Overview of Aboriginal People in Canada and Aboriginal Offenders in Federal Corrections*. Ottawa: Correctional Services Canada.

———. 2009. *Towards a Continuum of Care*. Ottawa: Correctional Services Canada.

Correctional Services Program. 2015. *Adult Correctional Statistics in Canada: 2013–2014*. Ottawa: Statistics Canada.

Cote-Meek, S. 2014. *Colonized Racism, Trauma and Resistance in Postsecondary Education*. Halifax: Fernwood Books.

Culhane, D. 1998. *The Pleasure of the Crown: Anthropology, Law and First Nations*. Burnaby: Talon Books.

Currie, C., T. Wild, D. Schopflocher, L. Laing, and P. Veugelers. 2013. "Illicit and Prescription Drug Problems among Urban Aboriginal Adults in Canada: The Role of Traditional Culture in Protection and Resilience." *Social Science and Medicine* 88: 1–9.

Currie, J. 2001. *Best Practices: Treatment and Rehabilitation for Women with Substance Abuse Problems*. Ottawa: Minister of Public Works and Government Services.

Dafnos, T. 2015. "First Nations in the Crosshairs." *Canadian Dimension* 49: 23–26.

Daschuk, J. 2013. *Clearing the Plains*. Regina: University of Regina Press.

Dauvergne, M. 2012. "Adult Correctional Statistics in Canada 2010/2011." *Juristat* 12: 1–27.

Davidson, D., and A. Hurley. 2007. *Oil Sands Development and Water Use in the Athabasca River-Watershed: Science and Market based Solutions*. Edmonton: Munk Centre for International Studies.

Day, S., and J. Green. 2010. "Indian Act Remedy Bill C-3 is Flawed." *Rabble,* May 21.

Dempsey, J. 2005. "Status Indian: Who Defines You?" In *Indigenous Peoples and the Modern State*, edited by D. Champagne, K. Torjesen, and S. Steiner, 134–47. Walnut Creek: AltaMira Press.

Department of Justice Canada. 2007. *The 2007 National Justice Survey: Tackling Crime and Public Confidence*. Ottawa: Department of Justice Canada.

Diabo, R., and S. Pasternak. 2011. *Canada: First Nations Under Surveillance*. Montreal: Global Research.

Dickason, O. 1992. *Canada's First Nations: A History of the Founding Peoples from Earliest Times*. Toronto: McLelland and Stewart.

Dion, P., and S. Coulombe. 2008. "Study: Portrait of the Mobility of Canadians in 2006: Trajectories and Characteristics of Migrants." *Report on the Demographic Situation in Canada, 2005-2006*. Statistics Canada Catalogue no. 91-209. Ottawa: Statistics Canada.

Dixon, E. 1999. "The First Colonization of North America." In *Bones, Boats, and Bison: Archeology and the First Colonization of Western North America*, edited by E. Dixon, 19–43. Albuquerque: University of New Mexico Press.

Dobyns, H. 1966. "Estimating Aboriginal American Population: An Appraisal of Techniques with a New Hemisphere Estimate." *Current Anthropology* 7: 395–416.

Droitsch, D., and T. Simieritsch. 2010. *Canadian Aboriginal Concerns with Oil Sands*. Edmonton: Pembina Institute.

Dumont, J. 2005. "Developing a Cultural Framework." First Nations Regional Health Survey. http://fnigc.ca/sites/default/files/ENpdf/RHS_General/developing-a-cultural-framework.pdf.

Duran, E. 2006. *Healing the Soul Wound: Counseling with American Indians and Other Native Peoples*. New York: Teachers College Press.

Duran, E., and B. Duran. 1995. *Native American Postcolonial Psychology*. Albany: State University of New York Press.

Duran, E., B. Duran, M. Yellow Horse-Brave Heart, and S. Yellow Horse-Davis. 1998. "Healing the American Indian Soul Wound," In *International Handbook of Multigenerational Legacies of Trauma*, edited by Y. Danieli, 341–54. New York: Plenum.

Dyck, R., H. Klomp, and L. Tan. 2001. "From 'Thrifty Genotype' to 'Hefty Fetal Phenotype': The Relationship between High Birth Weight and Diabetes in Saskatchewan Registered Indians." *Journal of Public Health* 92: 340–44.

Earle, L. 2011. *Understanding Chronic Disease and the Role for Traditional Approaches in Aboriginal Communities*. Prince George: National Collaborating Centre for Aboriginal Health.

Eberts, M. 2014. "Victoria's Secret: How to Make a Population of Prey." In *Indivisible: Indigenous Human Rights*, edited by J. Green. Halifax: Fernwood Publishing.

Ekos. 2001. "Highlights of First Nations Survey On-Reserve." www.inac.gc.ca/nr/prs/s-d2001.

Elsey. C. 2013. *The Poetics of Land and Identity among BC Indigenous Peoples*. Halifax: Fernwood.

Ennab, F. 2010. "Rupturing the Myth of the Peaceful Western Canadian Frontier." MA Thesis, University of Manitoba.

Environics. 2010. *Urban Aboriginal Peoples Study 2008–2011*. Scarborough: The Interprovincial Group.

Evans-Campbell, T. 2008. "Historical Trauma in American Indian/Native Alaska Communities: A Multilevel Framework for Exploring Impacts on Individuals, Families, and Communities." *Journal of Interpersonal Violence* 23: 316–38.

Eyford, D. 2013. "Forging Partnerships Building Relationships." Ottawa: Report to the Prime Minister Office.

Ferguson, S., and J. Zhao. 2013. *The Educational Attainment of Aboriginal Peoples in Canada*. Statistics Canada Catalogue no. 99-012-X2011003. Ottawa: Statistics Canada.

Findlay, I., and J. Russell. 2005. "Aboriginal Economic Development and the Triple Bottom Line: Toward a Sustainable Future?" *The Journal of Aboriginal Economic Development* 4: 23–45.

First Nations Centre. 2005. *National Aboriginal Health Organization First Nations Regional Longitudinal Health Survey (RHS) 2002/03: Results for Adults, Youth and Children Living in First Nations Communities*. Ottawa: First Nations Centre, National Aboriginal Health Organization.

First Nations Information Governance Centre (FNIGC). 2012. *First Nations Regional Health Survey (RHS) Phase 2 (2008/10) National Report on Adults, Youth and Children Living in First Nations Communities*. Ottawa: First Nations Information Governance Centre.

First Nations Leadership Council. 2013. *Advancing an Indigenous Framework for Consultation and Accommodation in BC*. Vancouver: First Nations Leadership Council.

First Nations Leadership Council and Ministry of Economic Development. 2011. *Journey to Economic Independence*. Vancouver: First Nations Leadership Council.

Fisher, R. 1977. *Contact and Conflict: Indian–European Relations in British Columbia, 1774–1890*. Vancouver: University of British Columbia Press.

Fisheries and Oceans Canada. 2006. *An Integrated Aboriginal Policy Framework*. Ottawa: Communications Branch.

Flanagan, T., C. Alcantara, and A. Dressay. 2010. *Beyond the Indian Act*. Montreal and Kingston: McGill-Queens University Press.

Flanagan, T., and K. Beauregard. 2013. *The Wealth of First Nations: An Exploratory Study*. Vancouver: Fraser Institute.

Foley, D. 2008. "Does Culture and Social Capital Impact on the Networking Attributes of Indigenous Entrepreneurs?" *Journal of Enterprising Communities* 2: 204–24.

Fontaine, T. 2010. *Broken Circle: The Dark Legacy of Indian Residential School: A Memoir*. Victoria: Heritage House Publishing.

Frideres, J., and R. Gadacz. 2010. *Native Peoples in Canada*. Toronto: Pearson.

Furgal, C., T. Garvin and C. Jardine. 2010. Trends in the study of Aboriginal health risks in Canada. *International Journal of Circumpolar Health*, 69: 322–32.

Furi, M., and J. Wherrett. 2003. *Indian Status and Band Membership Issues*. Ottawa: Political and Social Affairs Division, Library of Parliament.

Gallagher, B. 2013. *Resource Rulers: Fortune and Folly on Canada's Road to Resources*. Waterloo, ON: Lightning Source.

Garriguet, D. 2008. "Obesity and the Eating Habits of the Aboriginal Population." *Health Reports* 19: 1–13.

Giordano, P., S. Cerrkovich, and J. Rudolph. 2002. "Gender, Crime, and Resistance: Toward a Theory of Cognitive Transformation." *American Journal of Sociology* 107: 990–1064.

Gordon, C., and J. White. 2014. "Indigenous Educational Attainment in Canada." *International Indigenous Policy Journal* 5 (4). http://ir.lib.uwo.ca/iipj/vol5/iss3/6.

Graham, J. 2007. *Rethinking Self-Government: Developing a More Balanced, Evolutionary Approach.* Ottawa: Institute on Governance.

———. 2010. *The First Nation Governance System.* Policy Brief No. 36. Ottawa: Institute on Governance.

Graham, J., and F. Levesque. 2010. *First Nation Communities in Distress: Dealing with Causes, Not Symptoms.* Ottawa: Institute on Governance.

Green, J., ed. 2014. *Indivisible: Indigenous Human Rights.* Halifax: Fernwood Publishing.

Grekul, J. and P. LaRocque. 2011. "Hope is Absolute: Gang-Involved Women: Perceptions from the Frontline." *Aboriginal Policy Studies* 1: 132–60.

Guha, R. 1997. *Dominance without Hegemony: History and Power in Colonial India.* Cambridge: Harvard University Press.

Groves and Lukacs. 2011. "RCMP Spied on Protesting First Nations." *The Media Co-op,* December 5.

Guimond, E. 2003a. "Changing Ethnicity: The Concept of Ethnic Drifters." In *Aboriginal Conditions: Research as a Foundation for Social Policy,* edited by J.P. White, P. Maxim, and D. Beavon, 91–107. Vancouver: University of British Columbia Press.

———. 2003b. "Fuzzy Definitions and Population Explosions: Changing Identities of Aboriginal Groups in Canada." In *Not Strangers in these parts: Urban Aboriginal Peoples,* edited by D. Newhouse and E. Peters, 35–50. Ottawa: Policy Research Initiative.

Guimond, E., N. Robitaille, and S. Seneccal. 2009. "Aboriginal People in Canadian Cities: Why are they growing so fast?" *Canadian Issues* Winter: 11-17.

Halliday, W.M. 1935. *Potlatch and Totem: Recollections of an Indian Agent.* London and Toronto: J.M. Dent and Sons.

Hamilton, A., and C. Sinclair. 1991. *Report of the Aboriginal Justice Inquiry of Manitoba.* Winnipeg: Queens Printer.

Hanselmann, C. 2001. *Urban Aboriginal people in Western Canada: Realities and Policies.* Calgary: Canada West Foundation.

Hawthorne, H. 1966. *A Survey of the Contemporary Indians of Canada.* Ottawa: Department of Indian Affairs and Northern Development.

Health Canada. 2003. *Statistical Profile on the Health of First Nations in Canada.* Ottawa: Health Canada.

Health Council of Canada. 2005. *The Health Status of Canada's First Nations, Métis and Inuit Peoples: A Background Paper to Accompany Health Care Renewal in Canada: Accelerating Change.* http://healthcouncilcanada.

———. 2012. *Empathy, Dignity, and Respect.* Ottawa: Health Council of Canada.

———. 2013. *Canada's Most Vulnerable: Improving Health Care for First Nations, Inuit, and Métis Seniors.* Toronto: Health Council of Canada.

Hedican, E. 2013. *IPPERWASH: The Tragic Failure of Canada's Aboriginal Policy.* Toronto: University of Toronto Press.

Hellin, C. 2008. *Dances with Dependency: Out of Poverty through Self-Reliance.* Los Angeles: Ravencrest Publishing.

Henderson, J. 1997. "Interpreting *Sui Generis* Treaties." *Alberta Law Review* 36: 43–76.

———. 2008. "Treaty Governance." In *Aboriginal Self-Government in Canada*, edited by Y. Belanger, 20–38. Saskatoon: Purich Publishers.

Henderson, J. 2009. "Dialogical Governance: A Method of Constitutional Governance." *Saskatchewan Law Review* 72: 29–73.

Henderson, J., and R. Barsh. 1997. "The Supreme Court's Van der Peet Trilogy: Naïve Imperialism and Ropes of Sand." *McGill Law Journal* 42: 980–93.

Hoffecker, J., and S. Elias. 2007. *Human Ecology of Beringia*. New York: Columbia University Press.

Hoffecker, J., S. Elias, and D. O'Rourke. 2014. "Out of Beringia?" *Science* 28: 970–80.

Horn, C., and G. Halseth. 2011. "Seeing like a Circle: Perspectives on the Field from a Dialogue on Urban Aboriginal Economic Development." *Aboriginal Policy Journal* 1 (2): 101–31.

Howard, A, J. Edge, and D. Watt. 2012. *Understanding the Value, Challenges, and Opportunities of Engaging Métis, Inuit, and First Nation Workers*. Ottawa: The Conference Board of Canada.

Hughes, P., and M. Mossman. 2005. *Criminal Justice in Canada*. Ottawa: Department of Justice.

Human Rights Watch. 2013. *Those Who Take Us Away: Abusive Policing and Failures in Protection of Indigenous Women and Girls in Northern British Columbia, Canada*. Toronto: Human Rights Watch.

Hylton, J. 2010. *Aboriginal Sex Offending in Canada*. Ottawa: Aboriginal Healing Foundation.

Indian Affairs Branch. 2012 [1879–80]. *Report on Industrial Schools for Indians and Halfbreeds*. Ottawa.

INAC (Indian and Northern Affairs Canada). 1995. *Aboriginal Self-Government*. Ottawa: Public Works and Government Services Canada.

———. 2009. *Summative Evaluation of INAC's Economic Development Programs*. Ottawa: INAC.

Industry Canada. 2002. *Aboriginal Entrepreneurs in 2002*. Ottawa: Industry Canada.

Innes, R. 2013. *Elder Brother and the Law of the People*. Winnipeg: University of Manitoba Press.

Janz, T., J. Seto, and A. Turner. 2009. *Aboriginal Peoples Survey, 2006: An Overview of the Health of the Métis Population*. Ottawa: Statistics Canada.

Jedwab, J. 2006. "What Price do Aboriginals Pay for Preserving their Languages and Culture in Canada?" Paper presented at the Association for Canadian Studies, Ottawa.

Johnson, S. 2004. "Adult Correctional Services in Canada, 2002/03." *Juristat* 24 (10): 1–30.

Johnson, H., and M. Dawson. 2010. *Violence against Women in Canada: Research and Policy Perspectives*. Toronto: Oxford University Press.

Jordan-Fenton, C., and M. Pokiak-Fenton. 2014. *Fatty Legs: A True Story*. Toronto: Annick Press.

Jorgensen, M. 2000. "Bringing the Background Forward: Evidence from Indian Country on the Social and Cultural Determinants of Economic Development." PhD diss., Harvard University.

———, ed. 2007. *Rebuilding Native Nations: Strategies for Governance and Development*. Tucson: University of Arizona Press.

Jorgensen, M., and S. Cornell. 2007. *Resources for Nation Building*. Tucson: University of Arizona Press.

Kelly, E., D. Schindler, P. Hodson, J. Short, R. Radmanovich, and C. Nielsen. 2010. "Oil Sands Development Contributes Elements Toxic at Low Concentrations to the Athabasca River and Its Tributaries." *Current Issue* 107: 16178–83.

Kennedy, R., S. Kasi, and V. Vaccdarino. 2001. "Repeated Hospitalizations and Self-Rated Health among the Elderly." *American Journal of Epidemiology* 153: 232–41.

King, M. 2014, "Addressing the Disparities in Aboriginal Health through Social Determinants Research." In *Aboriginal Populations: Social, Demographic and Epidemiological Perspectives*, edited by F. Trovato and A. Romaniuk, 197–210. Edmonton: University of Alberta Press.

King, T. 2012. *The Inconvenient Indian*. New York: Random House.

Kirkness, V. 1999. "Aboriginal Education in Canada: A Retrospective and a Prospective." *Journal of American Indian Education* 39: 29–47.

Kirmayer, L., G. Brass, T. Holton, K. Paul, C. Simpson, and C. Tait. 2007. *Suicide among Aboriginal People in Canada*. Aboriginal Healing Foundation Research Series. Ottawa: Aboriginal Healing Foundation.

Kliewer, E., T. Mayer, and A. Wajda. 2002. *The Health of Manitoba's Métis Population and their Utilization of medical Services: A Pilot Study*. Winnipeg: Cancer Care Manitoba and Manitoba Health.

Knockwood, I. 2001. *Out of the Depths: The Experiences of Mi'kmaw children at the Indian Residential School at Shubenacadie, Nova Scotia*. Halifax: Rosewood.

Kondro, W. 2012. "Health Disparities among Income Groups Becoming More Pronounced," *Canadian Medical Association Journal* 184: E695–96.

Krehbiel, R. 2008. "The Changing Legal Landscape for Aboriginal Land Use Planning in Canada." *Plan* Summer: 1–4.

Kreuter, M. W., and McClure, S. 2004. "The Role of Culture in Health Communication." *Annual Review of Public Health* 25: 439–55.

Kroes, G. 2009. *Aboriginal Youth in Canada: Emerging Issues, Research Priorities, and Policy Implications*. Ottawa: Policy Research Initiative.

Kroskrity, P., and M. Field, eds. 2009. *Native American Language Ideologies*. Tucson, University of Arizona Press.

Ktunaxa/Kinbasket Tribal Council. n.d. *The Self Government Landscape*. Vancouver: BC Treaty Commission. http://www.bctreaty.net/files/pdf_documents/self_government_landscape.pdf

Kulchyski, P. 1994, *Unjust Relations: Aboriginal Rights in Canadian Courts*. Toronto: Oxford University Press.

———. 2005. *Like the Sound of a Drum: Aboriginal Cultural Politics in Denendeh and Nunavut*. Winnipeg: University of Manitoba Press.

Ladner, K. 2009. "Take 35: Reconciling Constitutional Orders." In *First Nations, First Thoughts: The Impact of Indigenous Thought in Canada*, edited by A. M. Timpson, 279–300. Vancouver: University of British Columbia Press.

Laframboise, S., and K. Sherbina. n.d. "The Medicine Wheel: Dancing to Eagle Spirit Society." http://www.dancingtoeaglespiritsociety.org/medwheel.php.

Lalonde, C. 2006. "Identity Formation and Cultural Resilience in Aboriginal Communities." In *Promoting Resilience in Child Welfare*, edited by R.J. Flynn, P. Dudding, and J. Barber, 52–71. Ottawa: University of Ottawa Press.

Lane, P., M. Bopp, J. Bopp, and J. Norris. 2002. *Mapping the Healing Journey: The Final Report of a First Nation Research Project on Healing in Canadian Aboriginal Communities*. Ottawa: Solicitor General of Canada, Aboriginal Corrections Policy Unit.

Langlois, S., and A. Turner. 2014. *Aboriginal Languages and Selected Vitality Indicators in 2011*. Ottawa: Statistics Canada.

Latimer, J., and L. Foss. 2004. *A One Day Snapshot of Aboriginal Youth in Custody across Canada: Phase II*. Ottawa: Department of Justice Canada.

Lavoie, J., and L. Gervais. 2010 "Towards the Adoption of a National Aboriginal Health Policy." In *Aboriginal Policy Research, Vol IX: Health and Well Being*, edited by J. White, D. Beavon, and N. Spence, 121-139. Toronto: Thompson Educational.

Lawrence, B. 2012. *Fractured Homeland*. Vancouver: University of British Columbia Press.

Lewis, M. and R. Lockhart. 2002. *Performance Measurement, Development Indicators and Aboriginal Economic Development*. Port Alberni: Centre for Community Enterprise.

Linnitt, D. 2012 *Alberta Finds Mismanagement of Errors Causes Fracking Water Contamination*. Victoria: Desmog.

Little Bear, L. 2000. "Jagged Worldviews Colliding." In *Reclaiming Indigenous Voices and Vision*, edited by M. Battiste. Vancouver: University of British Columbia Press.

Lix, L., S. Bruce, S. Joykrishna, and T. Kue Young 2010. "Risk Factors and Chronic Conditions among Aboriginal and Non-Aboriginal Populations." *Health Reports* 20: 4.

Llewellyn, J. 2002. "Dealing with the Legacy of Native Residential School Abuse in Canada, Litigation, ADR, and Restorative Justice." *University of Toronto Law Journal* 52: 253–300.

Llewellyn, J., and R. Howse. 1998. *Restorative Justice: A Conceptual Framework*. Ottawa: Law Commission of Canada.

Loh, S., and M.V. George. 2003. "Estimating the Fertility Level of Registered Indians in Canada: A Challenging Endeavour." *Canadian Studies in Population*, 30(1): 117–135.

Loppie-Reading, C., and F. Wien. 2008. *Health Inequalities and Social Determinants of Aboriginal Peoples' Health*. Ottawa: National Collaborating Centre for Aboriginal Peoples Health; Public Health Agency of Canada.

Lotz, J. 1999. "More About CED." *Community Connections* Spring.

Luffman, J., and D. Sussman. 2007. "The Aboriginal Labour Force in Western Canada." *Perspectives on Labour and Income* 8 (1): 13–27.

Lutz, J. 2008. *Makuk: A New History of Aboriginal–White Relations*. Vancouver: University of British Columbia Press.

Maaka, R. and A. Fleras. 2008. "Contesting Indigenous Peoples Governance." In *Aboriginal Self-Government in Canada*, edited by Y. Belanger, 69-104. Saskatoon: Purich Publishing.

McCarthy, S. 2013. "CSIS, RCMP Monitored Activist Groups before Northern Gateway Hearings." *Globe and Mail*, November 21.

MacDonald, D. 2014. "Aboriginal Peoples and Multicultural Reform in Canada: Prospects for a New Binational Society." *Canadian Journal of Sociology* 39: 64–86.

McKay, M. 2001. *Report on Canada's Compliance with the International Convention on the Elimination of All Forms of Racial Discrimination in Response to Canada's 13th and 14th Reports to the Committee on the Elimination of all Forms of Racial Discrimination*. Ottawa: Canadian Feminist Alliance for International Action.

McNeil, K. 2004. *The Inherent Right of Self-Government: Emerging Directions of Legal Research*. Chilliwack: BC First Nations Governance Centre.

———. 2006a. "Aboriginal Title and the Supreme Court: What's Happening?" *Saskatchewan Law Review* 69: 281.

———. 2006b. "What is the Inherent Right of Self-Government?" Presentation at the Governance Development Forum, Parksville, BC, October 3.

———. 2007. *The Jurisdiction of Inherent Right Aboriginal Governments*. Ottawa: National Centre for First Nations Governance.

————. 2010. *Common Law, Aboriginal Title.* Oxford: Clarendon Press.

Malenfant, E., and J.-D. Morency. 2011. *Population Projections by Aboriginal Identity in Canada.* Ottawa: Statistics Canada.

Mann. M. 2010. "Incarceration and the Aboriginal Offender: Potential Impact of the Tackling Violent Crime Act and the Corrections Review Panel." In *Aboriginal Policy Research, Vol 8: Exploring the Urban Landscape*, edited by J. White and J.Bruhn, 233–53. Toronto: Thompson Educational.

————. 2012. "Sentencing Aboriginal Offenders: The Honour of the Crown, Reconciliation and Rehabilitation of the Rule of Law." MLaws thesis, Queen's University.

Mao, Y., B. Moloughey, R. Semenciw, and H. Morrison. 1992. "Indian Reserve and Registered Indian Mortality in Canada." *Canadian Journal of Public Health* 83: 350–53.

Marchildon, G.P. 2005. *Health Systems in Transition: Canada.* Toronto: University of Toronto Press.

Masching, R. 2009. *Aboriginal Strategy on HIV/AIDS in Canada II.* Toronto: Canadian Aboriginal AIDS Network.

Mendelson, M. 2004. *Aboriginal People in Canada's Labour Market: Work and Unemployment, Today and Tomorrow*, Ottawa: Caledon Institute of Social Policy.

————. 2006. *Aboriginal Peoples and Postsecondary Education.* Toronto: Canada Caledon Institute of Social Policy.

————. 2008. *Improving Education on Reserves: A First Nation Education Authority Act.* Ottawa: Caledon Institute of Social Policy.

————. 2014. *A Second Look at the First Nations Control of First Nations Education Act.* Ottawa: Caledon Institute of Social Policy.

Milke, M. 2013. *Ever Higher, Government Spending on Canada's Aboriginals since 1947.* Vancouver: Fraser Institute.

Miller, J. 1989. *Skyscrapers Hide the Heavens: A History of Indian–White Relations in Canada.* Toronto: University of Toronto Press.

Miller, J.R. 2009. "Which 'Native' History? By Whom? For Whom?" *Canadian Issues* June: 33–36.

Milloy, J. 1999. *A National Crime: The Canadian Government and the Residential School System, 1879-1986.* Winnipeg: University of Manitoba Press.

Monture-Angus, P. 1999. *Journeying Forward: Dreaming First Nations' Independence.* Halifax: Fernwood Publishing.

Morehouse, T. 1987. "Native Claims and Political Development: A Comparative Analysis." Paper presented at the Annual Meeting of Western Regional Science Association, Kona, Hawaii, February 19.

Morellato, M. 2003. "The Existence of Aboriginal Governance Rights within the Canadian Legal System." http://epub.sub.uni-hamburg.de/epub/volltexte/2009/1045/pdf/Existence_governance.pdf

Morris, A. 1991 [1880]. *The Treaties of Canada with the Indians of Manitoba and the North-West Territories.* Calgary: Fifth House.

Morse, B. 2010. "Developing Legal Frameworks for Urban Aboriginal Governance." In *Exploring the Urban Landscape*, edited by J. White and D. Bruhn, 1–27. Toronto: Thompson Publications.

Morse, B., ed. 1989. *Aboriginal Peoples and the Law: Indian, Métis and Inuit Rights in Canada.* Ottawa: Carleton University Press.

Mosby, I. 2013. "Administering Colonial Science: Nutrition Research and Human Biomedical Experimentation in Aboriginal Communities and Residential Schools, 1942-1952." *Social History*, 46:1-15.

Munch, C. 2012. *Youth Correctional Statistics in Canada: 2010–2011*. Ottawa: Statistics Canada.

NAEDB (National Aboriginal Economic Development Board). 2011. *Recommendations for the Renovation of Aboriginal Economic Development Programs*. Gatineau: NAEDB.

———. 2012. *Recommendations on Financing First Nation Infrastructure*. Gatineau: NAEDB.

———. 2013. *Addressing the Barriers to Economic Development on Reserve*. Gatineau: NAEDB.

National Aboriginal Health Organization. 2012a. "Fact sheet." http://www.taam-emaad.montreal.ca/index.htm.

———. 2012b. "Integrating Traditional Medicines into Western Medical Treatment." http://www.naho.ca

National Aboriginal Law Section, Canadian Bar Association. 2010. *Bill C-3-Gender Equity in Indian Registration Act*. Ottawa: Canadian Bar Association.

National Association of Friendship Centres. 2009. *Urban Aboriginal Economic Development: A Friendship Centre Perspective*. Ottawa: NAFC.

National Centre for First Nations Governance, 2009. *Rebuilding Nations*. West Vancouver: National Centre for First Nations Governance.

National Collaborating Centre for Aboriginal Health. 2009–10. "Culture and Language as Social Determinants of First Nations, Inuit and Métis Health." Ottawa: Public Health Agency of Canada. http://www.nccah-ccnsa.ca

National Indian Brotherhood. 1972. Indian Control of Indian Education. Ottawa.

National Native Addictions Partnership Foundation. 2000. "NNADAP Renewal Framework for Implementing the Strategic Recommendations of the 1998, General Review of the National Native Alcohol and Drug Abuse Program." Draft, working paper. Muskoday, SK: NNAPF.

National Panel on First Nation Elementary and Secondary Education for Students on Reserves. 2012. *Nurturing the Learning Spirit of First Nations Students*. Ottawa: Aboriginal Affairs and Northern Development Canada.

Native Women's Association of Canada. 2007. "Aboriginal Women and the Legal Justice System in Canada." Paper presented at the National Aboriginal Women's Summit, Corner Brook, Newfoundland, June 21.

Naumann, D. 2008. "Aboriginal Women in Canada: On the Choice to Renounce or Reclaim Aboriginal Identity." *Canadian Journal of Native Studies* 28 (2):343–61.

Nettleton, C. 2007. "An Overview of Current Knowledge of the Social Determinants of Indigenous Health." World Health Organization symposium on the social determinants of Indigenous Health, Geneva, Switzerland.

Newhouse, D. 2005. "Notes for Native Aboriginal Economic Development Board." Discussion paper presented at Trent University, Peterborough, July 13.

Newhouse, D., K. Fitz-Maurice, T. McGuire-Adams, and D. Jetté. 2012. *Well-being in the Urban Aboriginal Community: Fostering Biimaadiziwin, a National Research Conference on Urban Aboriginal Peoples*. Toronto: Thompson Educational Publishing.

Nguyen, M. 2014. "Consulting Whom? Lessons from the Toronto Urban Aboriginal Strategy." *International Indigenous Policy Journal* 5 (1). http://ir.lib.uwo.ca/iipj/vol5/iss1/3

Nisga'a Lisims Government. 2002. "Self-Government: The Five Realities." In *The Changing Landscape*, 18–25. Vancouver: BC Treaty Commission.

Norberg-Hodge, H. 2010. "Breaking Up the Monoculture." *Bhoomi Magazine*. http://www.bhoomimagazine.org/article/breaking-monoculture.

Norris, M.J. 2003. "From Generation to Generation: Survival and Maintenance of Canada's Aboriginal Languages within Families, Communities and Cities." Paper presented at the seventh Conference of the Foundation for Endangered Languages, Broome, Western Australia, September 22–24.

———. 2006. "Aboriginal Languages in Canada: Trends and Perspectives on Maintenance and Revitalization" In *Aboriginal Policy Research: Moving Forward, Making a Difference*, edited by J. P. White, S. Wingert, D. Beavon, and P. Maxim. Toronto: Thompson Educational Publishing.

Norris, M., and S. Clatworthy. 2011. "Urbanization and Migration Patterns of Aboriginal Populations in Canada: A Half Century in Review: (1951-2006)." *Aboriginal Policy Studies* 1: 13–77.

Norris, M.J., and K. MacCon. 2003. "Aboriginal Language, Transmission and Maintenance in Families: Results of an Intergenerational and Gender-Based Analysis for Canada, 1996." In *Aboriginal Conditions: Research as a Foundation for Public Policy*, edited by J. White, S. Wingert, D. Beavon, and P. Maxim. Vancouver: University of British Columbia Press.

Norris, M., and M. Snider. 2008. "Endangered Aboriginal Languages in Canada: Trends, Patterns and Prospects in Language Learning, Personal Correspondence." In *Endangered Languages and Language Learning, Proceedings of the 12th Foundation for Endangered Languages Conference*, edited by T. de Graaf, N. Ostler, and R. Salverda. The Netherlands: Foundation for Endangered Languages/Fryske Akademy.

O'Donnell, V., and H. Tait. 2004. "Well-Being of the Non-Reserve Aboriginal Population." *Canadian Social Trends* Spring: 19–23.

O'Meara, D. 2014. "Why First Nations Groups Scoring Oil Sands Contracts is 'no longer a given.'" *Financial Post*, 4 July.

Office of the Correctional Investigator. 2006. *Annual Report of the Office of the Correctional Investigator 2005–2006*. Ottawa: Public Works and Government Services Canada.

Office of the Treaty Commissioner. n.d. *Aboriginal Rights and Title*. Saskatoon: Office of the Treaty Commissioner.

Oliver, L., and D. Kohen. 2012. "Unintentional Injury Hospitalizations among Children and Youth in Areas with a High Percentage of Aboriginal Identity Residents: 2001/2002 to 2005/2006." *Health Reports* 23 (3). Statistics Canada Catalogue no. 82-003-XPE.

Orr, J. 2013 "Defining and Measuring Aboriginal Economic Development Success." In *Aboriginal Measures for Economic Development*, edited by J. Orr, W. Weir, and Atlantic Aboriginal Economic Development Integrated Research Program, xii-xvi. Halifax: Fernwood Publishing.

Oster, R., J. Johnson, and B. Hemmelgarn. 2011. "Recent Epidemiologic Trends of Diabetes Mellitus among Status Aboriginal Adults." *Canadian Medical Association Journal* 183: E803–E808.

Palmater, P. 2011. "Stretched Beyond Human Limits: Death by Poverty in First Nations." *Canadian Review of Social Policy* 65/66: 112–27.

Parriag, A., and P. Chaulk. 2013. "The Urban Aboriginal Middle-Income Group in Canada: A Demographic Profile." *Aboriginal Policy Studies* 2: 34–63.

Peach, I. 2011. "Finding Your Allies Where You Can: How Canadian Courts Drive Aboriginal Recognition in Canada." *Aboriginal Policy Studies* 1: 106–31.

Pendakur, K., and Pendakur, R. 2011. "Aboriginal Income Disparity in Canada." *Canadian Public Policy* 37: 61–83.

Penner, B.K. 1983. Penner Report. Ottawa: Special Committee on Indian Self-Government.

Pennock, J., J. Park, M. Tjepkema, and N. Goedhuis. 2015. *Avoidable Mortality among First Nation Adults in Canada: A Cohort Analysis*. Ottawa: Statistics Canada.

Perreault, S. 2009. *The Incarceration of Aboriginal People in Adult Correctional Services*. Ottawa: Department of Industry.

————. 2011. *Violent Victimization of Aboriginal People in the Canadian Provinces, 2009*. Ottawa: Statistics Canada.

————. 2014. *Admissions to Adult Correctional Services in Canada 2011–2012*. Ottawa: Statistics Canada.

Perreault, S., and S. Shannon Brennan. 2010. "Criminal Victimization in Canada, 2009." *Juristat* 30 (2). Statistics Canada.

Perreault, S., and R. Kong. 2009. "The Incarceration of Aboriginal People in Adult Correctional Services." *Juristat* 29 (3). Statistics Canada.

Perrin, Thorau and Associates. 2009. *First Nations and Economic Prosperity in the Coming Decade*. Vancouver: Business Council of British Columbia.

Peters, E. 2010. "Aboriginal People in Canadian Cities." In *Canadian Cities in Transition: New Directions in the Twenty-First Century*, fourth edition, edited by Trudi Bunting, Pierre Filion, and Ryan Walker, 375–90. Toronto: Oxford University Press.

————. 2011. "Emerging Themes in Academic Research in Urban Aboriginal Identities in Canada, 1996–2010." *Aboriginal Policy Studies* 1: 78–105.

Peters, E., and C. Andersen. 2013. *Indigenous in the City: Contemporary Identities and Cultural Innovation*. Vancouver: University of British Columbia Press.

Peters, J., and J. White. 2009. "Aboriginal Education: Current Crisis and Future Alternatives." In *Aboriginal Education*, edited by J. White, J. Peters, D. Beavon, N. Spence, 109–16. Toronto: Thompson Books.

Poelzer, G. n.d. *Inherent vs. Delegated Models of Governance*. Prince George: University of Northern British Columbia.

Ponting, R., and C. Voyageur. 2001. "Challenging the Deficit Paradigm: Grounds for Optimism among First Nations of Canada." *Canadian Journal of Native Studies* 21: 2–18.

Porter, L., and D. Calverley. 2011. "Trends in the Use of Remand in Canada." *Juristat*. Catalogue No. 85-002-X.

Proulx, C. 2003. *Reclaiming Aboriginal Justice, Identity, and Community*. Saskatoon: Purich Publishers.

Public Health Agency of Canada. 2009. *Report from the National Diabetes Surveillance System: Diabetes in Canada*. http://www.phac-aspc.gc.ca/publicat/2009/ndssdic-sns-ddac-09/1-eng.php.

————. 2010. *What Determines Health?* Date Modified May 18, 2010. http://www.phac-aspc.gc.ca/ph-sp/determinants/index-eng.php.

Public Safety Canada. 2004. "Public Confidence in the Criminal Justice System." *Research Summary* 9 (6): 1–2.

Quann, N., and S. Trevethan. 2000. *Police Reported Aboriginal Crime in Saskatchewan*. Ottawa: Canadian Centre for Justice Statistics.

Randall, J., A. Harris, L. Svenson, D. Voaklander, and S. Parker. 2012. *Health Status of the Métis Population of Alberta*. Edmonton: Metis Nation of Alberta/University of Alberta.

Raphael, D., A. Curry-Stevens, T. Bryant. 2008. "Barriers to Addressing the Social Determinants of Health: Insights from the Canadian Experience." *Health Policy* 88: 222-35.

Ray, A. 1974. *Indians in the Fur Trade*. Toronto: University of Toronto Press.

————. 2011. *Telling It to the Judge*, Montreal/Kingston: McGill-Queens University Press.

RCMP (Royal Canadian Mounted Police). 2014a. *Criminal Threats to the Canadian Petroleum Industry*. Ottawa: Critical Infrastructure Intelligence Assessment.

————. 2014b. *Missing and Murdered Aboriginal Women: A National Operational Overview*, Ottawa: RCMP.

————. 2015. *Missing and Murdered Aboriginal Women: Royal Commission on Aboriginal Peoples: 2015 Update*. Ottawa: RCMP.

Reform Commission. 1991. *Report on Aboriginal Peoples and Criminal Justice: Equality, Respect and the Search for Justice as Requested by the Minister of Justice under Subsection 12(2) of the Law Reform Commission Act*. Ottawa: Law Reform Commission of Canada.

Reilly, J. 2010. *Bad Medicine: A Judge's Struggle for Justice in a First Nations Community*. Victoria: Rocky Mountain Books.

————. 2014. *Bad Judgment: The Myths of First Nation Equality and Judicial Independence in Canada*. Victoria: Rocky Mountain Books.

Restoule, Jean-Paul. 2005. "Male Aboriginal Identity Formation in Urban Areas: A Focus on Process and Context." PhD diss., Ontario Institute for Studies in Education (OISE), University of Toronto.

Roberts, L.W., R.A. Clifton, B. Ferguson, K. Kampen, and S. Langlois, eds. 2005. *Recent Social Trends in Canada 1960–2000*. Kingston/Montreal: McGill-Queen's University Press.

Robertson, D. 2014. *Sugar Falls: A Residential School*. Winnipeg: Portage and Main Press.

Romaniuc, Anatole. 2003. "Aboriginal Population of Canada: Growth Dynamics under Conditions of Encounter of Civilizations." *Canadian Studies in Population* 30: 128–45.

Romanow, R. 2002. *Future of Health Care in Canada*. Ottawa: Canada

Ross, M. 2003. *Aboriginal Peoples and Resource Development in Northern Alberta*. Calgary: Canadian Institute of Resources Law.

Ross, R. 1996. *Returning to the Teachings: Exploring Aboriginal Justice*. Toronto: Penguin.

Royal Commission on Aboriginal Peoples. 1996a. *Bridging the Cultural Divide: A Report on Aboriginal People and Criminal Justice in Canada*. Ottawa: Royal Commission on Aboriginal Peoples.

Royal Commission on Aboriginal Peoples. 1996b. *Looking Forward, Looking Back*, vol. 1 of the *Report of the Royal Commission on Aboriginal Peoples*. Ottawa: Supply and Services.

Royal Society of Canada Expert Panel. 2010. *Environmental and Health Impacts of Canada's Oil Sands*. http://rsc-src.ca/en/expert-panels/rsc-reports/environmental -and-healthimpacts-canadas-oil-sands-industry.

Rudin, J. 2010. "Aboriginal Peoples and the Criminal Justice System." http://www. archives.gov.on.ca/en/e_records/ipperwash/policy_part/research/pdf/Rudin.pdf.

Rustand, J. 2010. *Is Inherent Aboriginal Self-Government Constitutional?* Toronto: Canadian Constitution Foundation.

Saini, M., and A. Quinn. 2013. *A Systematic Review of Randomized Controlled Trials of Health Related Issues within an Aboriginal Context*. Prince George: National Collaborating Centre for Aboriginal Health.

Samson, C. 2003. *A Way of Life that Does Not Exist: Canada and Extinguishment of the Innu*. Saint John's: Institute of Social and Economic Research.

Sapers, H. 2014. *Annual Report 2013–2014*. Ottawa: Office of the Correctional Investigator.

Sawchuk, J. 2015. "Social Condition of Aboriginal Peoples." *Canadian Encyclopedia*. http://www.thecanadianencyclopedia.ca/en/article/native-people-social-conditions/.

Sellars, B. 2012. *They Called Me Number One: Secrets and Survival at an Indian Residential School*. Vancouver: Talon Books.

Shanks, G. 2005. *Economic Development in First Nations*. Ottawa: Public Policy Forum.

Sharpe, A., J. Arsenault, S. Lapointe, and F. Cowan. 2007. *The Potential Contribution of Aboriginal Canadians to Labour Force, Employment, Productivity and Output Growth in Canada, 2001–2017*. Ottawa: Centre for the Study of Living Standards.

Shih, M., D. Sanchez, and G. Ho. 2010. "Costs and Benefits of Switching among Multiple Social Identities." In *The Psychology of Social and Cultural Diversity*, edited by R. Crisp. Chichester: Blackwell.

Siggner, A. and R. Costa. 2005. *Aboriginal Conditions in Census Metropolitan Areas, 1981–2001*. Ottawa: Minister of Industry.

Silver, J., and J. Hay. 2006. *In Their Own Voices: Building Urban Aboriginal Communities*. Black Point, NS: Fernwood Publications.

Sinclair, J. 2010. "Trickster Reflections: Part I." In *Troubling Tricksters: Revisioning Critical Conversations*, edited by D. Reder and L. Morra. Waterloo: Wilfrid Laurier Press.

Sinha, V., and A. Kozlowski. 2013. "The Structure of Aboriginal Child Welfare in Canada." *The International Indigenous Policy Journal* 4 (2). http://ir.lib.uwo.ca/iipj/vol4/iss2/2.

Sisco, A., and N. Stewart. 2009. *True to Their Visions: An Account of 10 Successful Aboriginal Businesses*. Ottawa: The Conference Board of Canada.

Slattery, B. 1992. "First Nations and the Constitution: A Question of Trust." *Canadian Bar Review* 71 (2): 261–93.

Smylie, J. 2008. "The health of Aboriginal Peoples." In *Social Determinants of Health: Canadian Perspectives*, second edition, edited by D. Raphael, 281–301. Toronto: Canadian Scholars' Press Inc.

Solicitor General Canada. 2002. *Corrections and Conditional Release Statistical Overview*. Ottawa: Public Works and Government, Services Canada.

Standing Senate Committee on Aboriginal Peoples. 2011. *Reforming First Nations Education: From Crisis to Hope*. Ottawa.

Standing Senate Committee on Human Rights. 2007. *Children: The Silenced Citizens*. Ottawa.

Statistics Canada. 2002. *Aboriginal Entrepreneur Survey*. Ottawa: Statistics Canada.

———. 2004. *The Daily: Aboriginal Entrepreneur Survey*. Ottawa: Statistics Canada.

———. 2006a. *Aboriginal Peoples Survey 2001—Provincial and Territorial Reports: Off reserve Aboriginal Population*. Statistics Canada Catalogue no. 89-618-XIE.

———. 2006b. *Portrait of Canada*. Ottawa: Census 2006.

———. 2006c. *The Daily: Aboriginal People as Victims and Offenders*. Ottawa: Statistics Canada.

———. 2008a. *Aboriginal Peoples in Canada in 2006: Inuit, Metis and First Nations*. 2006 census http://www12statcan.ca/census-recensement/2006/as-sa/97-558-XIE 20060001.pdf.

———. 2008b. *Aboriginal Statistics at a Glance*. Statistics Canada Catalogue no. 89-645-X.

———. 2011a. *Aboriginal Languages in Canada*. Statistics Canada Catalogue no. 98-314 -X2011003.

———. 2011b. *Aboriginal Peoples and Language*. Ottawa: National Household Survey.

———. 2011c. *Aboriginal Peoples in Canada: First Nations People, Metis and Inuit*. Ottawa: National Household Survey. Statistics Canada Catalogue no. 99-011-X2011001.

———. 2011d. *Canada Year Book: Aboriginal People*. Statistics Canada Catalogue no. 11-402-X.

———. 2013a. *Aboriginal Peoples in Canada: First Nations People, Métis and Inuit*. Ottawa: Statistics Canada Catalogue no. 99-011-X2011001.

———. 2013b. *Education in Canada: Attainment, Field of Study and Location of Study*. Ottawa: Statistics Canada.

———. 2013c. *The Educational Attainment of Aboriginal Peoples in Canada*. National Household Survey 2011. Ottawa: Statistics Canada

Status of Women. 2002. *Assessing Violence against Women: A Statistical Profile*. Ottawa: Status of Women.

Task Force on Federally Sentenced Women. 1990. *Creating Choices*. Ottawa: Correctional Services.

Task Force on Urban Issues. 2002. *Canada's Urban Strategy: A Blueprint for Action*. Ottawa: Government of Canada.

Taylor, J. 1983. *Canadian Indian Policy during the Interwar Years, 1918–1939*. Ottawa: Queen's Printer.

Taylor, J., and J. Kalt. 2005. *American Indians on Reservations: A Data Book of Socio-Economic Change Between 1990 and 2000 Censuses*. Boston: Harvard Project on American Indian Economic Development.

Thorton, R. 2000. "Population History of Native North America." In *A Population History of North America*, edited by M. Haines, and R. Steckel, 156–93. Cambridge: Cambridge University Press.

Titley, B. 1986. *A Narrow Vision: Duncan Campbell Scott and the Administration of Indian Affairs*. Vancouver: University of British Columbia Press.

Tjepkema, Michael and Russell Wilkins. 2011. "Remaining Life Expectancy at Age 25 and Probability of Survival to Age 75, by Socio-Economic Status and Aboriginal Ancestry." *Health Reports* 22 (4). Statistics Canada Catalogue no. 82-003-X.

Tjepkema, Michael, R. Wilkins, S. Senecal, E. Guimond, and C. Penney. 2009. "Mortality of Métis and Registered Indian Adults in Canada: An 11-Year Follow-Up Study." *Health Reports* 20: 31–51.

Toledano, M. 2015. *Oil Activists Named as National Security Threats Respond to Leaked RCMP Report*. Vancouver: Vice.

Toronto Dominion Economics. 2011. *Debunking Myths Surrounding Canada's Aboriginal Population*. Toronto: TD.

———. 2012. *Estimating the Size of the Aboriginal Market in Canada, Toronto*. Toronto: TD.

Totten, M. 2008. *Promising Practices for Addressing Youth Involvement in Gangs*. Vancouver: Ministry of Public Safety and Solicitor General Victim Services and Crime Prevention Division.

———. 2010. "Involvement in Canada: A Gendered Approach." In *Exploring the Urban Landscape*, edited by J. White and J. Bruhn, 256–78. Thompson Educational Publishers.

Trovato, F., and A. Romaniuk. 2014. *Aboriginal Populations: Social, Demographic and Epidemiological Perspectives*. Edmonton: University of Alberta Press.

Truth and Reconciliation Commission of Canada. 2012. *Interim Report*. Winnipeg: TRC.

———. 2015. *Honouring the Truth, Reconciling for the Future*. Ottawa.

United Nations. 1978. *United Nations and Human Rights*. New York: United Nations.

———. 2007. Declaration of the Rights of Indigenous People. Geneva.

Urban Aboriginal Task Force. 2007. *Urban Aboriginal Task Force Final Report*. Toronto: Ontario Federation of Indian Friendship Centres, Ontario Métis Aboriginal Association, Ontario Native Women's Association.

Usalcas, J. 2011. *Aboriginal People and the Labour Market: Estimates from the Labour Force Survey, 2008–2010*. Ottawa: Statistics Canada, Minister of Industry.

Varcoe, C. 2011. *Harms and Benefits: Collecting Ethnicity Data in a Clinical Context.* Michael Smith Foundation for Health Research. http://www.ciqss.umontreal.ca/Docs/SSDE/pdf/Varcoe.pdf

Waldran, J. 2004. *Revenge of the Windigo: The Construction of the Mind and Mental Health of North American Aboriginal Peoples.* Toronto: University of Toronto Press.

Waldran, J., A. Herring, and T. K. Young. 2006. *Aboriginal Health in Canada: Historical, Cultural and Epidemiological Perspectives.* Toronto: University of Toronto Press.

Walter, M., and C. Anderson. 2013 *Indigenous Statistics: A Quantitative Research Methodology.* Walnut Creek: Left Coast Press.

Ward, T. 2005. "Institutional Constraints on Indian Farming on the Canadian Prairies, 1885–1920." Paper presented at the Canadian Economics Association Annual meetings, May.

Warry, W. 2007. *Ending Denial: Understanding Aboriginal Issues.* Toronto: University of Toronto Press.

Webster, C. 2012. "Prescription Drug Abuse Rising among Aboriginal Youths." *Canadian Medical Association Journal* 184 (12): E637-E648.

Weir, W. 2007. *First Nation Small Business and Entrepreneurship in Canada.* Saskatoon: University of Saskatchewan.

Wenman, W., M. Joffres, and I. Tataryn. 2004. "A Prospective Cohort Study of Pregnancy Risk Factors and Birth Outcomes in Aboriginal Women." *Canadian Medical Association Journal* 171: 585–89.

Wesley, M. 2012. *Marginalized: The Aboriginal Women's Experience in Federal Corrections.* Ottawa: Public Safety Canada.

Wesley-Esquimaux, C. and B. Calliou. 2010. *Best Practices in Aboriginal Community Development: A Literature Review and Wise Practices Approach.* Banff: Banff Centre.

Wherrett, J. 1999. *Aboriginal Self-Government.* Ottawa: Library of Parliament, Parliamentary Information and Research Service.

White, J., and J. Peters. 2010. "A Short History of Aboriginal Education in Canada." In *Aboriginal Education*, edited by J. White, J. Peters, D. Beavon, and N. Spence, 13–31. Toronto: Thompson Books.

Wilkins, R., S. Uppal, P. Finès, S. Senécal, É. Guimond, and R. Dion. 2008. "Life Expectancy in the Inuit-Inhabited Areas of Canada, 1989 to 2003." *Health Reports* 19 (1). Statistics Canada Catalogue no. 82-003-X.

Wilson, D., and D. Macdonald. 2010. *The Income Gap between Aboriginal Peoples and the Rest of Canada.* https://www.policyalternatives.ca/publications/reports/income-gap-between-aboriginal-peoples-and-rest-canada.

Wilson, D. and H. Northcott. 2008. *Dying and Death in Canada.* Toronto: University of Toronto Press.

Wilson, K. and E.J. Peters. 2005. "'You Can Make a Place for It': Remapping Urban First Nations Spaces of Identity." *Environment and Planning D: Society and Space* 23: 395.

Wood, D., and C. Griffiths. 2000. "Patterns of Aboriginal Crime." In *Crime in Canadian Society*, edited by R. Silverman, J. Teevan and V. Sacco, 250–62. Toronto: Harcourt Brace.

Woolford, A. 2005. *Between Justice and Certainty: Treaty Making in British Columbia.* Vancouver: University of British Columbia Press.

Yip, D., R. Bhargava, Y. Yao, K. Sutherland, J. Manfreeda, and R. Long. 2007. "Pediatric Tuberculosis in Alberta Epidemiology and Case Characteristics (1990–2004)." *Canadian Journal of Public Health* 98: 276–80.

Index